Raymond M. Costello, Ph. D.
Department of Psychiatry
University of Texas
Medical School at San Antonio
7703 Floyd Curl Drive
San Antonio, Texas 78229

therapy
in the ghetto

therapy in the ghetto:

political impotence and personal disintegration

barbara lerner

The Johns Hopkins University Press: Baltimore and London

For my grandparents, Jacob and Tzippa Turen, for my mother, Mary Turen Lerner, and for a shtetl called Kolonye where, for a time, orthodoxy and radicalism flourished together.

preface

In the strict sense, this book is the outgrowth of five years of research on outpatient psychotherapy with nontraditional clients, those who are severely disturbed or lower class or both. More broadly, it reflects a concern with a group of related psychosocial, professional, and, yes, political issues, issues which first began troubling me in the mid-fifties when I worked as a subprofessional with neglected client groups; they have continued to trouble me, in one way or another, throughout my professional career. More specifically, this book involves an attempt to test a conviction which grew out of that work, a conviction that individual psychotherapy, under appropriate conditions, can be an effective method of helping not only those classical clients traditionally served by this method, but also, those nonclassical clients who have rightfully become the main focus of community mental health endeavors.

To my mind, one's attitude toward the treatability of such clients has profound and far-reaching implications. Thus, in addition to presenting the research itself, its background, hypotheses, measures, and results, I have attempted to spell out the implications of divergent attitudes in considerable detail and to present extensive clinical examples. My own bias on this key issue is strong and positive, and my way of dealing with it is to make that explicit, here at the outset, and I hope, wherever necessary throughout this work. In addition, I have attempted to make it possible for others to reach their own conclusions by being as specific as possible about the methods of data collection and by presenting as much of the data itself as possible.

Despite these precautions, there are those who may be tempted to dismiss this book and its findings out of hand because they define objectivity as the absence of bias rather than as the explicit awareness and acknowledgment of it. I would urge such readers to reconsider on two bases. First, what looks like objectivity in the form of neutrality is often only an unrecognized bias, usually in favor of the status quo. Second, the mental health field has suffered greatly as a result of a tendency for professionals to dichotomize themselves into two groups: those who are willing to make personal commitments but unwilling to test them, and those who are unwilling to make any commitments but are willing to test anything. In my view, significant numbers of psychologists, psychiatrists, and social workers must be willing to do both before the common ideals of our separate professions can begin to be realized in a meaningful way.

The fifteen therapists of the Blank Park Center who participated in this study are such people. Deeply committed to individual psychotherapy, they nonetheless took the risk involved in exposing themselves, their work, and their beliefs to extensive testing, committing their time and talents under difficult circumstances and without official recognition or reward. I am deeply grateful to them and to their forty-five clients for making this research not only possible but genuinely pleasurable as well.

In attempting to relate the work made possible by their efforts to the broader context of community mental health, I have been greatly influenced by years of discussion and collaborative work with Sheppard Kellam and Jeanette Branch of the Woodlawn Mental Health Center in Chicago, and with Mary Riley Williams, formerly of Mobilization for Youth in New York, later Director of the Deprived Areas Recreation Team in Detroit, and currently Director of the Professional Skills Alliance, also in Detroit. All of these people have helped to stimulate and sharpen my thinking in this area, but none of them are in any way responsible for the outcome as I have presented it here.

The manuscript itself was read and criticized by two mentors who have played a significant role in my scientific, clinical, and general education: Donald Fiske of the University of Chicago and Ralph Heine of the University of Michigan. I am indebted to each of them for numerous valuable suggestions, both substantive and stylistic, and I owe an additional debt to Donald Fiske for his thoughtful advice on methodological problems, statistical handling of the data, and interpretation of the results.

All statistical computations and tests were independently redone by at least two people—originally, by myself and Winfield Fish, a very helpful and conscientious research assistant, and later, with the aid of Khazan Agrawal, chief statistician of the Woodlawn Mental Health Center. Again, however, responsibility for the final product is strictly my own.

Funds to have the data scored and analyzed were provided by Ohio University, and this part of the work was greatly aided by the sympathy and support of my colleagues and students there. Sensitive and reliable blind scoring of the data, using a number of complex clinical scoring systems, some created for this study as well as some more tried and tested older ones, was provided by the following people: Margery Baittle, Jack Vognsen, and Karol Weinstein in Chicago, Illinois; Neal Warren in Pasadena, California; Larry Pacoe and Arthur Van Cara in Pittsburgh, Pennsylvania; and the staff of the Arkansas Research and Rehabilitation Center, under the direction first of Charles Truax and, later, of Frank Lawlis in Fayetteville, Arkansas.

In addition to requiring the generous assistance of so many people, testing the commitments and beliefs expressed in this book and controlling for bias in the process required some specialized methods. As a result, the book is heavily technical in a few places, most notably in some sections of Part 2 (e.g., chapter 5) and Part 3 (e.g., the first half of chapter 8). I sincerely hope that this will not deter professionals who are not research specialists or people who are not professionals at all from reading this book. Technical problems aside, the substantive issues involved here are far too important to be considered, let alone decided, by professionals alone or, worse still, by any small subgroup of us. The book as a whole is, I think, quite comprehensible, even if one skims or skips some of the technical parts, and for this, much credit is due to people already mentioned. I would also like to express my appreciation to Billie Paige, who typed, retyped, and copyread the manuscript with patience and precision, and to her husband, George, for his frequent hospitality and forbearance during the process.

In addition, I am grateful to Czatdana Tomicious-Baxter, an expert on matters of technical style and organization in Greek, Turkish, Italian, and, fortunately for me and the readers of this book, English: she prepared the subject index for this volume with maximal speed and efficiency, and with minimal help from me.

Finally, to clear up any remaining doubt about the overall trend of this book, I should perhaps mention that I initially thought of subtitling it "The Radical Clinician's Handbook." I decided not to because, for better or for worse, it is only my liberal acquaintances who regard me as a radical; my radical acquaintances generally regard me as a liberal. In light of this, it seemed better to leave the book politically unlabelled in the hope that its readers might struggle for themselves with the meaning of these terms in relation to the current professional and social scene and with their own place in it, as well as with the place of this book.

contents

list of tables

therapy
in the ghetto

part I:

background of the research

the research problem

PSYCHOTHERAPY, STATUS, AND NEED

From its inception, psychotherapy has been, in essence, a medicine for mandarins, designed and prescribed primarily for mildly to moderately disturbed middle and upper class individuals. Freud, the first psychotherapist, was very clear about this fact, reiterating at frequent intervals (e.g., Freud, 1935, 1959a, 1959b, and 1963) that while his personality theory was all inclusive, the method of treatment he derived from it was quite exclusive. He was equally clear, albeit regretful, about who was excluded: the poor and the psychotic.

Psychotherapy has developed apace since Freud founded it at the turn of the century. In the subsequent multiplicity of schools and orientations, one can find a forthright challenge to virtually every Freudian tenet of treatment. Therapists disagree, and disagree sharply, as to the how, why, what, when, and where of treatment (e.g., Harper, 1959; Rogers, 1966), but with regard to the who, there is a striking degree of consistency over time, across professions and between orientations. Regardless of whether researchers investigate who is most likely to be considered a desirable client (e.g., Goldman and Mendelsohn, 1969; Knapp, Levin, McCarter, Wermer, and Zetzel, 1960), who is most likely to receive psychotherapy (e.g., Hollingshead and Redlich, 1958; Gallagher, Sharaf, and Levinson, 1965; Michael, 1967), who is most likely to remain in therapy (e.g., Auld and Myers, 1954; Imber, Nash, and Stone, 1955; Overall and Aronson, 1963; Winder and Hersko, 1955), or who is most likely to be judged as having profited from therapy (e.g., Barron, 1956; Bloom, 1956; Garfield and Affleck, 1961; Grey, 1966; Hunt, Ewing, LaForge, and Gilbert, 1959; Katz, Lorr, and Rubinstein, 1958; Lohrenz, Hunter, and Schwartzman, 1966; Miles, Barrabe, and Finesinger, 1951; Sulli-

3

van, Miller, and Smelser, 1958), results are essentially the same: mildly or moderately disturbed middle and upper class people are good clients; severely disturbed and/or lower class people are poor ones, rejected by and rejecting of professional therapy and therapists.

Exceptions, of course, exist, particularly with regard to the severely disturbed. Beginning with the work of people like Federn (1952), Sullivan (1962), Fromm-Reichman (1950), and Sechahaye (1951), and continuing to the present day in the work of such figures as Will (1961), Searles (1965), and, most recently, Rogers (Rogers, Gendlin, Kiesler, and Truax, 1967), a relatively small but significant handful of clinicians has challenged longstanding and widespread beliefs about the unsuitability of psychotics for individual psychotherapy. These more hopeful clinicians have produced results that seemed, to them at least, to provide some support for their optimism. Despite this, most therapists remain profoundly pessimistic about the severely disturbed and prefer to refer them elsewhere.

With regard to lower class clients, the situation is even worse. No really significant group, with the possible exception of the behavior therapists (e.g., Graziano, 1969), has arisen to challenge what is generally regarded as a basic lack of aptitude for individual psychotherapy among the poor.[1] Most professionals assume this lack of aptitude and go on from there, if they go on at all, to try to explain it, usually in terms of various intellectual and emotional shortcomings thought to be endemic among the lower classes. In sum, if personal preferences were the only factors involved in client selection, the poor and the psychotic would get very short shrift indeed from the vast majority of professional therapists.

However, one's ability to act in accord with one's personal preferences is largely determined, in the mental health field as in other social arenas, by one's position within a status hierarchy. In general, high status professionals with long experience and training have tended to be able to enforce their preferences and to work only or mainly with "good clients," relegating "bad clients" to those subordinate to them in status, due to lack of training or lack of experience or both. Thus, in most instances, the poor and the psychotic do not get psychotherapy at all, and when they do, they are likely to get it from relatively inexperienced and/or untrained therapists who work with them by default rather than by choice and with not very sanguine expectations about results.

The common rationale for this state of affairs has been that since the poor and the psychotic are generally unable to profit from therapy anyway, scarce professional resources should not be wasted upon them but should instead be concentrated where they can do the most good, on the treatment

---

[1] Graziano's article is an unusually honest and courageous description of the way an established mental health power structure responded to such a challenge.

of mildly or moderately disturbed middle and upper class individuals. For many decades, this rationale sufficed. Most mental health professionals accepted it and practiced their craft upon a very select sample in a relatively untroubled fashion.

With the advent of the community mental health movement, the situation began to change, at least to the extent that the profession can no longer be described as untroubled. Briefly, what community mental health workers have discovered and documented is that both the incidence and the severity of psychological disorder is highest among the lowest class in the population (e.g., Dohrenwend and Dohrenwend, 1965; Phillips, 1967; Roman and Trice, 1967). Moreover, if one moves beyond the narrow and dated "illness model" and views psychological functioning in broader and more positive human terms (e.g., Albee, 1969; Maslow, 1962; Szasz, 1960), it becomes apparent that lower class people are generally more hampered in fulfilling their psychological and social potential than are their middle and upper class counterparts. Thus, mental health professionals can fairly be described as having systematically concentrated their efforts in the area of least pressing need, ignoring areas of greatest need and failing to meet their social responsibilities.

Agreement on this point is not unanimous among mental health workers but it is widespread and growing, as is a determination at least to attempt to change the situation. Here, however, agreement ends and controversy over methods of change begins. The current situation, in fact, is one in which both the demand for clinical services and the conflict over clinical methods have reached new high points. To be sure, controversy over approaches to treatment is not new to the clinical field. Arguments about the utility of psychotherapy in particular have been going on for a long time (e.g., Astin, 1961; Bergin, 1963; Cartwright, 1955; DeCharms, Levy, and Wertheimer, 1954; Denker, 1946; Eysenck, 1952, 1960; Friess and Nelson, 1942; Landis, 1937; Luborsky, 1954; Strupp, 1963), but they have been greatly intensified by the growing emphasis on community mental health. Critics of the psychotherapeutic approach point out that research has yet to document convincingly its effectiveness for any group of clients, least of all for the poor and the severely disturbed. In fact, such studies as currently exist seem to indicate that psychotherapy is least effective with precisely those latter two groups. As a result, a large and increasing number of professionals (e.g., Albee, 1965; Hunt, 1960; Orlinsky, 1966) argue that psychotherapy has no legitimate role to play in community mental health programs and should be replaced by wholly new approaches to mental health problems.

Certainly, new approaches are needed. Leaving aside, for the moment, the question of its effectiveness, psychotherapy has two basic limitations as a mental health tool, one practical and one philosophical. The first has to do with sheer numbers: troubled people vastly outnumber trained therapists and all responsible studies of manpower realities, past, present, and prospective. indicate that this will always be so (e.g., Albee, 1959; Arnhoff, Rubinstein, and Speisman, 1969; Schofield, 1964). Briefer forms of therapy and briefer training for therapists, including the training of nonprofessionals as therapists, can reduce but not eliminate the problem. As long as therapy remains the sole weapon in the mental health armamentarium, need will always greatly exceed the resources available to meet it.

Even if this were not so, the other basic limitation referred to above would still militate against an exclusive focus on therapy in the strict sense. The other limitation, the philosophical one, has to do with assumptions about the basic causes of psychological malfunctioning and distress.

As previously cited epidemiological studies show, and as ecological studies beginning with the classic work of Faris and Dunham (1939) further illustrate, psychological malfunctioning and distress are not randomly distributed. They are highest in the lowest class in the population, highest that is among the poor—and the poor tend to be concentrated in particular geographical areas. Moreover, as Harrington (1963) has so forcefully illustrated, the poor today are not a random, ever-changing group; nor is their condition a temporary one. The poor in America have become a permanent, physically and socially isolated underclass, comprised primarily of minority group members who have been neglected and rejected as groups by the larger society over many generations. The specific groups which comprise this underclass are many and diverse, for example, Appalachian whites, American Indians, and Puerto Rican and Mexican Americans. A consideration of each of these groups is, however, beyond the scope of this volume. Instead, this book focuses selectively on one particularly crucial group of exemplary social victims: impoverished Blacks in urban ghettos.

The center in which the research was done was in such a neighborhood and a majority of the clients in the research are such people. In that particular community, as in others like it across the nation, most residents are functioning below their psychological capacity and many are deeply distressed, but to view it as a community of "patients" is both depreciating and inaccurate because it implies that the basic problem of the ghetto is the personal pathology of its residents. Actually, the best evidence we have indicates that the reverse is true: the social pathology of the society in which ghetto dwellers live is the basic problem and gives rise to the personal difficulties with which they struggle. In such settings, treating "patients" without attempting to modify the social conditions which produce them is a Sisyphus-like task, somewhat analogous to treating malaria victims in a mosquito-infested swamp. Treating those already afflicted is a humane, even a heroic endeavor, but a rather futile one unless there is a simultaneous effort to drain the swamps to prevent new infections. In addition to psychotherapy, programs of primary prevention aimed at changing the social conditions which produce the need for psychotherapy must also be initiated.

PRIMARY PREVENTION AND PARTICIPATORY DEMOCRACY

How and by whom is this to be done? Obviously, mental health services alone, whatever form they take, cannot solve all the problems of the ghettos, nor of the society which created and maintains them, but mental health professionals should be able to make a significant contribution in the area of primary prevention, and despite what some critics say, they should be able to do it without going outside their field of expertise. Granted, the intrapsychic approach of most schools of psychotherapy, useful as it may sometimes be for individuals, does not, by itself, provide an adequate basis for work with communities. However, at least one relevant new body of theory, research, and practice does exist. Generally referred to as milieu therapy, this new approach has grown out of the efforts of social scientists and practitioners in inpatient settings over the past few decades. What these workers have learned and demonstrated is that day-to-day client-staff interaction around reality issues can be a potent cause of psychological malfunctioning (e.g., Caudill, 1958; Goffman, 1961) and that alteration of that interaction in the direction of a therapeutic community can be a potent cure for psychological malfunctioning (e.g., Cumming and Cumming, 1962; Jones, 1953; Stanton and Schwartz, 1954). Although many variations exist, the essence of a therapeutic community is simple enough to be summed up in two familiar, nontechnical words: participatory democracy.[2]

Participatory democracy exists when there is open communication and shared decision-making among all parties affected by an event. Both elements are essential because neither can exist without the other. In small groups, participatory democracy can be achieved through the direct participation of everyone involved, and in larger groups, it can be achieved through representative leadership, responsive to the wishes of those who are being represented.[3] At this point, some readers may be tempted to comment that milieu therapy is nothing but the rediscovery and renaming of what sensible people

[2]This summarization is generally applicable to pioneering efforts in this realm, such as those described in the references cited; it is obviously not applicable to more recent attempts to control and manipulate inpatient environments through the use of token economies and other behavioral modification techniques, although proponents of these strategies have tended to use the same term—milieu therapy—to refer to their own very different approaches.

[3]Some proponents of participatory democracy have insisted on defining the term so as to exclude representative leadership, a position which seems to me unnecessary and unwise. Surely, it is possible to fight against the evils of unrepresentative leadership without attacking the concept of representative leadership itself, and with it, all possibility of any organization larger than that of the face-to-face group.

already know. Perhaps, but the fact is that until very recently most people did not grasp the therapeutic efficacy of this simple principle and did not apply it to psychotics or to poor people.

Prior to the advent of milieu therapy, the social system of the typical mental hospital was usually strictly authoritarian, with official decision-making power in the hands of a few members of the medical profession. Membership in this profession was like caste membership in that it guaranteed one a permanent position at the top of the hierarchy and closed off any possibility of mobility for nonmedical people. Medical people made unilateral decisions about the operation of the ward and the treatment of the inmates that affected every aspect of the work life of other staff members and the total life of the inmates.

In this situation, covert and overt dissatisfaction and disagreement among different groups of staff members and between staff and inmates were rampant. Communication was extremely poor because, as long as decision-making was not shared, communication was generally both futile and dangerous; and, as long as communication was poor, decisions were based on inadequate data and tended to be inappropriate. This deplorable reality situation was demoralizing for staff members at all levels and fostered confusion, impotence, depersonalization, and deterioration in inmates. However, such results were interpreted as reflections of personal pathology because behavior was seen as a product of internal psychological forces and not of the interaction between individual psychology and current social reality.

When social scientists finally shifted their focus and began to study the social world of the mental hospital as well as the psychological worlds of its inmates, they learned that even the most regressed chronic psychotics are at least as responsive to changing external reality as to timeless internal fantasies, that altering reality alters behavior, and that, given a chance to participate in making decisions that affected their lives, inmates generally did so in a responsible manner and with constructive results for all concerned—for staff as well as for themselves.

The point of all this for community mental health in deprived urban Negro neighborhoods is that ghettos are very much like unreconstructed mental hospitals, not because the fantasies of poor Blacks are like those of psychotics but because social reality in the two settings is similar. The basic psychosocial problem of the ghetto, like that of the old hospital, is the absence of participatory democracy. Ghetto institutions are generally administered by officials who are neither representative of nor responsive to the people they are supposed to serve. These officials are usually white "experts" who live outside the Black community and do not share decision-making with local residents, although nowadays, they sometimes ask selected residents to rubber stamp their decisions after the fact. This failure to share decision-making cuts off the possibility of open communication, and without open communication, shared decision-making is impossible—and so a vicious cycle is set in motion. Officials feel maligned and mistreated, increasingly isolated in an unreasoningly hostile world—after all, they are only trying to do what is "best" for the community; residents feel increasingly frustrated, depreciated, and enraged—after all, they are only trying to get some "decent" service.

A few mental health experts who understand milieu theory as well as individual dynamics and are courageous enough to accept its implications are now acting as consultants to such embattled institutions, helping them to become representative of and responsive to those they serve by facilitating open communication and shared decision-making. For example, on the south side of Chicago, at the Woodlawn Mental Health Center, an agency supported but not strait-jacketed by the City of Chicago Board of Health, with additional financial assistance from the University of Chicago, the Federal Government, and the State of Illinois, professionals began their work by developing an advisory board made up of local residents and representing the widest possible variety of community interests and opinions (Kellam and Branch, 1970; Kellam, Branch, Agrawal, and Grabill, 1970; Kellam and Schiff, 1966, 1967, and 1968; Kellam, Schiff, and Branch, 1968). They then asked their board to determine with them a set of priorities for mental health programs in the Woodlawn area, offering their technical expertise not to dictate those priorities but to translate them into action.

Because Woodlawn is an urban Negro ghetto with the usual low general level of income and education, many board members were poor and poorly educated.[4] Yet, what they requested was a first priority program with far more positive potential than the usual keep-the-walking-wounded-walking type of "crisis" program which focuses only on those already afflicted. They asked for a program of primary prevention aimed at the young and focused on helping them develop to their fullest. The result was a program in the schools of Woodlawn centered around first-grade children, their teachers, and their parents, a program with a potential for breaking down old barriers and opening up new opportunities for self-fulfillment for everyone involved in it.

In the Woodlawn community, of course, professionals began with a distinct advantage. Unlike most poor communities, Woodlawn was highly organized, with a democratic and representative neighborhood organization (Brazier, 1969; Sanders, 1970; Silberman, 1964). Thus, it was *relatively* easy to identify genuinely representative individuals, to negotiate a plan with them, and to approach the educational bureaucracy not as supplicants or

---

[4]Many, but not all. Woodlawn, like many urban ghettos, contains a significant minority of residents who have "made it," educationally, vocationally, and financially, and who have chosen to remain in the community, an important group often overlooked by outsiders observing the ghetto.

sycophants but as independent intermediaries with a genuine mandate from the people of the community, a mandate that deserves and gets respect for obvious practical, as well as for moral and intellectual, reasons.

In areas where democratic and representative neighborhood organizations do not exist, professionals have helped to create and strengthen them by offering the people in these areas a real opportunity to make their wishes known to and, if necessary, their power felt by recalcitrant bureaucrats. This is what Mobilization for Youth attempted to do in New York (e.g., Brager and Purcell, 1967; Cloward and Ohlin, 1960; Marris and Rein, 1967) and what the Deprived Areas Recreation Team (DART) and the Professional Skills Alliance (PSA) are trying to do in Detroit (Williams, 1969, 1971).

PSYCHOTHERAPY RECONSIDERED

At this point, many readers may be wondering what the immediately pre-ceding pages have to do with the problem with which this chapter began. What, after all, has all this to do with an argument in favor of a role for individual psychotherapy in community mental health programs in impov-erished areas? Has it not, in fact, strengthened the hand of those who argue against such a role, insisting that the focus should be on social change rather than on individual treatment?

In my view, the answer to that question depends upon what one thinks psychotherapy is and what it attempts to do. If one thinks of psychotherapy as a technique or set of techniques by which an expert attempts in his wisdom to improve, enlighten, plan for, or manipulate a recipient in his ignorance, then the answer is clearly nothing. On the other hand, if one defines psychotherapy as an attempt by one human being with specialized training to establish a genuinely meaningful, democratic, and collaborative relationship with another person in order to put his special knowledge and skills at the second person's disposal for such use as he chooses to make of it, then I think the answer is everything.

Flatly stated, the viewpoint which animates this book is that the poor need programs of psychotherapy and of social change and need to have both sorts of programs administered and staffed by the same sorts of people—people with a democratic and not an elitist or authoritarian outlook and approach. The corollary to this point of view is that those who cannot treat the poor as individuals because they are unable to establish meaningful com-munication and unwilling to share decision-making with them cannot treat them as groups either. They cannot plan with the poor or help the poor to implement their own plans, but can only plan for them, imposing from above their own usually inaccurate and often demeaning conception of what the poor "should" have, want, do, and be, much as the supposedly liberal experts of the Kennedy and Johnson administrations have attempted to do with the people of Viet Nam (e.g., Chomsky, 1969). Unpalatable as it may seem, this analogy is an accurate one. In the domestic as in the foriegn sphere, experts too often attempt to mold people into an elite image of what is desirable instead of serving them in their attempt to develop and implement their own image of themselves and the world.

Contemporary experts who attempt to mold rather than to serve their clients usually defend their right to do so in terms of their superior knowledge as a result of their scientific training. The fallacy in that defense is that decisions about what individuals and groups of individuals *should* be, have, want, and do are decisions which involve values, and in this area every man is a legitimate expert for himself and no man is a legitimate expert for others. Science can help men to achieve the goals they value and to judge the success of their efforts, but that is all it can do. There is not and cannot be a scientific basis for deciding which goals have value or how much. Hence, the choice is not between expert and nonexpert ways of making choices; it is between relatively democratic and relatively undemocratic ways of making choices.

From the perspective detailed here, the conflict over individual versus group methods in community mental health rests on a false dichotomy because the essential nature of constructive psychotherapy and social action is the same. So too are the goals of both: to promote effective action in one's own behalf, in the former case by removing internal psychological obstacles to such action and, in the latter, by removing external social obstacles to it. Even the methods, in a general conceptual sense if not in a narrow technical one, are not all that different. Good psychotherapists, as defined above, usually attempt to achieve their goals by restoring meaningful psychological contact with other individuals (starting with the therapist), by facilitating insight into psychological problems, and by promoting ego-strengthening through internal organization and individual problem-solving. Similarly, good community workers, as defined above, usually attempt to achieve their goals by restoring meaningful social contact between members of groups, by facilitating insight into group social problems and by group strengthening through social organization and collective problem-solving. According to this view, the only real dichotomy is between those who work on and those who work for their clients.

Is it possible to work successfully for the poor and the severely disturbed? Throughout this chapter, examples of individuals and agencies who feel that it is have been presented. I hope that it has also been made clear that such individuals are a minority. Most therapists see the poor and the severely disturbed as untreatable, except by the manipulative techniques of the grosser forms of behavior therapy, and most community mental health proponents seem to see them as objects of social manipulation to be planned for, not with. Moreover, a number of previously cited research studies seem to show that, at least as far as individual psychotherapy is concerned, the majority is right and the minority wrong. Psychotherapy, according to these studies, is simply not effective with the poor and the severely disturbed. It is time to take a closer look at that research.

When one does, two major problems emerge. The first bears on the soundness of the data and has to do with the outcome problem. No really satisfactory method of assessing the results of psychotherapy—or, for that matter, of any other form of treatment or intervention with individuals or with groups—has yet been devised. Thus, the effectiveness or lack of effectiveness of psychotherapy with any population remains an open question. In this context, the fact that by present measurements the poor and the psychotic seem to fare less well in individual treatment than others becomes a less than convincing finding. To mention only one of several possibilities, researchers may simply have been less good at assessing relative change in the poor and the severely disturbed because of a lack of appropriate group standards and experience. In other words, usual outcome criteria are not only unsatisfactory for a number of technical reasons to be detailed in later chapters, they may also be severely biased.

The second major problem with studies purporting to show the ineffectiveness of psychotherapy with the poor and the psychotic has to do with their fairness as tests. As was noted earlier, the professional status of a clinician has tended to be highly correlated with the social status of the clients he served. As a result, very few highly trained and motivated professionals worked extensively and by choice with severely disturbed lower class individuals. Thus, studies of the effects of psychotherapy with this group have generally had to rely either on therapists with little training or on therapists with little experience with such clients. In light of the overall situation, it seems reasonable to assume that many of these therapists approached the task with some rather negative attitudes and expectations. The potentially crucial influence of expectations on outcome, as illustrated by Goldstein's work (1962) and, more generally, by the Rosenthal effect (Baez, 1968, Burnham and Hartsough, 1968; Rosenthal, 1966; Rosenthal and Jacobson, 1968), suggests, at the very least, that studies using such therapists may not provide a fair test of the ability of nonclassical clients to profit from psychotherapy.

In the present study, a concerted effort was made to deal with both of the problems detailed above in such a way as to make possible a fair test of the major hypothesis of this study: that individual therapy under appropriate conditions can be an effective method of helping not only those classical clients traditionally served by this method but also those nonclassical clients who have become the main focus of community mental health endeavors. To do this, the first requirement was to find an appropriate setting, one in which large numbers of such clients were treated by well-trained therapists, experienced in dealing with them and with some reasonably positive expectations as a result of that experience. An institution, hereafter referred to as the Blank Park Center, in a large midwestern city, hereafter referred to as Stock City, was such a setting.

In the next chapter, an attempt will be made to describe that setting in some detail because, in addition to providing necessary information on the context of the present research, it also serves as a concrete clinical example of the general problems and processes discussed in this first chapter. More specifically, it provides an illustration of the importance of participatory democracy for professionals as well as for the people they serve and of the consequences of its absence. Thus, what follows is intended as a case study of an institution and of the professional politics which led to its emergence and, later, to its decline.

Material on which this case history is based was obtained by the participant-observer method during the period from 1965 to 1968, when the author was employed at the center as research co-ordinator and clinical supervisor, and for a short period in 1968, as co-ordinator of community-based services for the Blank Park Project. In collecting these data, every effort was made to achieve objectivity in the sense of historical accuracy. No attempt was made to achieve objectivity in the sense of attitudinal neutrality—the author resigned in protest against the events described near the end of chapter 2.

CHAPTER **2**

the research
setting

PSYCHOTHERAPY AND PROFESSIONAL POLITICS
AT THE CENTER

Prior to 1969, the Blank Park Center, a facility of the Midwest State Department of Mental Health, was a very large outpatient clinic with well over one hundred professional staff members and just under one hundred business, clerical, and maintenance people, serving approximately 7000 clients a year. Located in Blank Park, a hungry Black ghetto just outside of the downtown area, the center had a long history of providing service to the city's poor and severely disturbed. Unlike most such institutions, it often provided service of a surprisingly high quality—surprising because, until very recently, it was not fashionable to work with the poor or the severely disturbed. As a result, such clients tended to get a kind of depression-based maintenance service through public welfare agencies or the kind of minimal custodial care that was provided by the old human-warehouse type of state hospitals. Of course, even these typical institutions generally contained a few especially motivated and dedicated staff members who managed to provide quality care despite the multiple obstacles that overwhelmed most of their peers, but usually such people were a tiny minority who had relatively little effect on the flavor of their institutions.

The Blank Park Center was different, largely because of its special role in relation to the professional caste system referred to in the preceding chapter, a caste system which placed psychiatrists at the top of the hierarchy, psychologists in the middle, and social workers at the bottom. Based on the erroneous view that most psychological problems have an organic etiology, this caste system resulted in a situation in which social workers are frequently expected to relate to psychiatrists as nurses to physicians, playing the role of doctor's handmaiden rather than functioning as independent agents. Among social workers with a heavy investment in treatment, the more intelligent and independent ones naturally have tended to reject this role and to seek arenas in which they can be judged on the basis of competence rather than caste position.

As a result of such seeking (by psychologists as well as social workers)—plus a high level of demand for therapeutic services and a shortage of trained therapists—great cracks in this caste system began to appear, first on the west coast and then on the east coast. In the conservative midwest, however, it altered more slowly—so slowly, in fact, that for many years one of the few large institutions in the Stock City area where social workers functioned without pretense and without apology as primary therapists was at the Blank Park Center. Consequently, this institution tended to attract some of the better social workers in the Stock City area, and it attracted relatively large numbers of them—the social work staff of the adult clinic alone generally included between twenty and thirty social workers, all with master's degrees, most of which were attained at the better Stock City area universities where, ironically, Sigmund Freud had long since dethroned Jane Addams as king of the curriculum.

Because of the ghetto setting of the center, these social workers found themselves in the relatively unique situation of having to apply their generally classical psychoanalytic training to large numbers of distinctly nonclassical clients. Some quietly opted out of this dilemma by regarding intake as a sieve with which to sort out the few "good clients," the mildly disturbed middle class ones, from the many "bad clients," those who were lower class and/or severely disturbed. An impressive number, however, responded to the challenge and struggled to combine Freudian insights with Addams' style of social awareness, modifying classical therapeutic methods so as to make them meaningful and useful to nonclassical clients.

There were three major results of this struggle. Result one was the development of a group of practitioners convinced that the general professional pessimism with regard to the treatability of the poor and the psychotic was unfounded and resulted more from the lack of motivation and experience of professionals than of clients. Result two was a "let a hundred flowers bloom" atmosphere where strict orthodoxy withered and creative modifications of traditional therapy flourished. Of course, this setting, plus the job protection of civil service, allowed weeds as well as flowers to grow; but on the whole, in contrast to the deadly ideological conformity of most therapeutic centers which tended at the time to be dominated by one "school" or orientation, the atmosphere was refreshing and the results constructive. Result three was a degree of social consciousness and practical commitment rare among professional therapists. Specifically, instead of avoiding the poor and the severely disturbed or treating them only by default, many of these therapists treated them by choice and, as will be illustrated in later chapters, did it rather well.

By and large, the three results listed above applied mainly to the numerically dominant social service staff. In fact, in terms of professional credentials and talent and resultant professional standing outside the institution and the department, the usual hierarchical pyramid was inverted at the center. Here, with a few exceptions, social workers were at the top, psychologists in the middle, and psychiatrists at the bottom. This inversion was implicitly recognized within the center and outside it in a variety of ways. For example, with regard to training functions, the center was officially approved as a placement center for social-work field-work students from all major Stock City area universities; it also had a psychology internship program which did not, however, have American Psychological Association approval, although it sought it repeatedly; it had no psychiatric trainees whatsoever.

Explicitly and officially, however, the old caste system still prevailed, with the result that the formal administrative apparatus was neither representative of nor responsive to the staff of the center and was dominated by members of professions other than social work. This domination was so complete that even the training committee was chaired and staffed mainly by psychiatrists and psychologists. As long as the major function of the center was individual psychotherapy, this undemocratic state of affairs was annoying but relatively unimportant because formal administrative functions were largely irrelevant to the real work of the institution. Administrative decisions did not seriously affect the relationship between client and therapist, and administrative co-ordination was not vital in facilitating such relationships. Thus, a small group of psychiatrists, psychologists, and others got a salve for their egos, and social workers got their freedom, a bargain not unlike that made by the couple who divided their responsibilities by letting the husband make all of the important decisions—whether to recognize Red China—and the wife make all of the minor ones—where they should live and work and how the children should be raised.

A NEW SYSTEM AND OLD PROBLEMS

This was the scene at the old Blank Park Center when its parent organization, the Midwest State Department of Mental Health, acquired a new director and launched a heavily funded drive to institute a community mental health approach within the state. The highly centralized new state administration began its drive with the avowed intention of maximizing service and minimizing travelling time for service recipients. At the time, there were two major state-owned and -operated service facilities for psychologically disturbed adults in the Stock City area, the Blank Park Center and Stock State Hospital. In contrast to the former, the latter is a large inpatient hospital located in a comfortable white neighborhood far north of the downtown area. The main local result of the statewide reorganization was the creation of two costly new inpatient-outpatient facilities, the X Zone Center, located immediately adjacent to Stock State Hospital, and the Y Zone Center, located far west of the city. Negroes who managed the long trip to either of these places (Y is almost inaccessible to Stock City residents without cars and is on the outskirts of Brickville, a town famous in the history of the northern civil rights struggle for its bitter and violent opposition to Black people) travelled through and to neighborhoods which were strongholds of white racism. Thus, while services were initially made more accessible to the city's affluent whites, this was hardly the case for its poor Blacks.

Of course, sites for mental health facilities should not be chosen simply with regard to the amount of poverty or pigmentation in a community but with regard to the extent of need for such services. In general, need is not easy to determine with any degree of precision because studies of the incidence of psychological disorder in untreated populations are plagued by the criterion problem. Mental health experts trying to arrive at a workable and meaningful definition of a "case" are not too much better off than that group of financial experts who ended up by defining their key word, "income," as, "Income is income from all sources." As a result of this state of affairs, each new epidemiological survey tends to conflict with those that have preceded it, with estimates of the general incidence in society at large, for example, ranging from under one percent to over sixty percent (Dohrenwend and Dohrenwend, 1965). In this chaotic context, it is especially striking that virtually all epidemiological studies agree on one point: the incidence of psychological disorder is highest among the lowest class in the population.

There are those who nonetheless reject this finding on the grounds that it reflects the middle class bias of the investigators who did the research. Such critics take a relativist stance, arguing that the high rate of disorder found among the poor is a product of the application of inappropriate middle class standards to lower class behavior. No attempt is here being made to deny the existence and importance of class-linked subcultures in our society, but to say that much of the behavior in question is normal is like saying that it is normal for the poor to be miserable—a notion that the twentieth-century poor are rejecting with a vehemence that even the most insular can no longer ignore.

Thus, the best evidence available to date indicates that the need for mental health services is greatest in the poorest neighborhoods, and in Stock City, as in most of the larger urban areas, the poorest neighborhoods are Black. Despite this, the State Department of Mental Health not only built its expensive new facilities in areas far removed from Stock City's Black poor but also, for several years, poured the bulk of its time, money, and energy into these new facilities.

Development of the first of the new Stock City area State Centers, X, began with a lot of high level "planning" and with an impressive physical plant, but with a shortage of both professionals, aside from "chiefs," and clients. Department officials initially attempted to deal with their personnel shortage by recruiting—at the Blank Park Center! Their efforts were enormously successful in the psychology department, less so in the psychiatry department, and a total failure among social workers. To a man, the social work staff of the Blank Park Center refused to desert the central city ghetto for the new northside facility. They remained and continued to "do their thing," a decent, meaningful, and worthwhile thing, but, for reasons spelled out in chapter 1, hardly a total answer to the mental health problems of the community which surrounded them, or of any other human community.

Meanwhile, X gradually managed to solve its professional staffing problems, in part, with workers from other state facilities interested in what initially looked like an opportunity to gain access to higher status clients in a physically impressive new setting. The client problem, however, proved more refractory. Confronted by a dearth of service applicants, administrators complained that they were in an area of "low psychiatric awareness," rather than inferring that they might be in an area of "low psychiatric need." On the basis of this assumption, they began to plan and implement a public relations campaign to encourage greater use of the facility by the relatively affluent and successful community surrounding it, a campaign which risked encouraging the kind of psychological hypochondriasis that Schofield (1964) warned against so eloquently in his book, *Psychotherapy: the purchase of friendship.*

The campaign had no immediate effect, and government and welfare officials outside the department grew impatient enough with the by now heavily staffed but still essentially clientless facility to bring external pressure to bear. As a result of this pressure, the extended planning idyll was abruptly ended and X was charged with what had formerly been the responsibility of the old County Psychopathic Hospital, becoming the new intake point for Stock State Hospital. Having planned for a small number of middle class and mildly to moderately disturbed clients, staff and administrators at X were now confronted with a flood of severely disturbed lower class clients, and they went through a painful period of reorientation and readjustment with much staff turnover. During this period, department officials were too busy with the problems of X to intervene to any significant extent in the affairs of the old Blank Park Center.

Busy or not, the statewide reorganization effected by the new administration had placed officials at X in a hierarchically superior position to those at the Blank Park Center. Becuase X was a "zone center"[1] and the Blank Park Center was not, the old institution lost its autonomy and became subordinate, first in name and later in fact, to the newer one. This subordination took a curious form. The crisis forced upon X by the sudden influx of initially unwanted "bad clients" was eventually resolved by a kind of conversion experience. Officials and staff who remained at X embraced the new clients, became advocates of new methods of treating them and of a particular brand of community mental health. Shortly thereafter, they began sending missionaries to preach the new gospel at the old Blank Park Center.

CONSULTANTS, THE SYSTEM, AND THE CENTER

Initially, the missionaries functioned like consultants, and they will hereafter be referred to as the new consultants, although they often had different titles. Consultation as such was not new to the Blank Park Center; it had long had an extensive consultation program, not from but to its staff, and long-standing problems with it. Briefly, the trouble was that the old consultants were primarily classical conservatives, psychoanalysts who were, for the most part, in the peculiar position of having higher status and less knowledge than the staff. Ironically, they had higher status because they were presumed to know more and often they did, in particular areas. The catch, of course, was that their knowledge usually derived from work with an altogether different client population. Generally, their experience, while lengthy and intensive, had been largely confined to work with middle and upper class neurotics and their experience with the poor and the psychotic was extremely limited. Yet, it was precisely with regard to these latter clients that they were now required to give expert advice.

Usually, they were aware that treatment as they practiced it would not work with the majority of these new clients, but they were not aware of or adept at modifications which would make it work nor, because of their strong vested interest in a particular treatment technique, were they deeply interested in exploring the possibilities for such modifications. Instead, they

---

[1]Ironically, the zone center form of organization was touted by its originators as a form of decentralization in which a regional authority is set up to mediate between local institutions and the central state authority. In point of fact, however, as long as zone center leadership is representative of and responsive to central authority superiors and not to local institutions and communities, decentralization exists only in a geographic and not in an organizational sense, and top-down orders rather than two-way communication is still the order of the day, only at closer quarters and, hence, more oppressively.

tended to handle the resultant problems by deciding, usually after a long and involved discussion of dynamics, either that the clients in question were untreatable or that they were suitable only for supportive therapy, without any real clarification of what that meant or of what, in particular, was to be supported.

With treatment recommendations as crude, unuseful, and unvarying as these as the predictable outcome of most such dynamic discussions, the discussions themselves began to seem, to many of the therapists at the center, more like time-wasting pomposity than profundity. Therapists concerned with treating needy clients and not with abstract theorizing or professional "climbing" often became impatient, particularly when they not only knew more about what could be done with certain types of clients but also knew which staff members were particularly skilled at meeting the needs of particular sorts of clients.

This bad situation was made worse by the fact that the classical conservative consultants were not regarded by the administration and did not regard themselves as serving a temporary function. Success was not judged by the speed and efficacy with which a consultant could train people so that they no longer needed his help. On the contrary, the usual goal was to develop a permanent personal following, forever dependent upon the forever superior wisdom of the consultant. Some therapists did, of course, welcome such a relationship and members of this minority tended to establish rather similar relations with the few "good clients" they could garner, judging the success of each endeavor not by its outcome but by its length and "depth." Most therapists, however, rejected such consultation, either from the outset or after a period of time, and there was continual tension between administrators trying to Russian-volunteer an audience for the consultants and staff members trying to be left alone to do their work in peace.

When the new crop of consultants arrived they entered as additions to rather than as replacements for the old crop. And indeed, they were not replacements but a different breed, taking a whole new tack. The new consultants were primarily young turks who saw themselves as community mental health advocates, and their approach was the opposite of that taken by the analytic consultants. Whereas the conservative analysts tended to cling to classical therapeutic procedures and to reject new clients, the turks tended to accept the new clients and to reject the old procedures. Convinced, albeit without experience or evidence, that the poor and the psychotic could be reached and helped, they were enthusiastic about various new ways of doing this.

Even from so brief and oversimplified a description as this, it is apparent that the young turks had much in common with the dedicated therapists of the Blank Park Center, hereafter referred to as "the old radicals," since both shared a genuine concern for and a relative optimism about the treatment potential of traditionally rejected clients. Thus, the new consultants entered with a natural basis from which to elicit the sympathy and support of old radicals. The institution they entered was badly in need of new consultants to help the staff supplement its own effective but limited approach and to turn the Blank Park Center into a truly comprehensive and creative center for social as well as for psychological change. Unfortunately for everyone concerned, and especially for the people of Blank Park, this did not happen. Instead, despite their common concern, the young turks and the old radicals failed to make common cause and wound up working at cross purposes.

On the surface, there were two main reasons for this negative outcome. The first had to do with the attitude of the young turks toward individual therapy and the second with their attitudes toward the old radicals who practiced it at the center. With regard to the latter point, because the notion that the poor and the psychotic are treatable was a relatively new idea to most of the turks and because the intellectual justification for their superordinate status rested upon this newness, they tended to assume that it was new to all professionals. Thus, when they attempted to convey their "news," they frequently sounded like missionaries bringing Christianity to the heathens, an approach which may have been more-or-less appropriate when addressing conservative analytic colleagues or reactionary staff members at typical poor peoples' institutions but was quite inappropriate and, often, downright offensive for an audience dominated by old radicals.[2] Often, the old radicals had been working on the problem of creating rapport and establishing means of communication which circumvented class barriers for a decade or more. With this background, a less than optimal salary scale, and a surfeit of disproportionately well-paid and rather irrelevant consultants, they were unlikely to respond without ambivalence to what looked to them like a group of self-important Johnny-come-latelys.

Nonetheless, if this were the only difficulty, it could probably have been resolved. No one likes to be underestimated, misjudged, and condescended to, but all other things being equal, the staff might have been pleased that at last people in positions of power shared their goals, and they might have worked to make the new consultants aware of this to attain recognition for what they were doing. However, all other things were not equal. In particular, there were real disagreements about methods.

[2] A typical incident involved a lecture delivered at a specially called meeting by a consultant who urged the assembled professional and nonprofessional staff of the Blank Park Center to go out and visit the homes of the poor to see what their lives were really like, a suggestion that fell rather flat since most of the professionals had already spent years doing just that. The other half of the audience, the nonprofessionals, did not need to "visit" such homes either; most of them had grown up in them and many still lived there.

The treatment methods favored by the center's radicals tended to be highly individualized, empathically developed modifications within the conventional two-person framework. Because they felt that they had managed to achieve their goals within that framework, they were understandably loath to abandon it. Usually, however, they were pressured to do just that, and the new forms of treatment favored by the turks were presented as replacements for rather than additions to the old methods. Insult was added to injury when the staff were asked to assume the role of beginners to learn new ways of achieving their own goals without receiving any recognition for the fact that they not only held those goals long before the arrival of the turks but also achieved them without using "turkish" methods. Understandably, many refused to play the game by these rules and, inevitably, many superior players were thereby lost.

Even under more ideal circumstances, however, the new methods championed by the turks were not geared to excite the enthusiasm of either the radicals or the community they served. In the psychological realm, the turks rejected individual therapy simply because they were convinced, without study and despite protests from staff, that it did not and could not work with nonclassical clients. What they substituted for it was hardly revolutionary. Group, family, and crisis therapy were the methods they most frequently favored. Ironically, none of these methods were new to the staff; all had been in flexible use at the center for many years as optional alternatives and/or additions to individual therapy. None, however, had previously been seen as panaceas which were inevitably superior to one-to-one treatment, and none had been bureaucratized into formal courses and discrete programs.

Similarly, in the social realm, the turks and the administration they represented rejected primary prevention, a strategy which necessarily involved social change. Instead, they favored indiscriminate consultation to and for institutions in, but not of, the ghetto. They did this without first establishing a solid democratic basis for such consultation by conferring seriously and at length with indigenous and representative community people to ascertain their views, wants, and needs. Instead, after a few perfunctory nods, the turks bypassed the community and sent its bureaucrats out to establish rapport with other bureaucrats, judging their success not by the response of the community, which usually varied from indifference to irritation, but by the response of other bureaucrats. Since these other bureaucrats were also more eager to plan for the community than to contact it and to create real possibilities for planning with it, their response was generally favorable. Needless to say, such consultation inevitably focused upon the deficiencies of the poor and the disturbed and not on the deficiencies of the society that created them, many of which were exemplified by these very bureaucrats and their very bureaucratic institutions.

Not surprisingly, most of the old radicals saw the new work opportunities created by the turks as meaningless and the initial conditions for participation in them as demeaning. As a result, few of them participated fully, some were peripherally involved, and the majority ignored them entirely, or tried to. Rejection of the new consultants, however, proved much more difficult than it had been with the old consultants.

In a practical if not in a moral or intellectual sense, the new consultants had more to offer than did the old ones. Generally, the old consultants were outside the system with a circumscribed position and no particular leverage in it. The new consultants, however, tended to be new Department of Mental Health employees with close ties to and considerable leverage and backing from the central administration. Empowered to change the internal structure of the institution and to mete out position, power, and higher salaries as well as more evanescent rewards like prestige, they made little impact on the community but did gradually make a strong impact on the staff, an impact that created deep divisions among staff members.

All of this proved but a preamble to later events. The Blank Park Center was distressed but not disintegrating as long as the influence from the growing hierarchy above it took the form of consultation. Consultants, after all, have other things to occupy their time, and thus their influence, while often powerful, is seldom constant or pervasive. This was particularly true in this situation because the consultants were mainly interested in their home base and seat of power—usually at X—which was considered by far the more important of the two institutions. As a result, their interest in the Blank Park Center was, if no longer peripheral, at least still secondary.

A FAILED COMMUNITY MENTAL HEALTH EFFORT

Eventually, however, the threat of ghetto riots and the encouragement of federal funds for community mental health programs aimed at the urban poor encouraged department officials to focus their full attention on the centrally located Blank Park Center and the ghetto community which surrounded it. Armed with some $2.8 million in federal funds earmarked for a community mental health program in Blank Park, zone officials took direct control of the center and began reorganizing it in earnest.

Despite the dissatisfaction, distrust, and division among old and new professional staff members, consultants, and administrators, the need for a more intensive and varied program in Blank Park and for constructive use of the large sums of money made available for that purpose was so great and so apparent that significant numbers of professionals from all camps made an earnest, last-ditch effort to co-operate with one another in order to get the Blank Park Program off the ground. Co-operation, cash, and fanfare notwithstanding, the program proved impossible to launch.

Individual therapists may relate to individual clients, faulty administration or no, but mental health institutions relate to communities—and there, administration is crucial. Just as an individual therapist cannot truly help his clients with their problems until he has achieved some insight into his own, so a mental health institution cannot truly help a community with its social problems without first recognizing its own. Governed by a state administration which, however benevolent its intentions, was intrinsically authoritarian and administered by officals who were neither representative of nor responsive to the needs and wishes of its staff or the community around it, the Blank Park Center was a sick institution. Its sickness showed up with painful clarity when it attempted to relate as an institution to a community, as shown by the events that took place during the week in which Martin Luther King was murdered.

While attempting to launch the Blank Park Project, a much touted and heavily funded community mental health program ostensibly aimed at helping poor Blacks, the State Department of Mental Health was paying very low wages to poor Blacks in its own employ, a number of whom lived in Blank Park. The irony of this was not apparent to department officials but it was to many members of the American Federation of State, County, and Municipal Employees, which finally decided to strike against the department on Thursday, April 4, 1968.

The union membership was made up largely of nonprofessionals—clerks, hospital attendants, dietary and laundry workers, and maintenance men. Most of these people were Black, many of them had ten or more years of service with the state, and none of them was rich. Although the mental health budget in the state had been greatly increased in the recent past, thanks largely to the enlightened leadership of Governor Oak, the union members were not asking to become rich: one of the basic financial demands of the union was a $15.00 a month raise for employees earning *less* than $4,800 a year. In addition, they made a number of nonfiscal demands which were, in effect, a request for a modest degree of participatory democracy.

The department responded to the strike by seeking an injunction against the strikers and by ordering professional staff members to act as strikebreakers. The day the strike began, the department's director issued a memo advising that failure to work as directed would be considered insubordination and would constitute grounds for dismissal. Despite this intimidation, union members continued to picket, and at the Blank Park Center, large numbers of nonunion professionals declined to cross their co-workers' picket-lines. On Friday, April 5, departmental strategy shifted. The Blank Park Center, an exclusively outpatient facility, was ordered closed, and its professional staff was ordered to deploy itself to various inpatient units throughout the state in order to meet "emergency" needs there. Staff members who crossed picket-lines at several of these hospitals,[3] not out of lack of sympathy for the strikers nor out of fear of department reprisals, but out of concern, lest helpless inpatients be deprived of food, shelter, and elementary safety and comfort, found that no discernible emergency existed. Some left in disgust, others tried to find some useful service to perform, and a few wasted the day on such nonessential assignments as sheet-folding and coffee-drinking.

Meanwhile, the westside ghetto, initially immobilized by the murder of Dr. Martin Luther King on Thursday, the day the strike began, was coming to violent life. Rioting, looting, and especially arson began on Friday, increased on Saturday, and by Sunday, as a result of numerous raging fires, many westside residents were without food, shelter, or elementary safety and comfort. Many of the victims were Blank Parkers, some were Blank Park Center clients, and the center was in an ideal position to provide emergency aid for them. Located in the heart of the westside ghetto with a large physical plant, a fully equipped kitchen, its own body of experienced and happily unarmed guards, and a genuine eagerness to help on the part of the majority of its staff members, professional and nonprofessional, union and nonunion alike, the center remained closed.

The Director of the Department of Mental Health met with the director and deputy director of Zone X, which includes the Blank Park Center, the X Center, and Stock State Hospital (the last-named official was also acting as superintendent of the center and director of the Blank Park Program), and agreed it would be "too dangerous" to reopen the center. A meeting of the executive committee of the Blank Park Center was then called, the decision to keep the center closed was presented as a *fait accompli*, and, with one dissenting voice—a social worker's—the committee acquiesced. No member of the Blank Park community and no official member of the Blank Park Project staff was consulted, and protests were to no avail. The center remained closed Sunday, Monday, and Tuesday. It finally reopened on Wednesday, April 10, but its night clinic remained closed. Vehement objections from staff finally led to its reopening the week of April 15.

Administration officials seemed genuinely surprised at the profound grief, anger, and shame of the center's staff over this chain of events. Apparently they had not anticipated that staff members might have strong feelings about providing service when it was most needed in spite of the possible danger involved. Was the staff's courage quixotic? Of course, no one can be certain what would have happened had the center been opened during the crisis, but it is a fact that a number of other social agencies in and near the riot-stricken

[3]The feeling among many union members against what they considered scab labor by professionals from outside their institutions ran so high that at some locales police protection was required for those who crossed the picket lines.

area did function during this period, including the Blank Park Project's city-sponsored sister agency. Staff members at these other facilities helped and were not hurt, while the Blank Park Center, the institution with the largest staff and the lion's share of the resources, did nothing.

Several staff members, including the present author, resigned in protest. Others began to drift away, demoralization increased, and eventually, the administration came up with a new plan which involved transferring most of the remaining staff to other facilities, some already existing and some newly created. Thus, the Blank Park Center ceased to be a major center for psychological change and failed to become a major center for social change. Until that unhappy outcome, however, it provided, among other things, an unusually appropriate research setting in which to test the efficacy of psychotherapy for poor and severely disturbed clients. It is on that research that the next sections of this book will focus.

AN ANALYSIS OF THE FAILURE

Before doing that, however, it seems worthwhile to try to summarize the basic reason for the failure of the initial Blank Park Program and to tease out its implications, particularly because outcomes like this are not unique. Community mental health failures are, in fact, common enough to have caused several prominent champions of the "third revolution" (e.g., Albee, 1965; Smith, 1968) to express deep concern lest the whole movement suffer paralysis before its promise can be realized. These authors argue that continuing adherence to the medical model of illness and treatment is the chief threat to the health of the movement and that its recovery and progress would be relatively uncomplicated if this threat were removed.

My own view is that the basic problem is deeper and more general than that and that, as a consequence, a more radical solution is required. With regard to the example presented here, each reader may judge for himself, but for me, the implication is that systems and institutions with authoritarian structures cannot effectively mobilize the therapeutic potential of any community, not even of their own, and that this is true regardless of whether the institutions in question are medical, educational, recreational or what-have-you.

In the present example, while a tradition of arbitary medical dominance initially contributed to the organizational and administrative difficulties of the Blank Park Center, it was hardly responsible for the ultimate failure of the Blank Park Program. In fact, the new state administration was markedly more liberal than its predecessors in meting out positions of power to non-medical professionals and has been, in some quarters, harshly and unfairly criticized for doing so. The real problem, it seems, is that although individuals in new categories acquired power, there was no real change in the nature of that power because the system remained an authoritarian one.[4] As a result, new officials within the system tended to behave like old ones, regardless of their professional category. As representatives of a centralized, hierarchical bureaucracy, jealous of its authority and eager to increase and extend it, they did not favor participatory democracy for professional staff members, nonprofessional staff members, or the client community.

With regard to the future, the promise of community mental health for Blank Park and areas like it still exists, and officials in such areas frequently have good intentions and substantial resources. Can these—will these—be used effectively if there is no major change in administrative structures? Many people, professionals and politicians alike, seem to think so. In Midwest State, as in other states and places, it is easier to hang the man than the system, and the future is likely to bring repeated shifts in personnel at the tops of heavily centralized, hierarchical, and authoritarian pyramids. Those who feel that such shifts will suffice seem to assume that events and behaviors like those involved in the sequence described above reflect peculiar personal failings of specific administrators rather than typical responses of average professionals in authoritarian systems. Perhaps, but if so, we are a badly flawed group and, despite the heterogeneity of our characters, our flaws seem remarkably homogeneous.

To take only the most obvious and factual of examples, consider the paradox of attempting to fight poverty and poverty-related conditions predisposing to psychological difficulties and deficits while, at the same time, creating and maintaining those very conditions by underpaying and ignoring the nonprofessional employees of the poverty-fighting agencies. Perhaps this obvious paradox should have been apparent to officials of the Midwest State Department of Mental Health from the outset. Perhaps, if they were more sensitive and more responsive individuals, it would have been. Yet, their failure to recognize and resolve the paradox is hardly atypical.

Community mental health agencies are generally government, hospital, and/or academic institutions or, at least, closely related to one or more such institutions. In all three of these institutions, nonprofessional employees are often poorly paid, poorly protected, and poorly treated. Martin Luther King died trying to organize government employees in Memphis, and his successor, Ralph Abernathy, risked his life to organize hospital workers in Charleston. If we, as professionals, cannot relate constructively to one another and to the poor within our own institutions, what promise can we hold out for the poor outside our walls?

---

[4]More specifically, it shifted from a traditional authoritarian system to a bureaucratic authoritarian system, a shift which is taking place in mental health institutions all across the nation. See chapter 11 for a more detailed analysis of bureaucratic organization and its implications.

CHAPTER **3**

the design
of the study

RESEARCH RESOURCES AND RESISTANCE AT THE CENTER

Until the problems detailed in the preceding chapter submerged it, the Blank Park Center provided a fairly ideal setting for the present research because of the characteristics of both its therapist and its client population. With regard to therapists, the center contained a sizeable group of well-trained and experienced professionals, many of whom *chose* to work frequently with poor and/or psychotic clients. With these therapists, it seemed possible to make a fairer test of the efficacy of psychotherapy for such clients than had heretofore been made. Because this group of therapists was quite heterogeneous with regard to therapeutic orientation—almost every major school of therapy was represented—it seemed probable that the results of such a test would have wider than usual applicability. Moreover, since the center had both a psychology internship program and a social-work field-work program, the possibility of obtaining comparative data on the results of therapy achieved by inexperienced therapists also existed.

With regard to clients, the center provided a fairly ideal setting because it had large numbers of extremely poor and grossly psychotic clients who were being treated on a strictly voluntary, outpatient basis. In addition, it also had an adequate supply of middle class and nonpsychotic clients and a sprinkling of upper class clients.[1] Thus it seemed possible to obtain comparative data on the relative efficacy of psychotherapy with different types of clients as well as with different types of therapists and to explore the interaction between

---

[1] Because of its easily accessible, central location just outside the downtown area, the center drew its clientele from all parts of Stock City and not just from the Blank Park area.

28

client factors, therapist factors, time factors, and outcome in a more differentiated way than had heretofore been attempted.

Before any of this rich research potential could be tapped, however, it was necessary to elicit therapist co-operation—no easy task for a newcomer to the center whose specialty was clinical research. For one thing, the center was already surfeited with newcomers touting a variety of professional products (see chapter 2), and for another, like the majority of clinicians everywhere and despite obvious need and constant exhortation (e.g., Glover, 1952; Raimy, 1950; Ward and Richards, 1968), most therapists at the center had little interest in research. In fact, the image of research current at the center was an extremely negative one. There was a widespread feeling that research in general and quantification in particular was at best irrelevant and at worst antithetical to the clinical enterprise. Among social workers especially, this feeling typically seemed to have originated in a brief, unsatisfactory, and unpleasant exposure to research in graduate school and to have been intensified by later experiences with what might be described as bureaucratic research.

The phrase bureaucratic research is used to designate studies with one or more of the following characteristics: (a) they are designed by distant officials for purposes that are not made clear to participants; (b) no attempt is made to explore researchable clinical questions which are of concern to participants; (c) participation is mandatory, not voluntary; (d) professionals are required to perform time-consuming clerical tasks for the researchers; (e) professionals are expected to make alterations in their methods of treatment without regard to their views on how this might affect their clients; (f) no adequate channels are provided to enable staff to question, criticize, or suggest changes in the research procedures; (g) no additional compensatory help, time, money, or stimulation is provided for participants; (h) no meaningful feedback on the results of the research is given.

In this project, a sustained effort was made to change the image of research held by the therapists of the center and to provide a basis for a mutually satisfying and productive collaboration with them. To do this, some fifteen months were spent in studying, observing, and informally interviewing staff members. During this period, efforts were directed toward designing a research proposal that would be meaningful to the staff and to their clients, as well as scientifically valid. With a tentative research plan formulated, the next step was to devise a vehicle that would allow staff members to reevaluate their views on the role of research in the mental health field, to reconsider their own attitudes towards it, and to examine the specific research project in which they were ultimately being invited to participate. To this end, the psychotherapy research workshop was designed.

THE PSYCHOTHERAPY WORKSHOP

Intended as a training as well as a research and recruitment vehicle, the workshop was formally initiated in January 1967. Participation in it was on a strictly voluntary basis and heavy emphasis was placed on the fact that the training to be provided was not aimed at turning clinicians into researchers. Participants were told that in the workshop director's view, all clinicians did not need to become researchers, any more than all physicians did, but that because psychosocial research might prove as important to clinicians as biomedical research has been to physicians, it was important to help clinicians become intelligent research critics, consumers, and collaborators. Thus, senior therapists who participated in the workshop were not to be viewed as novice researchers but as experts, learning about the role other experts could play in facilitating their joint goals and exploring possibilities for maximizing their effectiveness through collaboration with such experts.

In its initial phase, the workshop took the form of an advanced post graduate seminar for senior clinicians, complete with a course outline and list of readings (see Appendix A). During this phase, the focus was on exploring such issues as the lack of communication between scientists and humanists generally, its social and psychological bases, and its implications in the mental health field. With this background in mind, the focus shifted to a consideration of new trends in the mental health field, the conflicts they produce for clinicians, and the role of research, actual and potential, in both creating and resolving these conflicts.

Next, the focus shifted to discussion of the specific research proposal with which this book is concerned. Discussion centered first on the situation at the Blank Park Center. Therapists expressed their awareness of the low esteem in which their work was held by the new administrators of the system in which they worked and their concern that these administrators would eventually make it impossible for them to continue with their work by gradually eliminating individual therapy from the list of legitimate programs at the center.[2] Some therapists expressed deep cynicism about administration motives, arguing that the changes administrators seemed determined to force through had no basis in concern for the welfare of clients but resulted solely from a vested interest in change for the sake of personal aggrandizement. This view was usually predicated on the conviction that individual psychotherapy was of obvious benefit to significant numbers of clients, including severely disturbed lower class ones, and that administrators knew this but did not

---

[2] Actually, individual therapy never really constituted a discrete, formal, properly packaged, and hierarchically organized program at the center. It was just something that most people did because they and their clients chose to do it and felt it was beneficial. As such, it never had true bureaucratic legitimacy but was now in danger of achieving true bureaucratic illegitimacy.

care. In the workshop, it was suggested that while it was possible to develop a vested interest in change as well as in the status quo, administrators might really not know that individual therapy was effective with severely disturbed lower class clients and that indeed its effectiveness was not an established fact but open to serious question.

Workshoppers were told that while the researcher personally shared their convictions about therapeutic efficacy and would, in fact, be a therapist in the study herself, both she and they might prove to be wrong. The question was whether we were willing to put our convictions to a test, one that might produce results favorable to our convictions but might also produce results unfavorable to them. It was explained that the researcher would have no more control over the final outcome of the study than other participants because all subjective scoring of the test data to be collected would be done by neutral outsiders, unaware of our personal hopes and fears and of our evaluations of the cases they considered.

The research proposal itself was presented as an intensive, complex, and multidimensional study of outcome in psychotherapy and of the relation of client factors, therapist factors, and time factors to outcome. It was explained that as such, the study included a large number of hypotheses specific to each group of factors studied and to the interrelations between factors within and between groups, but that all of these were subhypotheses which could be subsumed under the one main hypothesis of the study: that individual psychotherapy, under appropriate conditions, could be an effective method of helping not only those classical clients traditionally served by this method but also those nonclassical clients who have become the main focus of community mental health endeavors.

Workshop participants were told that in addition to meeting the usual scientific standards, this proposal was designed to satisfy the following four criteria: (1) maximal relevance to the specific professional interests and concerns of its participants; (2) minimal interference with the treatment process and individual style of treatment of each of its participants; (3) maximal benefit for every client in the research; and (4) minimal extra work for participants and no purely clerical or other work of the sort that could be performed by less highly trained people. Participants were encouraged to evaluate the research in terms of these four criteria and to make a commitment to participate in it only after they were fully informed about every detail of the research procedure as it affected them and their clients and only if they were fully satisfied that it met the four criteria outlined above.

THE THERAPIST AND CLIENT SAMPLES

Because the general research strategy involved the intensive study of a relatively small number of cases and because more therapists volunteered to participate than it was practical to include,[3] research participation was limited to therapists in the adult clinic of the Blank Park Center; selection among volunteers was made on the basis of one of the therapist factors to be studied, experience. Two groups of therapists were involved: a highly experienced and a highly inexperienced group. For the experienced group, the criterion was a minimum of five years of experience as a therapist, during which time a minimum of fifty clients had been treated, at least one-third of whom had been psychotic and one-third lower class. For the inexperienced group, the criterion was trainee status as either a social-work field-work student or a psychology intern. The final sample entering cases in the research consisted of fifteen therapists, eight experienced and seven inexperienced. Data on the age, sex, race, professional affiliation, and therapeutic orientation of these fifteen therapists is summarized in the table below.

Inspection of Table 1 indicates that the fifteen therapists in this study are a highly varied group in terms of therapeutic orientation, using eight different labels to describe themselves. In terms of professional affiliation, there is a

Table 1
Therapist Characteristics: General Description

Groups	Age	Sex	Race	Professional Affiliation	Therapeutic Orientation
Experienced Therapists $n = 8$	$\overline{X} = 40.1$ Range: 27–54	5 F 3 M	8 W 0 B	3 Psychologists 5 Social workers	2 Psychoanalytic 2 Interpersonal 1 Client-centered 3 Other*
Inexperienced Therapists $n = 7$	$\overline{X} = 28.1$ Range: 23–34	3 F 4 M	7 W 0 B	3 Psychologists 4 Social workers	2 Psychoanalytic 2 Ego psychology 1 Client-centered 2 Other*
Totals $n = 15$	$\overline{X} = 34.5$ Range: 23–54	8 F 7 M	15 W 0 B	6 Psychologists 9 Social workers	4 Psychoanalytic 2 Interpersonal 2 Client-centered 2 Ego psychology 5 Other*

*"Other" orientations listed by experienced therapists were Existential, Experiential, and Jungian; by inexperienced therapists, Existential and Learning Theory.

[3] Reliance on volunteers does not automatically consign one to the acceptance of a nonrepresentative sample. In this setting, for example, the most experienced group of therapists were the supervising social workers and all but two of them agreed to participate in the study and to encourage, but not to require, their fieldwork students to do so. Co-operation from the students of these therapists was 100 percent: there were four such students and all four of them participated in the study. Similarly, the three psychology interns in the study constituted a 100 percent sample of that group.

slight preponderance of social workers over psychologists, a fairly even division between men and women, and uniformity of race—all of the therapists were white. Further inspection indicates that the two groups of therapists are reasonably well matched on all characteristics except age: as would be expected, experienced therapists are generally older than inexperienced ones.

These fifteen therapists entered a total of forty-five cases in the research. The method of case selection reflected a desire to make the study as naturalistic and unartificial as possible. Therapists were asked to make no changes in their methods of case selection for the research but to accept cases for treatment in their usual way and at their usual rate and to enter every client with whom they made a therapeutic contract into the study from the time they agreed to participate until the time they had completed three cases for the study, or until data collection ceased, whichever point came first. The importance of their accepting every client they would ordinarily accept and of their including all such clients without exception in the research was heavily stressed, and the therapists clearly understood that rejection of high-risk cases would defeat the whole purpose of the research. To discourage further any possible tendency to bias the selection of research cases by eliminating "bad clients," therapists were also told that all drop-outs could be replaced and that no onus would be attached to the number of drop-outs a therapist had. At the point when data collection ceased, each of the fifteen therapists had entered at least one case into the study and some had entered as many as five cases to make up the final sample of forty-five clients.

These forty-five clients are much too heterogeneous for any facile generalizations about typical problems. They included a Black Muslim incapacitated by an illness that had no physical basis, a suicidal prostitute, a welfare mother who abused her children, an unwed pregnant teenager who was withdrawn and hallucinating, a man trying to pick up the pieces of his life after his tenth hospitalization, a woman who had struggled free of crushing financial burdens to pursue her lifetime ambition and then found herself paralyzed by depression, a man who realized his lifetime ambition and then found that his achievement made his life a misery, a child molester fearful of the police, a graduate student unable to complete his dissertation, a school teacher struggling to establish a satisfactory heterosexual relationship, a factory worker who felt that people on television were ridiculing him and broadcasting his deficiencies, and so on.

The one thing all of these people had in common was a sense that something inside themselves prevented them from struggling effectively to realize their full psychosocial potential. None of them discounted real and often terrible external obstacles to such a realization, but all of them were dissatisfied with their ability to mobilize their own resources in the struggle against external obstacles. In the next chapter, the phrase "psychosocial potential" will be defined, and in later chapters, these clients will be redescribed in terms of where they started out and where they ended up along a scale of psychosocial potential and in terms of other more conventional client measures. For the present, however, a brief presentation of some general descriptive characteristics will have to suffice. These characteristics are summarized in Table 2 below, which includes data on the age, sex, race, marital status, and treatment history of the forty-five clients who participated in this study.

Table 2 is particularly interesting for what it reveals about the previous treatment history of clients in this sample. Many studies of psychotherapy automatically exclude clients who have had prior treatment, in the interests of a laboratory-like purity. No such attempt was made in the present study with its naturalistic orientation, and the results seem worthy of special note. In this sample, two-thirds of the clients have had some type of treatment before. Thus, if the results of this study have any generality at all, the purist approach may seriously reduce the relevance of findings by eliminating the typical client from consideration.

Table 2
Client Characteristics: General Description

Groups	Age	Sex	Race	Marital Status*	Previous Treatment	Concurrent Treatment
Experienced Therapists' Clients n = 24	$\overline{X}$ = 28.5 Range: 19–42	19 F 5 M	16 B 8 W	4 M 10 D–S 10 S	7 None 5 Inpatient 10 Outpatient 2 Both	17 None 7 Drug therapy 0 Drug & activities therapy
Inexperienced Therapists' Clients n = 21	$\overline{X}$ = 33.5 Range: 16–57	10 F 11 M	7 B 14 W	8 M 4 D–S 9 S	8 None 6 Inpatient 3 Outpatient 4 Both	11 None 7 Drug therapy 3 Drug & activities therapy
Totals n = 45	$\overline{X}$ = 30.9 Range: 16–57	29 F 16 M	23 B 22 W	12 M 14 D–S 19 S	15 None 11 Inpatient 13 Outpatient 6 Both	28 None 14 Drug therapy 3 Drug & activities therapy

*M = married
D–S = divorced or separated
S = single

With regard to generality, the present sample is limited because it contains a higher than usual number of severely disturbed and lower class clients (see Part 3 for precise figures), but additional data on the personal treatment history of the therapists[4] in this study—a nonpsychotic middle and upper

---

[4]The phrase "personal treatment history of the therapists" is used, here and throughout the book, to refer to a therapist's experience(s) *as a client*. See chapters 6 and 9 for a fuller discussion of this issue.

class group—indicates that many of them have also had more than one course of treatment. Results of another study of therapists using a much larger and more generally representative sample drawn from different sections of the country and including psychiatrists as well as psychologists and social workers (Henry, Sims, and Spray, 1971) also indicate that multiple treatment experiences are hardly exceptional. Thus, the prevalent conception of therapy as a once-and-for-all, make-or-break operation may be quite erroneous.

The other information in Table 2 might be briefly summarized as follows: the typical client in this sample is an unmarried person in his late twenties or early thirties who has had previous treatment but is not receiving any concurrent treatment other than psychotherapy. In the sample as a whole, females outnumber males and Blacks outnumber whites. There are, however, some fairly marked differences between clients of experienced and inexperienced therapists. With regard to the four characteristics which are conventionally expected to have some bearing on outcome, experienced therapists' clients have the advantage on two measures. They tend to be slightly younger and to have been hospitalized less frequently as a result of their psychological difficulties. On the other hand, inexperienced therapists' clients are also ahead on two conventional prognostic measures: more of them have managed to get and stay married, and more of them are receiving some form of help in addition to psychotherapy—either drug or drug plus activities therapy.

The other two client characteristics listed, sex and race, are not generally considered to be prognostic characteristics in and of themselves, but it is interesting to note that experienced therapists in this sample have more female and more Black clients. These findings become more meaningful if they are considered in a pair context. Female therapists predominate over males in the experienced group, and the reverse is true in the inexperienced group, but all therapists are white. Thus, same-sex, client-therapist pairs predominate for both groups, but cross-racial pairs predominate only in the experienced therapists group.

In considering the possible prognostic significance of these findings, it should be noted that many contemporary observers, professional and nonprofessional, Black and white, feel that cross-racial contacts are more likely to generate tension, distrust, and distance than are contacts between persons of the same race. If this is true, then experienced therapists in this study would be at a distinct disadvantage in this respect. Again, however, potential advantages and disadvantages between groups of therapists in this sample seem to balance out. Previous research (e.g., Cartwright and Lerner, 1963) suggests that experienced therapists may do better with same-sex clients, whereas inexperienced therapists may do better with opposite sex clients. If this is so, then the experienced therapists have a compensating advantage over the inexperienced ones.

THE RESEARCH DESIGN

The research was deliberately designed to be as naturalistic as possible: relevance to the rich variety inherent in real life settings and situations was the guiding principle throughout. Thus, heterogeneity in the client sample, obvious even from the initial, surface description presented above, was not only accepted but welcomed. The aim was to account for variance through careful measurement of multiple factors rather than to eliminate it. No client was rejected because he posed problems for the research. Clients receiving some other form of treatment concurrent with their therapy are a case in point. The obvious question raised about such clients is whether changes, if they occur, are to be attributed to psychotherapy, to the other forms of treatment (in this study, drug and/or activities therapy), or to some combination of these. Instead of handling the problem by eliminating the clients, the procedure followed here was to attempt to answer the question, insofar as it was possible, by simply comparing outcomes achieved in cases receiving psychotherapy plus additional treatment with those receiving psychotherapy alone.

To stress the fact that the study is a naturalistic one is not to imply that it lacks scientific controls. Such a sacrifice was regarded as neither desirable nor necessary. Measurement of multiple potential sources of variance in the context of a priori hypotheses was the method used to attain control without interference with or distortion of the objects of the study.

This process may best be illustrated with regard to the problem touched upon above, that of deciding whether there is likely to be a causal or merely a coincidental relationship between changes taking place in clients and the treatment or treatments which accompany them. This problem is a real one, even with clients receiving psychotherapy alone, and efforts to deal with it have usually involved the inclusion of external controls in the form of an untreated comparison group.

Unfortunately, in the area of psychotherapy research, this classical procedure often raises more problems than it solves because adequate control groups do not really exist. This is especially true when dealing with clients receiving therapy on a voluntary, outpatient basis. Those who do not need treatment are obviously noncomparable; those who do but do not voluntarily seek or accept it are, for that reason, noncomparable; and those who need and seek treatment but are made to wait before receiving it are affected by the waiting period itself and/or by the expectations engendered and the nonspecific professional attention (intake interviews, testing sessions) received during it in ways that also make them demonstrably different (e.g., Barron and Leary, 1955; Cartwright and Vogel, 1960; Endicott and Endicott, 1963; Goldstein, 1960).

The strategy of internal controls in the context of a priori hypotheses, as suggested by Imber, Nash, Frank, Stone, and Gliedman (1957) and by Waterson (1954), provides a way out of this morass. This strategy involves identifying in advance the specific factors presumed to lead to successful therapeutic outcomes and comparing cases high on those factors with cases low on those factors, predicting that the former will improve to a significantly greater extent than the latter.

In more technical terms, cases low in specific therapeutic ingredients hypothesized to be relevant to positive treatment outcome constitute the control group, and cases high in those same ingredients constitute the experimental group. This solution to the problem of controls not only insures comparability insofar as members of both groups need, want, and get psychotherapy, it also avoids making unjustified assumptions about the homogeneity of psychotherapy, focusing instead on precise and specific elements in therapy rather than on a global entity defined so loosely as to court meaninglessness. Thus, the internal control solution has the added potential advantage of teaching us not only about whether psychotherapy works, but also about why it works—vital information if we are to test, refine, and communicate our treatment methods.

In the present study, five specific therapist factors were hypothesized to contribute to successful therapeutic outcomes: experience, democratic values, concurrent and predictive empathy, and subjective expectations of success. Each of these factors was defined and measured and its influence tested; all are discussed in detail in the chapters which follow. They are simply enumerated here because the aim at this point is to give a brief overview of the study as a whole. In attempting to grasp this overview, it is important to note that the present study is as much an attempt to cast doubt on certain widely held notions as it is to provide support for other less widely held ones. Accordingly, in addition to these five major positive hypotheses, there are three main groups of negative hypotheses.

The most significant of these has to do with client factors which the present research hypothesized would not be related to successful outcome. Five basic factors are involved here. In addition to social class and severity of psychological impairment, they include measures of authoritarianism, of pretherapy Rorschach patterns, and of initial in-therapy behavior. All five of these factors are generally regarded as trustworthy prognostic elements because they have predicted therapeutic failures and rejects with consistent success in past studies. The point of hypothesizing that they will not predict outcome in the present study is not to gainsay the fact that they have done so in previous ones. Rather, it is to suggest that previous results may have stemmed from the attitudes of the therapists in those studies toward clients with such attributes and not from the attributes per se. The underlying assumption that is being tested here is that success in psychotherapy is primarily a function of therapist variables, with client variables assuming major influence on outcome only in the absence of appropriate therapeutic conditions.

If the above-listed hypotheses are borne out, it will indicate that individual psychotherapy can be an effective method of helping "bad clients" as well as "good" ones, but it will not indicate whether it is, in even the grossest sense, a practical method. This is so because rational decisions about what is practical must take some account of costs as well as of gains, and costs, in this field, are not just matters of dollars and cents but have to do with the availability of resources. Therapeutic sessions are generally referred to as "hours," and rightly so, because time is the basic thing a therapist gives his clients. It is the necessary, although obviously not the sufficient, condition for therapeutic progress. Because of manpower as well as monetary shortages, the question of how much time is needed is a vital one.

Many therapists believe that there is a strong positive relationship between treatment length and treatment outcome and that constructive changes are much more likely to occur in cases of long duration than in those of short duration. This is thought to be especially true for deep level as opposed to superficial change and for severely distrubed as opposed to mildly or moderately disturbed clients. If these assumptions are correct then, given the extent of need, programs of individual psychotherapy would be extremely impractical in the community mental health arena. In the present study, these views were assumed to be incorrect and it was hypothesized that there would be no positive relationship between either severity of disturbance or amount of improvement and treatment length, as measured by either the number of months or the number of sessions involved. If these negative hypotheses are borne out, it will not indicate that psychotherapy alone is a practical solution to community mental health problems, but it will suggest that therapy is not nearly so impractical a component for such programs as it is often assumed to be.

Finally, if therapy proves to be potentially effective and practical, then it becomes important to know which therapist factors are significant in permitting the realization of that potential and which are irrelevant. Therapist factors believed to be among the most significant have already been listed and noted as a series of positive hypotheses. There is also a third group of negative hypotheses having to do with therapist factors which other observers have regarded as significant but which were hypothesized to be irrelevant in the present study. These include the therapists' categorization as a Whitehorn-Betz type A or type B therapist, his initial subjective liking for, understanding of, and interest in each of his clients, and his self-rated appraisal of the helpfulness of his own personal treatment (his experience as a client).

In addition to these major hypotheses about client factors, therapist factors, and time factors, the study was also designed to explore a subsidiary question having to do with the relations between client and therapist goals and severity of disturbance. The study was also designed to facilitate the exploration of clients' attitudes toward treatment in general and toward time factors in treatment in particular.[5] Altogether then, the study involved some fifteen major hypotheses plus a number of minor hypotheses, subhypotheses, and special questions (see chapter 7 for a complete listing).

Before any of these hypotheses and questions could be meaningfully tested and explored, however, it was essential to find a valid measure of therapeutic outcome. The outcome problem is a stubborn, difficult, and complex one which has plagued psychotherapy research since its inception. Numerous attempts at a solution have been made and knowledgeable observers vary in their evaluation of these efforts: some regard them as totally unsuccessful and some regard them as partially successful, but very few competent observers are fully satisfied. Professional reaction to this situation has been different at different times, but in recent years, many researchers have chosen to handle the dilemma by focusing on process rather than on outcome research. Process research involves attention to what happens in therapy rather than to what happens as a result of therapy, and it has produced some very interesting data.

Unfortunately, at present, it is difficult to know just what to make of these data. Ultimately, its evaluation must depend upon its relation to outcome because, however well specified the therapeutic process may be, its usefulness—its goodness or badness, if you will—can only be judged by the results it produces. The point is clearly, if cruelly, brought home by the old gag line, "the operation was a success but the patient died." Thus, as Paul (1967), Cartwright (1968), and others have indicated, process research may be interesting and worthwhile in its own right, but it does not and cannot obviate the need for a solution to the outcome problem. In a study like the present one, no option existed. It was necessary to tackle the outcome problem head on. The result was a new measure of outcome which is described and discussed in chapters 4 and 5 and tested against a variety of criteria in chapter 8.

RESEARCH PROCEDURES

What remains to be done in this chapter is to give some overall idea of the data sources and data collection methods of this study. Briefly, data for the study consisted of test and questionnaire material collected from each client

---

[5] These data were not analyzed in time for inclusion in this book and will be reported separately.

and each therapist at pre-therapy and at post-therapy sessions, and of tape recordings of early, intermediate, and late therapy sessions for each case. More specifically, the test battery for clients included the following items:

1. A modified Q-sort Self-description
2. A form of the F-scale
3. The Rorschach
4. A 10-card TAT consisting of six of Murray's original cards plus four new cards designed for this study
5. A client goal selection form (used only at pre-therapy)
6. A client outcome rating form (used only at post-therapy).

Data collected from therapists included the following items:

1. An extended self-description form
2. The Lorr form of the Whitehorn-Betz A-B Scale
3. A specially designed test of professional attitudes
4. Two independent measures of empathic ability at pre-therapy and at post-therapy
5. A client description and goal selection form
6. A therapist's outcome rating form
7. A therapy attendance form
8. Tape recordings of therapy sessions.[6]

Each of the above listed tests and measures, and the scoring and categorization systems derived from them, are discussed in detail in the chapters which follow; new forms devised for the study are reproduced in Appendix B. For now, it is enough to note that in addition to providing a wealth of descriptive data on each client and each therapist in the study, the data sources outlined above provided the basis for four independent measures of outcome, five main measures of client factors, ten main measures of therapist factors, and two objective measures of time factors in treatment. With all of these data, it was hoped that it would be possible to specify with some degree of precision what sorts of clients might be helped by what sorts of therapists under what conditions and in what period of time. Particularly, it was hoped that it would be possible to learn whether "bad clients," those who score poorly on any or all of the prognostic measures used to define them, are really untreatable or simply require therapists who are more experienced (in a task-specific as well as a general sense) and skilled and who bring more constructive attitudes to the task.

Finally, the test batteries were constructed, ordered, and administered in ways that were intended to make them as useful, interesting, and non-threatening to participants as possible. For example, therapists were asked to

---

[6]Therapists were asked to tape any one of the first five sessions and every tenth session thereafter. A shortage of tape recorders obviated the possibility of tighter controls here, e.g., insisting that the first tape always be of the first session.

refer their clients for initial testing only after a clear therapeutic contract[7] had been made so that no client need fear that test results might lead to the rejection of his treatment application. All testing was done by the same person (the investigator) and was presented to the client as an attempt to help him clarify his own feelings and aspirations, as well as to contribute to knowledge in the area. To dissuade clients from the widely held notion that testing is an effort to strip away defenses and expose them as wholly inadequate, inferior, and/or evil beings, the initial test in the client battery at both pre- and post-therapy, the modified Q-sort Self-description, specifically asked the client to pay as much attention to those self-attributes which he regarded with satisfaction as to those he regarded with dissatisfaction. Succeeding tasks progressively helped him to focus on first his general attitudes and beliefs (the F Scale), his internal images and associations (the Rorschach), his interpersonal perceptions (the first part of the TAT), and his attitudes toward and goals in treatment (the specially designed second part of the TAT and the goal selection form at pre-therapy or the outcome rating form at post-therapy).

Both clients and therapists were encouraged to offer feedback to the investigator on their feelings about the tests, the tester, and the process of testing and to make whatever comments and criticisms occurred to them as freely as possible either orally or in writing, whichever they preferred. Feedback from the investigator to the therapists on the results of testing could not, of course, be given for fear of biasing the research, but clients were encouraged to share with their therapists any discoveries they made about themselves during the course of testing which they considered important. It was explained to them that such sharing was their prerogative and theirs alone and that the researcher would not communicate their test results to their therapists during the course of treatment nor to any other person who could identify them. Ultimately, no client refused to be tested, although one very frightened psychotic lady required extensive and patient preparation, including an opportunity to meet with the tester in her therapist's presence before agreeing to come alone for a regular testing session. This then concludes the outline of the study, an outline which will be filled out in the chapters which follow.

---

[7]The term "therapeutic contract" is here used to designate a clear commitment on the part of a therapist to work with a client which is clearly expressed to that client so that he understands that he is not just being interviewed, processed, or diagnosed but has been offered treatment by the person he is seeing and has accepted that offer.

part II:

issues, hypotheses, and measures

4

the need for new measures

In the preceding chapters, mental health bureaucracies were criticized for being authoritarian rather than democratic structures, and it was suggested that without some form of genuine democracy, the therapeutic potential of communities and individuals could not be fully mobilized. Democracy alone, however, is not sufficient to insure the effective utilization of a mobilized potential. The fact that individuals or groups freely and fairly decide upon relevant goals ensures the sincerity but not the success of their efforts to achieve those goals. Meritocracy must be combined with democracy if there is to be excellence in the pursuit of goals as well as freedom and fairness in the choice of them.

According to a growing number of post-Weberian writers (e.g., Blau, 1963; Gouldner, 1952; Merton, 1940; Peter and Hull, 1969), the typical bureaucracy is no more meritocratic than democratic. The reasons are many and complex, but in the mental health field, one major problem is the absence of valid measures of treatment outcome, a situation which makes it impossible to create a truly meritocratic system, with or without either bureaucracy or democracy.

The consequences of this lack are particularly far-reaching in a period like the present, when acceptance of new groups of clients and new goals has produced an avalanche of new treatment approaches, including the quite seriously suggested use of computers (Colby, Watt, and Gilbert, 1966) and dogs (Levinson, 1961) as therapists and auxilliary therapists. As these examples are intended to suggest, the diversity in current methods is so fantastic that it seems unlikely that all are equally effective, but without a meaningful standard by which to judge results, there is no objective way to separate the wheat from the chaff. In this situation, the temptation to adopt one of two extreme stances is great: to condemn everything new or to reject everything old. In order to ensure what is so badly needed, healthy growth rather than either stagnation or rank proliferation, a widely applicable and widely acceptable measure of treatment outcome is of crucial importance.

PROBLEMS IN ASSESSING IMPROVEMENT

The chances of any single measure achieving wide acceptability and being widely applied, already slim because of numerous technical difficulties, are made slimmer still by philosophical differences. Such differences have caused researchers attempting to construct measures of treatment outcome to follow two divergent paths. Analytically and phenomenologically oriented researchers have tended to focus on internal changes—achievement of insight or increased self-acceptance—and behavioristically oriented researchers have tended to focus on external alterations—removal of symptoms or return to work.

Internal states and processes are difficult to measure and are inevitably value laden, but a number of efforts have been made over the years, with the result that we now have a variety of techniques for assessing internal change as seen from the perspective of each of the participants in the treatment situation and from an outside perspective, usually that of a tester. There are, however, drawbacks to each of these measures, one of the main ones being that they usually fail to correlate with one another and distressingly often produce flatly contradictory results. For example, it is not at all uncommon for a treatment recipient to be judged improved by his therapist, unchanged by himself, and deteriorated on the basis of some test. Since no one measure is clearly superior to the others, in such a situation one is at a loss in seeking an objective basis on which to decide which conclusion to accept, which to reject, or how to reconcile the disparities.

Difficulties like these have lent added weight to the behaviorists' argument that internal change is a nonscientific will-of-the-wisp, seducing its followers deeper and deeper into a shadowy swampland. Such researchers urge the use of clearly observable criteria, behavioral facts on which everyone can agree, no matter what their perspective. This is an attractive argument but a misleading one because behavioral measures are only superficially clear. As Kafka demonstrates so excruciatingly, the external facts of a situation may be crystal clear and yet shed only a feeble ray of light on their meaning—and it is meaning, after all, that counts.

Because the replacement of internal with external measures is currently very fashionable in the mental health field, it seems worthwhile to develop this point at some length by using a highly regarded behavioral measure as an example: hospitalization. With regard to hospitalization, the chief fact to be noted is that sheer chance plays a large role in determining which individuals will be institutionalized as a result of their psychological difficulties. "Railroading" of normal individuals is not the problem here. At least in this country at the present time, very few well-functioning individuals spend time in mental hospitals. The problem is that there are at least as many very poorly functioning individuals outside of hospitals as there are in them. In more technical terms, using hospitalization as a criterion, one ends up with few or no false positives but with an inordinate number of false negatives.

These facts are particularly apparent in a setting like the center where this research was done. In the research sample, for instance, only about one-third of the clients had ever been hospitalized, but among the nonhospitalized group, approximately one-fifth had frankly psychotic symptoms—full-fledged auditory or visual hallucinations, gross somatic or persecutory delusions, and so forth. Such evidence of pathology will be immediately convincing to some but not to others. The unconvinced—proponents of a purely social rather than a psychosocial definition of "mental illness" (e.g., Roman and Trice, 1967), as well as some behaviorists who pride themselves on being "hard-headed"—are likely to present some variant of an argument that goes like this: however "crazy" they may seem to certain professionals, nonhospitalized psychotics must have something going for them that hospitalized people don't. After all, they manage to maintain themselves in the community, and that is a better test of their adequacy than some mystic clinician's evaluation of their internal state—or is it?

The case of one of the clients in this research may help to answer that question. Joe Johnson,[1] a man in his early thirties, was brought to the center by his elderly mother at his insistence. An extremely frightened and guarded man, he was very erratic about keeping appointments and very slow to reveal any of his feelings or any of the facts of his situation. Gradually, however, his therapist learned that although his physical health was excellent and his intelligence normal or better, he had left school at the age of 16 and had never been gainfully employed since, except for a brief period in military service which ended with his premature discharge after he went AWOL in a fugue state.[2] Totally isolated from other human beings, with the exception of his mother, Mr. Johnson spent most of his time at home working on his extensive collection of guns. On the few occasions when he did venture outside, he was likely to end up in a fight with strangers in a bar, or even on the street, and to

---

[1] Names of clients here and throughout this volume are totally fictitious, and any resemblance to the names of actual persons living or dead is purely coincidental.

[2] Mr. Johnson thought his fugue state was precipitated by a blow on the head delivered from behind by an unseen stranger for unknown reasons. Perhaps, but if so, he was a very strange stranger. Questioning elicited the fact that he did not take Mr. Johnson's money, watch, or ring; only his cross and his name—an inexpensive crucifix from around his neck and his I.D. bracelet. At least, these were the things he found missing when he "woke up" on a bus headed for Washington, D.C., and assumed that the stranger had stolen them.

inflict considerable damage upon them. Despite his overwhelming ability to defend himself—he was an expert marksman as well as a formidable fist-fighter—his fears, always intense, had grown so great in recent years that he spent most of his time locked in a closet in his mother's home, not eating for days and relieving himself on the floor. Upon learning this, his therapist recommended hospitalization. Working with skill and sensitivity, he brought the client to a point where his rational hopes for relief outweighed his irrational fears of harm, and he voluntarily agreed to seek admission to the nearest state hospital.

Now, a number of studies have pointed up the inadequacy of the typical hospital environment (see chapter 1), stressing the antitherapeutic effects it can create. As a result, there have been some improvements in hospital conditions generally and, in a few inpatient settings, something approaching a truly therapeutic milieu has been created. The transformation of a custodial institution into a therapeutic milieu is, however, a difficult undertaking, especially when it involves far-reaching changes in the hospital's authority system and redistribution of decision-making power on a more egalitarian basis. An easier way to respond to the challenge is to decide that since hospitals often seem to be bad for people, people should not be hospitalized, and to act on this premise by refusing admittance whenever possible and by discharging those who are admitted as soon as possible. This is the policy many state hospitals currently follow, judging their therapeutic success by the degree to which they are able to reduce their inmate populations and justifying their approach by contending that clients are always better off in the community.

It was this policy with which Mr. Johnson was confronted when he finally screwed up his courage and made a timid bid to get out of his closet by getting into the state hospital. If one is willing to grant that living in a closet is a less adequate adjustment to society than interacting with staff and inmates on a hospital ward, then acceptance of his bid would have been a success for Mr. Johnson. Unfortunately, rejection of it counted as a success for the hospital, a statistical plus, another person saved from inmatehood and returned to "society." In so unequal a contest, the outcome can come as no surprise. His therapist's outcries notwithstanding, hospital admission workers spent a short time with this quiet, polite, neatly dressed man and sent him home, whereupon he dropped out of treatment and returned to his closet.

Of course, anecdotal evidence like that presented above can be terribly misleading as a basis for generalizations, and, at first glance, the case of Joe Johnson may seem particularly vulnerable to this charge. Obviously, very few people spend their lives in actual closets. The question, however, is not how many people live in closets but how many people are locked into environments as stifling as closets. Considered in this light, Joe Johnson may be more typical than we like to think. After all, people from free, spacious, and growth-promoting environments do not tend to become psychotic. Rather, it is people from narrow, restrictive, and impoverished environments who are psychosis-prone. Thus, individual psychotics are not usually social mutants arising by chance out of their otherwise healthy communities but are reasonably faithful reflections of the familial and societal pathology which spawns them.

If one accepts this reasoning, then it follows that simply returning a client to his community of origin without seriously attempting to alter that community or his capacity to survive and flourish in spite of it is hardly a solution for any mental health problems, with the possible exception of a few short-range financial ones. To put it as plainly as possible, the demonstrated fact that the environment provided by many mental hospitals is a poor one does not mean that any particular nonhospital environment is necessarily a good one, even in the most relative of senses. Accordingly, as things stand now, some psychotic people are probably better off at home, but a good many others may well be better off in hospitals, even under present conditions. Many hospital inmates at least seem to think so. The popular image of mental hospitals as places filled with people clamoring to get out is actually quite false, and the old joke about locking hospital doors to keep outsiders out rather than to keep insiders in has more than a grain of truth in it.

This is not intended as an argument in favor of wholesale hospitalization, even of volunteer inmates, as a solution to mental health problems. Instead, it is a plea for a truly therapeutic response to mental health problems, a comprehensive response which would involve simultaneous and sustained efforts to improve communities inside and outside hospital walls and to free and strengthen individuals on both sides of those walls.

The implication of all this for the issue which this chapter focuses upon is that external measures alone cannot solve the problem of assessing treatment outcome. Their presence or absence may be clear but their meaning is not, and they are as value-laden as internal measures. This does not mean that external measures can be discarded. Internal measures that do not relate to external measures in any meaningful way pose just as many problems as external measures unrelated to internal ones. A rich and satisfying inner life is one thing; autism is another. What good is insight, depth, or openness unless it bears some real and measurable fruit in the external world in at least a significant number of instances? One's answer to such a question depends, in part, upon one's epistemological assumptions, which cannot be explored here without going too far afield, but perhaps it will suffice to suggest that a phenomenological approach which never burdens itself with "hard" data can easily degenerate into a solipsistic one. Conversely, as the preceding pages have tried to demonstrate, a behavioristic approach which ignores "soft" data easily becomes mechanistic and meaningless.

What is needed is a sensitive internal measure that correlates, at least roughly, with those crude but essential external measures. In this study, an effort to develop such a measure was made, and the result was the Rorschach Psychological Functioning Scale (RPFS). The choice of Rorschach's Test as the basis for this scale is not likely to be a popular one. There is a ponderous body of literature on failures of the Rorschach technique (e.g., Berg and Adams, 1962; Jensen, 1964; Kelley, 1954; Meehl, 1960), and as a result of these failures, plus the ascendancy of phenomenological and behavioristic schools of thought which reject many of Rorschach's assumptions about the existence of an externally comprehensible inner reality, the inkblot test has been in a state of declining grace for some time (e.g., Thelen, Varble, and Johnson, 1968). At present, even its most official proponents (e.g., Molish, 1968; 1969) are expressing concern over its future.

To deal adequately with all of the criticisms levelled at the Rorschach would require a separate volume, but a couple of very general points can be made here. First, most Rorschach research has been badly flawed, but the flaws are of two types: relatively minor ones that are inherent in the technique, and absolutely major ones that are endemic to the field. Getting rid of the Rorschach will get rid of the first set of problems but not of the second. Until these latter problems are squarely faced, there is likely to be progression without progress; a succession of new tests but no new solutions to stubborn old problems.

PROBLEMS IN ASSESSING IMPAIRMENT

A prime example of these stubborn old problems is the whole question of the classification of psychological disturbance. The Rorschach has most often been found wanting because it failed to predict category of disturbance in the sense of discriminating between various diagnostic labels in common use. This failure is real but relatively unimportant because the diagnostic labels themselves are of such limited utility as to be practically, if not historically, of minor importance.

The historical importance of conventional labelling derives from the fact that in the eighteenth, nineteenth, and early twentieth centuries, serious psychological disturbances were thought to be reflections of specific organic pathologies, amenable, like other diseases, to specific medical treatment, once the organic factors underlying each "mental illness" were isolated. Thus, labelling began as an effort to classify each disease in terms of its characteristic symptoms as a precondition for searching out and correcting its presumed physical basis. Originally, this conception represented a great advance over previously prevalent notions of causation which focused on perversity, sin, and the supernatural. The result was a general trend toward more humane treatment of those with serious psychological difficulty and, in a few dramatic instances—for example, the relation between treponema pallidum and tertiary syphillis—the discovery of a specific cause and a specific treatment for a few small groups of disordered personalities.

For the overwhelming majority of psychological problems, however, the initially progressive belief in an organic etiology soon proved a great impediment to further progress in understanding and treatment. Freud, following in the footsteps of his great predecessors, Charcot and Janet, was among the first to challenge this notion, arguing that many psychological disorders not only had a basically psychological rather than a physiological etiology but that the presumed invariant relationship could even be reversed, with psychological disorders producing physical ones. In his view, early experiences, centered around the expression and satisfaction of universal human sexual needs, determined both ordinary "normal" psychological development and specific forms of maldevelopment. Accordingly, Freud superimposed a whole new system of diagnostic categorization, based on specific problems with specific forms of sexual needs that arose at specific points in what he took to be a universal, biologically ordained form of development.

This new system was an improvement over the old one but still contained many flaws, chief among them being retention of the notion that psychological distress was closely analogous to physical distress, in that specific symptoms always reflected specific etiological factors which, while now seen as largely psychological rather than physiological, were still viewed as invariant and universal because they stemmed from man's common biology. A half century of work, begun by the neo-Freudians and continued by a host of anthropologists, sociologists, social psychologists, and others, has made it abundantly clear that while human biology may be universal, human cultures are fantastically diverse. It is the unique interaction of general biology with a particular culture and not biology per se which defines and shapes human needs and our experience as well as our expression of them, not only in the first five years but all through life.

Thus, the presumably universal and invariant categories of "psychological disease" which Freud identified have proved not to be universal or invariant at all, the most obvious example being classical hysteria, a syndrome highly prevalent in Freud's Victorian society and relatively rare in our own very different era. Moreover, research has totally failed to substantiate any invariant connection between specific responses to childhood sexual needs—for example, breast-feeding versus nonbreast-feeding—and later forms of psychological distress or lack of it. Specific examples aside, in theoretical terms, the basic problem here, which has been clearly and eloquently underlined by

Albee (1969), Szasz (1960), and others, is that most psychological "diseases" are not only not reflections of physical pathology but are not diseases at all nor even closely analogous to diseases.

Retention of the analogy and of the classification system based on it has become a major source of confusion, hypocrisy, and obfuscation, as well as the misallocation of energy, power, and money. The plain fact is that despite more than a hundred years of biopsychological research and God knows how many hundreds of millions of dollars in research funds, the vast majority of people who fail to fulfill their psychosocial potential badly enough to notice it with distress themselves or to be noticed with dismay by others are not "sick." Despite countless revisions, a classification system which is deeply rooted in the old medical model is of quite limited utility in understanding or helping them.

In immediate practical terms, two problems are paramount. First of all, too many human beings fall between the stools; no existing diagnostic category adequately describes them. As a result, the determined conventional categorizer spends much of his time forcing round pegs into square holes. Second, even when an individual does seem to fit reasonably well into one of the traditional niches, we have learned very little about him when we label him. For instance, the relationship between diagnostic label, severity of impairment, and area of dysfunction is tenuous and imprecise to the point of uselessness. Moreover, labelling a person by his presumed weaknesses tells us very little about his probable strengths and almost nothing about how we should go about trying to help him. We simply do not have specific treatments for specific problems as defined by the conventional categorization system.

Faced with this situation, many therapists have decided to discard not only the Rorschach and the traditional diagnostic labelling system but the very principle of categorization itself. Unfortunately, it is not really possible to do that unless one is also willing to forego efforts to assess internal improvement as a result of therapeutic intervention. Internal measures of improvement are always simultaneous measures of impairment because improvement cannot be judged except in relation to impairment. Usually, however, outcome measures are evaluated only in terms of their ability to indicate change or improvement, and their adequacy as measures of impairment is assumed, a risky assumption that was not made in the present study.

The emphasis here was on developing a scale which would provide a testable basis for rank-ordering all adults along a single continuum having to do with the adequacy of psychological functioning and covering the entire range from grossly impaired to totally unimpaired functioning. Interest was thus centered on the scale's adequacy as a measure of impairment, and reliance on its efficacy as a measure of improvement was made conditional upon its prior success as a measure of impairment. The hope was that such a scale would possess more validity than other measures of outcome and would be a fairer test of relative improvement in the severely disturbed than previous measures. Of course, a scale like this would also have diagnostic utility and, with appropriate sampling, would be a valuable tool in epidemiological research.

Details on the technical specifics of the RPFS itself and on the external criteria against which the empirical validity of the RPFS was measured are provided in the following chapter. Data on how well the RPFS satisfies all of these criteria are presented in chapter 8. In the remainder of this chapter, an attempt will be made to discuss the theoretical adequacy of the scale as a measure of improvement and impairment and then to consider the value implications of the resultant definitions of psychological adequacy and inadequacy.

A REDEFINITION OF IMPROVEMENT AND IMPAIRMENT

With regard to theoretical adequacy, it has already been suggested that an adequate measure of improvement is dependent upon an adequate measure of impairment. In addition, it should be noted that an adequate measure of impairment presupposes an adequate measure of nonimpairment; that is, an operational conception of a fully functioning human being. Such a conception can be derived either from a knowledge of what is or from a sense of what ought to be. In the first case, the result is a normative conception, and in the second, an ideal conception. Those who prefer to use a normative approach generally stress man's common social nature, focusing on the extent to which he is shaped by his society; those who prefer to construct an ideal generally emphasize man's unique psychological attributes, focusing on his potential for shaping his society. In the present research, the intrinsic validity of both approaches was accepted, and man was defined as a psychosocial entity with equal emphasis on both the psycho and the social aspects of that combination.

Accordingly, adequate psychological functioning was defined as having two basic aspects, structural soundness and functional richness. Structural soundness is seen as a product of successful socialization resulting in a type of psychological organization which permits adequate contact and communication with the external world. It involves the ability to think and perceive the world in consensually validated terms and to achieve a satisfactory degree of integration, control, and balance in thought and feeling. Thus, standards for assessing structural soundness are heavily dependent upon normative data, with general conformity to these norms being regarded as positive and marked deviation from them as negative.

Functional richness, on the other hand, is seen as a result of freedom rather than discipline, freedom which permits adequate contact with and access to one's own highly personalized and emotionally charged inner world. It involves openess to private emotional and cognitive experience, and its hallmarks include spontaneity, energy, variety, affectivity, originality, and creativity.

Both structural soundness and functional richness are seen as vital for adequate psychological functioning, the first in dominantly social terms and the second in dominantly personal terms. In general, individuals weak in structure are likely to be characterized chiefly by poor adjustment to the external world, and individuals weak in function are likely to be characterized chiefly by poor adjustment to themselves. Actually, however, these two aspects of psychological adequacy are interdependent, in that persons low in structure are likely to be overwhelmed by, rather than in good contact with, their own inner lives; persons low in function are likely to exhibit a hollow and mechanical conformity rather than a meaningful adaptation to the external world. Each subscore thus represents a potential, the realization of which is dependent upon the relative adequacy of its complementary subscore.

The point in separating these two aspects of psychological functioning, despite their acknowledged interdependence, lies in what is hoped to be the ultimate utility of the distinction in suggesting appropriate courses of action and appropriate criteria for assessing the effectiveness of action. For example, when therapy is involved and the client has a high degree of structural soundness but a low degree of functional richness, the most appropriate goal would seem to be to free the personality, and the most appropriate criterion for evaluating the success of treatment would seem to be an increase in functional richness. On the other hand, when the client is one with a low degree of structural soundness and a high degree of functional richness, the most appropriate goal would seem to be to strengthen the personality, and the most appropriate criterion for evaluating success would seem to be an increase in structural soundness.[3]

What this analysis suggests is that, ideally, treatment goals should not be determined a priori and for everyone on the basis of the general values and particular psychotherapeutic orientation of the therapist, but should instead be specific to the client and based on an assessment of his major area of dysfunction. It also suggests that, instead of regarding psychological adequacy or inadequacy as unitary and expecting successful treatment always to result in across-the-board improvement on any and all presumed positive measures, an attempt be made to tailor outcome measurement to treatment goals, as-

---

[3] In either case, the scale would indicate areas of relative strength as well as areas of weakness and thus alert the therapist to client resources which could be mobilized in the therapeutic endeavour.

sessing results on measures specific to the dysfunction that most requires a remedy.

Such refinements are, however, largely a matter for future research. In the present study, therapists were not given their clients' test results and treatment proceeded quite independently of scale-based evaluations of its most appropriate direction. Moreover, most clients in the research entered therapy with serious defects in both areas. Thus, it seemed wisest to use the scale more crudely in this initial test of its efficacy and to count any pre- to post-therapy improvement in a client's combined structure-function score as a gain. Some preliminary work on the relation between client and therapist goals and overall severity of impairment was done, however, and that work will be explained more fully in chapters 5 and 10.

At this point, before discussing the value implications of the scale and before going on to present the scale itself and to consider preliminary aspects of its technical adequacy, having to do with administration, scoring, and reliability, it is necessary to emphasize my very heavy debt to the work of Ned Gaylin. Gaylin's thoughtful prior analysis of the different assumptions underlying different groups of Rorschach scores (1966) constituted a major and much needed clarification and provided the essential basis on which the RPFS was constructed. Thus, although the personality theory, therapeutic recommendations, and values underlying the present scale are quite different from Gaylin's, and although the suggested uses and specific components of the RPFS are also different, Gaylin's structure-function nomenclature was retained to underline his signal contribution.

A detailed discussion of all of the differences between Gaylin's scale and the RPFS would be beyond the scope of this chapter, but two very general points can be made here. First, the RPFS maintains Gaylin's basic distinction between normative and non-normative scores but attempts to sharpen, extend, and purify the division and to simplify the scoring process. Second, Gaylin's exclusive emphasis on the importance of the function score was replaced by an emphasis on the importance of both scores in an attempt to ensure the relevance of the scale for severely disturbed as well as for moderately disturbed clients. Moderately disturbed adults generally enter treatment with quite adequate structure scores. As a result, barring an unlikely and precipitous structural decline, relevant changes tend to take place, if at all, in their function scores. On the other hand, severely disturbed clients often enter treatment with very low structure scores,[4] the consequences of which

---

[4]Psychotics who have been hospitalized in authoritarian institutions for a long time and then released are the major exceptions to this generalization. They tend to have maximal discrepancies between their subscores involving high structure scores and rock bottom function scores, a pattern of personal impoverishment which seems more reflective of institutional effects than of psychosis per se.

are usually so painful that neither they nor their therapists are likely to regard treatment as very successful unless some improvement takes place in that area. The RPFS was designed to be appropriate for both types of client.

VALUE IMPLICATIONS OF THE DEFINITION

Despite the cool, objective tone of the preceding section, there is no such thing as a value-free definition of psychological adequacy or inadequacy. There are only variations in the degree of sophistication and candor with which one treats this issue. In what follows, I will try to lay my value cards on the table as best I know how so that the reader may understand how and why the RPFS is stacked as it is. First, with regard to the two halves of the scale, in a very rough and general way, structure might be thought of as corresponding to what others have called adjustment, and function to what others have called creativity. In this scale, both receive approximately equal stress. Many other people would prefer to weight them differentially, or to focus on only one, because they esteem the values implicit in one and denigrate those implicit in the other.

Those who value adjustment over creativity are usually rather conventional and conservative individuals, strongly oriented toward social approval and/or social order. They tend to be people with an underlying belief that while the status quo is not perfect and may need some alterations, it is basically sound, being a product of much past experience and experimentation involving many esteemed people and, as a result, not easily bettered and not lightly to be altered. Such people tend to have a high respect for tradition, however they define it, and to have a considerable distrust and fear of reckless tampering, destruction, and upheaval. A subscriber to these values might reasonably point to Nazi Germany as an example of how easily the search for a utopian new order, kindling and rekindling the fires of youthful idealism, may degenerate into an auto-de-fe of savagery and barbarism.

On the other hand, those who value personal creativity and innovation over adjustment are likely to ask, along with one of their recent predecessors, Gordon Allport: "Are not animals well adjusted to their environments and creative human beings seldom so?" (Powers and Witmer, 1951). Critical, restless, more hopeful and less humble, keenly aware of both suffering and stagnation, they are likely to see constraints on individual action or defense of tradition as reflecting a stultifying and calloused complacency. In the interests of what they interpret as compassion, freedom, justice, and the individual, such people are inclined to champion rapid growth and change and radical revision. With equal reasonableness, subscribers to these values might point to Nazi Germany as an example of how easily an accepted social order may become a repository of viciousness and corruption by whose standards a squeamish Gestapo agent would be regarded as psychologically inadequate while his more comfortably bestial brothers earn the tarnished and bloody medal of adjustment.

In constructing the RPFS, I have chosen to give equal weight to both adjustment—or adaptation as I prefer to call it—and creativity, not in an attempt to reach some sort of a neutral compromise between the two value stances crudely sketched above, but because I truly believe in both and in their essential complimentarity. More specifically, I believe that adaptation without the freedom of creativity becomes deadening and potentially deadly conformity, and that creativity without the discipline of adaptation becomes chaotic, meaningless, destructive to self and, potentially, to others. What is needed, in my view, is creative adaptation or adaptative creativity.

Sloganized in this fashion, the word creativity needs no defense: even those who, in practice, reject it totally generally claim to endorse it in the abstract, so long as its exercise does not upset any apple carts. On the other hand, the words adjustment and adaptation are sometimes vehemently re-jected by people who see that a creativity which never upsets anyone's apple cart is no creativity at all. Such people tend to feel that since creativity cannot exist in permanent subservience to adjustment in the usual sense of that word, it is basically incompatible with it.

Two points need to be made here. First, I am talking about a moving, dynamic balance, a productive tension between creativity and adjustment, not a permanent hierarchical arrangement. Second, the usual definition of adjustment, increasing the goodness of fit between self and surroundings by changing oneself to suit one's environment, is quite arbitrarily limited and slanted. Actually, as Hartmann (1951) among others has pointed out, one can also adjust or adapt by changing one's surroundings to better suit oneself or by searching out and switching to a new environment more in keeping with one's wishes. In the vernacular, the point of stressing adjustment as well as creativity is not to sell out but not to cop out or drop out either.

For those who still fear or hope that any combination of adaptation with creativity will produce a dominantly conservative hybrid with political impli-cations to match, I would like to be explicit about the fact that creative adaptation as defined above and reflected in the RPFS does not imply that moderate action is necessarily good and extreme action necessarily bad, or that short-range external success is the "true" measure of adequacy. With regard to the first point, the sort of action that is most appropriate or "best" depends upon one's interpretation of the personal and social situation one finds oneself in; with regard to the second point, what the RPFS measures is capacity for successful adaptation, not success itself. Apropos of this latter point, a perfect correlation between potential and actual adaptive success would only exist in a perfect society. By the same token, a zero correlation would be likely only in a totally corrupt and crazy society, and imperfect though ours is, we have yet to achieve perfect perversity for all citizens, although, of course, we have gone a long way in this direction in our treatment of selected minorities.

To better grasp some of the underlying issues involved in this discussion, one might regard the competing value stances described above, my own included, as reflecting different views on original sin. Psychologists, like theologians and philosophers before them and like their contemporaries in all walks of life, today divide on this issue as people have always done, although nowadays we tend to use different words for it. By whatever name, the problem of evil and its origins remains real and constant, insofar as we continue to hurt our fellows, to be hurt by them, and to wonder why.

Those who, like Freud, favor adaptation as an ideal, tend to locate original sin within, believing that man is instinctively evil (aggressive and selfish) and that society (or civilization as he preferred to call it) is the basically good restraining force, albeit sometimes overzealously so. Conversely, those who, like Rogers, favor creativity tend to locate original sin without, seeing man as basically good and society as the evil, corrupting force. With regard to the Freudian position, it seems reasonable to ask, if man is so bad, how did society get to be so good; with regard to the Rogerian position, it seems equally reasonable to ask, if man is so good, how did society get to be so bad?

In attempting to answer such questions, both Freud and Rogers have again followed time-worn paths, starting from the ancient tripartite division of the human psyche into thought, feeling, and sensation. Their paths diverge sharply, however, when it comes to valuing these three basic faculties, envisioning their ideal relationships and their potential for good and evil. Freud, like St. Paul before him, locates the source of evil in the human body, with its distracting sensations and preemptory urges. He differs mainly in feeling that bodily instincts are too compelling to be denied and in recommending controlled satisfaction rather than, for instance, celibacy. In the Freudian schema, although the instincts are accorded the healthy respect due to powerful adversaries, it is intellect which is elevated to sovereignty and seen as offering potential salvation through its dominance over the other faculties ("where id was, there ego shall be").

Emotion, in this formulation, tends to be seen as a mere concomitant of biological drive or a response to its thwarting and to get short shrift as a faculty in its own right. Such attention as it does receive tends to be condescending—emotions, like instincts, are seen as inherently irrational and id-tainted, in contrast to the rational intellect or ego, and hence properly to be subordinated to it, along with the id of which it is a part. Carl Rogers, on the other hand, appears to value emotion above all else and to see sensation as a sort of secondary concomitant of emotion. Despite his own brilliant intellectual achievements in making psychotherapy a field for scientific inquiry rather than authoritative pronouncement, he appears to see intellect and the intellectual proclivity for setting standards and making distinctions in terms of those standards as the primary source of evil in the world. In his method of therapy, cognitive elements are as relentlessly subordinated to affective ones as they are superordinated in the Freudian system.

Carried to its logical extreme, this Rogerian slant on the problem leads to a view of original sin as separate consciousness itself, a view in which intellectual structures are seen as a set of chains holding man to the mundane earth and barring him from the gates of heaven. Such a view has deeper roots in Eastern religion than in the Judeo-Christian tradition, and it is to the East that younger members of our society and their gurus usually turn in search of justification when they take this extreme position, insisting not only that the intellect and its prodigal son, science, is the source of all evil but that all cognitive structure and discipline is bad and only the total breakdown of cognitive structure achieved with certain forms of madness represents true freedom and goodness. The British psychiatrist, Ronald Laing, probably expressed this stance most clearly when he concluded a recent book with the prayer, "If I could turn you on, if I could drive you out of your wretched mind, if I could tell you I would let you know" (1970, p. 190).

My own feeling is that the intellect is no more evil or dirty than the body, that madness of the sort Laing celebrates in his book is exceedingly painful and unproductive and should not be glamorized any more than the opposite form of madness that Laing and his fellows rightfully deplore—the form which involves superconventional rationality to the exclusion of everything else. Such an unqualified celebration of disorder and rejection of structure seems to me to reflect a failure to differentiate between order and discipline which is internal, intrinsic, and essential, and that which is external, extrinsic, and arbitrary. The former may limit vision but the latter is essential in providing us with something to see. Without it, we have first chaos, a busy nothingness, and then entropy, a still nothingness. In my view, from nothing nothing comes, least of all enlightenment.

My own belief is that grossly unequal divisions within and between human beings are the source of sin and suffering in the world. To ask which divisions came first seems a chicken-egg sort of question, but in any case, the trouble lies both within and without. To deal with it we must struggle to change ourselves and the world we live in. To do that, we need to develop and utilize all of our faculties to the fullest extent possible, an achievement which seems doomed to failure if we start out by advocating a grossly hierarchical arrangement of faculties in which one is deified while others are denigrated. The need, as I see it, is to embrace the whole human package as an integrated totality and a potentially harmonious one, in which each faculty retains enough strength, autonomy, and integrity to make its own particular contribution, enhancing and enriching a whole in which synthesis is not synonymous with subordination but involves a kind of internal democracy which compliments and is complimented by external democracy.

RORSCHACH'S TEST, TEST BIAS, POVERTY, AND RACISM

How well does the RPFS succeed in embodying these values? Are both ideals and all three human faculties fairly represented in the specific components which make up its two major subscales? Readers trained in the specialized lore of the Rorschach can read the next chapter, examine the scale reproduced in it, and decide for themselves. Readers without such training are in a fix—and so am I in trying to reach them. The Rorschach is not so complex as the Talmud; still, it cannot be learned while one stands on one foot, and I am no Rabbi Hillel when it comes to extracting essences. The best I can do is to try to give some general background information on the test from which the RPFS is derived, the Rorschach, and on the man who devised it, Hermann Rorschach.

Rorschach and his test are among the best known and least understood phenomena of our century. The man's personal fate was erratic and ultimately tragic. Thus far, his instrument does not seem to be faring much better. Misunderstanding, neglect, and exploitation notwithstanding, Rorschach was a brilliant original thinker, and his test is the most ingenious psychological instrument we possess. That statement is not so excessive and partisan as it may sound to the uninitiated. Debate exists about the validity of Rorschach's ideas but not about their originality and ingenuity; even his detractors usually grant that. Indeed, the assumptions and hypotheses underlying the test are so refreshingly nonobvious that it is one of the very few psychological tests that cannot be accurately second-guessed and, hence, deliberately faked, even by very sophisticated subjects, unless they are specifically trained in the technique.

Basically, the test involves the use of a standardized, nonrepresentative set of inkblots which provide a uniform evocative stimulus with a minimum of built-in structure, allowing each person to create his own and, in so doing, to demonstrate not only some of the contents of his mind but also his own unique method of structuring and responding to the worlds within and around him. It is first and foremost a superb data-generating machine, capable, under optimal conditions, of providing a remarkably good external sample of any sighted person's internal milieu, of his cognitive and emotional style, and of the ways in which his thought, feeling, and bodily perceptions are related to one another, to common social views, and to unique personal vision and experience.

Thus, the test is a uniquely suitable instrument for reflecting the definitions and values explained in preceding sections, making it possible for a researcher who selects and weights components appropriately to assess both adaptive and creative resources in terms of thought, feeling, and bodily perception. Ways of controlling for examiner bias, assuring an adequate sample of responses and enhancing the test experience for both subject and tester are described in the next chapter, along with a detailed explanation of the ways in which the validity of the final resultant RPFS scale was empirically tested.

In what remains of this chapter, an attempt will be made to consider the amount of latitude these built-in values allow for individual and group differences. Comfortable for me and those who share my views, are they a straight-jacket for others? Clearly, a garment is there, but as I shall attempt to show, it is an extremely loose-fitting one which can be worn with style by very different psychological and social types. This catholicity is made possible by a virtue largely inherent in the method of analysis Rorschach devised for his test, a method so abstract and, at the same time, so zeroed in on fundamentals, that it can allow without prejudice for literally an infinite number of personal and subcultural variations.

Thus, in terms of psychological types, it is obvious that some people are gregarious extroverts who cultivate a large number of relatively superficial relationships, while others are introverted privacy-seekers who prefer a much smaller number of relatively intense relationships. Differences like these abound but have nothing to do with psychological adequacy or inadequacy, let alone with sickness or health. On the Rorschach generally, and on the RPFS particularly, such differences show up as just that, differences, not automatic virtues or failings. On this test, an extrovert loses points only if he fails to evidence any capacity for looking inward; an introvert loses points only if he shows no capacity to relate affectively to anyone outside himself.

In terms of social types, the same sort of variance exists, and again, the same sort of latitude is provided. For instance, minority groups in this country—Jews, Negroes, South Americans, and Southern and Eastern Europeans—have tended to encourage intense emotionality and, in the case of Jews, hyperintellectuality, while their Anglo-Saxon cohorts seem more inclined to distrust excess and to prefer more moderate and stable cognitive and affective styles (e.g., Erikson, 1963; Lerner, 1968; Singer and Opler, 1956). Modal or culturally quintessential personalities in any of these groups can and do attain perfect scores on the RPFS because it is an instrument which allows for the fact that there are any number of different ways of achieving the same end, the full realization of the human potential.

This does not mean that all groups would necessarily produce identical or even similar group averages. In fact, my own guess is that they would not because, while each of these cultures may be equally good, each cultural group is not equally well treated and, as a result, members of groups that bear the heaviest burdens of maltreatment and discrimination are more likely to be psychologically scarred, stunted, and crippled.

This point needs to be spelled out in some detail because it is currently very fashionable automatically to attack any test on which minorities perform poorly as a biased and discriminatory test. Since discriminated-against minorities do tend to perform poorly on many tests, this has produced a general antipathy to testing among earnest but ill-informed liberals and radicals, including some professionals who should know better. Some tests are invalid but many others are not. Testing is essential for any realistic and objective appraisal of the problems we face and of the merits of various attempts to solve them. Alas, the cause of testing has received even crueller blows from some of its proponents, the prime current example being Arthur Jensen, a psychologist who argues that the persistent differences in average I.Q. between whites and Blacks may be accounted for by the hereditarily inferior potential of Blacks (Jensen, 1969). [5] Obviously, with friends like that, testing needs no enemies to discredit it. Discrediting testing will not, however, solve the terribly real problem here; it will only deprive us of necessary problem-solving tools.

What needs to be discredited are fallacious interpretations of test findings and both the anti- and the pro-testing positions described above are thoroughly fallacious. Quite simply, if a *valid* test[6] shows that poor people or Black people do less well than rich people or white people, the correct interpretation is not that the tests must be biased and bad or that poor people and Black people are no good: it is that poverty, prejudice, and racism are bad for people, and indeed, we have overwhelming evidence from multiple, irrefutable sources that this is so.

Ironically, many of the very people who speak out most eloquently against the evils of poverty, prejudice, and racism then turn around when considering victims of these forces and insist that they see no adverse effects, as if life were like a Hollywood movie in which an overwhelmingly outnumbered and outgunned hero is viciously attacked, yet emerges unscathed and even unmussed from the fray. Only in the movies. In reality, real deprivation and brutality produce real scars and deformities which hurt and are not pretty to look at.[7] Discarding the tests which point up those scars and de-

---

[5] See SPSSI (Society for the Psychological Study of Social Issues) Council statement on race and intelligence (1969) for a brief but lucid account of the major scientific flaws which render the Jensen thesis untenable.

[6] Empirical standards for assessing the validity of the RPFS are described in the next chapter.

[7] Of course, good tests, properly administered and interpreted in appropriate settings are also capable of pointing up unsuspected actual and potential strengths, attributes, and resources—another reason why they should not be discarded.

formities will not heal the sufferers or protect those upon whom they inflict pain in their madness and rage. No amount of denunciation of the establishment and romanticization of its victims will gainsay the fact that these victims, in turn, victimize their fellow victims with sickening regularity. Those that don't often sink into an apathy which is hardly revolutionary and not always curable solely by impassioned rhetoric directed against "them."

People like Martin Luther King, Jr., and Malcolm X are beautiful in spite of and not because of the injustices they and their people have suffered. If successors to such people are to become successful revolutionaries rather than martyred saints, they must recognize and attack the ugly and crippling effects of the system on the personalities of their brothers, as well as the even uglier features of the system which disfigures them and prevents them from realizing their potential for psychological fulfillment and social action. Efforts in both directions must proceed simultaneously, and when they do, each will compliment and accelerate the other.

5
the rorschach psychological functioning scale (rpfs)

SCIENCE, ABSTRACTION, AND HUMANISM

The RPFS which is presented in this chapter is not only a highly technical instrument, incomprehensible in its specifics to laymen, but one which transforms the concrete reality of each person's responses into a total abstraction presented in numerical fashion, a set of scores and subscores. In our age of mass-produced depersonalization, when scientific methodology seems capable of serving the state and its minions but not man and his community, many understandably outraged individuals have begun to react against science itself, and to reject all mathematical abstractions, especially in the social sciences, as dehumanizing.

Actually, science and the numerical abstractions it requires are not in and of themselves dehumanizing, any more than valid tests are racist. In both cases, it is the uses to which these tools are put which creates their effects. In this book, numerical abstractions are used to make possible a real test of real commitments with regard to a vision of human potential and of the capacity of psychotherapy to help poor and severely disturbed people toward the realization of that potential. The willingness to subject one's commitments to such a test is not a concession to antihumanistic forces. It is one way of trying to stay on the right side of the line between genuine humanism and a head-in-the-sand self-indulgence which easily degenerates into sloppy and self-righteous sentimentality or authoritarian pronouncements.

In addition to requiring quantification, this method of staying on the right side of the line also requires one to state one's beliefs as precisely as possible in the form of hypotheses, specific bets made in advance of the game, and in a manner amenable to statistical testing. That is the essence of the scientific method. It makes for somewhat difficult reading, but there is no way of sugarcoating that difficulty without compromising the integrity of the method. Thus, the material which follows the presentation of the RPFS in this chapter and in five of the six chapters which come after it is more technical and difficult to read than the material in preceding chapters. Unlike the RPFS manual itself, however, most of this material is not incomprehensible for lay readers.[1] Since I have gone to a great deal of trouble to try to make that so, I hope that such readers will expend the time and energy necessary for comprehension.

In the effort to sustain one's attention during the process, it may help to remember that a real test is one in which the possibility of failure is really present, and thus, the likelihood that at least some of these carefully stated hypotheses will turn out to be false is very great. In general, hypotheses are stated with the certainty and explained with the intensity with which I felt them at the point when I devised them, but the reader needs to remain on guard and to refrain from accepting them as probable truths until he sees the results of the tests in chapters 8, 9, and 10. He also needs to use his imagination and sympathy to keep the human beings behind these numerical results in clear focus, at least until he gets to the last subsection of chapter 8, which deals with score changes and their human meaning and presents individual case histories rather than group statistics. First, however, here is the principal abstracting instrument of this study, the RPFS. Readers untrained in the Rorschach should skip the next subsection and go on to the following one.

THE RORSCHACH PSYCHOLOGICAL FUNCTIONING SCALE

RPFS Subscales, Elements, and Components

The overall scale has a total of 14 components divided into two subscales: a structure scale consisting of 8 components and a function scale consisting of 6 components. The structure subscale is designed to measure the structural soundness of personality, and the function subscale is designed to measure the functional richness of personality.

---

[1] Some statistical points, some of the tables in the section on results, and some parts of Chapter 8 may be incomprehensible to those without research training. Readers who find them so are encouraged to skip them without fear of losing the sense of the book or its continuity.

Structural soundness is defined as involving four basic elements: (1) gross reality contact; (2) specific perceptual accuracy; (3) emotional control and integration; and (4) cognitive balance. Each of these four elements of structure is assessed by two Rorschach measures, thus comprising the eight components of this subscale.

Functional richness is defined as involving two basic elements: (1) affective richness, and (2) cognitive richness. Each is assessed by three Rorschach measures, thus comprising the six components of this subscale.

The two subscales with all 14 of their specific components are presented below.

Structure Scale

Basic elements	Specific Components
Gross Reality Contact	1. *Number of popular responses* scored according to Beck (1961). This is thought to be a measure of gross reality contact, in that it assesses the subject's ability to perceive what is common to his culture and to be aware of at least some of its central stereotypes and norms. It is not, in and of itself, a measure of conformity because, as Beck has pointed out, awareness does not necessarily imply acceptance.
	2. *Bizarreness.* Scoring on this item is heavily dependent on clinical judgment. The crucial distinction here is between what is merely fanciful, imaginative, and unusual, and what is truly autistic, confused, and pathological. Records may be rated as bizarre on the basis of the form and/or the content of responses and also on the basis of verbalization accompanying responses. See appendix at the end of Table 3 for further details.
Specific Perceptual Accuracy	3. *Rorschach's F+* scored according to Beck (1961). This is thought to be a measure of the overall accuracy of perception of reality in the absence of manifest affect. Pedantic precision and/or hypercautious guardedness are not required here, only a reasonable degree of freedom from distortion.
	4. *Lerner's B+* (1968) scored according to Beck's form standards. This is thought to be a measure of the overall accuracy of perception of reality in the presence of manifest affect. Again, what is required here is not extreme accuracy but only the absence of consistent bias.
Emotional Control and Integration	5. *Number of pure C,Y,T, and/or V responses.* All such responses are seen as indicating failures in the internal integration and the external control of outwardly directed affect. Responses in which affect is dominant but

form is still present are not seen as representing failures of this type, nor even as necessarily tending in this direction; total absence of form is required here.

6. *Number of disturbed M responses.* M is defined in Beck's sense, referring mainly to human precepts, but also including animals and inanimate objects when these latter are anthropomorphized. M is considered disturbed when it is scored minus according to Beck's tables and/or when it would be classified in Lerner's system (1966; 1967) an Mb, FMb, Mfm, or BD response. M is also considered disturbed when it occurs more than once in an isolated body part rather than a whole figure.

Cognitive Balance

7. *Affective ratio and approach type.* Affective ratio refers to the extent to which productivity is affected by color and shading and approach type refers to the efficacy and flexibility of cognitive structuring. Affective ratio is considered satisfactory so long as the subject neither "freezes" nor "floods" in response to ordinary environmental stimuli; approach type is counted as satisfactory so long as the subject demonstrates a reasonable capacity to generalize (W production) and a relative freedom from obsessive intellectual narrowing and constriction (Dd production).

8. *Preoccupation and primary space.* Preoccupation refers to excessive focus on a particular content area or theme; primary space as defined and interpreted by Fonda (1960) and Lerner (1966) reflects excessive resistance to internal pressure stemming from ego-alien content in the form of rejected fantasies. Scoring on preoccupation is heavily dependent on clinical judgment (see appendix at the end of Table 3), and scoring on primary space on Fonda's standards.

Function Scale

Basic elements	Specific Components
Affective Richness	1. *Number of movement responses*, using Beck's definition of movement. Movement per se is considered an index of affective richness because it represents affect directed inward and lived out in fantasy, indicating a capacity for inner living of an affectively vital sort, regardless of its "quality" in any good-bad sense of that term. Thus, all movement responses are included in this count and counted equally, without regard to whether they are human, animal or inanimate, plus or minus, passive or

Function Scale

Basic elements	Specific Components

Affective Richness Continued active, so long as they meet Beck's standards for classification as movement.

2. *Number of color responses.* Color per se is also considered an index of affective richness since it too represents an emotional response, in this case directed outward, toward, and in response to, environmental stimuli. Again, sheer quantity without regard to quality is the criterion: all responses involving color whether in the form of pure C, CF, or FC, and whether pleasant or unpleasant, plus or minus, are counted and counted equally.

3. *B%* This is the percentage of total responses which involve affective determinants of any sort (M,C,Y,T, and V) and in any combination (form dominant, subservient, or absent). It is similar to Beck's Lambda and the converse of Rapaport's F% and is considered an index of affective richness because it illustrates the extent to which the subject responds emotionally to his world, as opposed to responding in purely intellectual terms unenlivened by affective overtones.

Cognitive Richness 4. *Total number of responses.* Sheer productivity is considered an aspect of cognitive richness in that it suggests intellectual liberation, energy, and freedom from constriction sufficient to allow for a variety of responses involving alternative ways of intellectually structuring and defining a stimulus.

5. *Number of separate content categories,* using Beck's system of content categorization. Diversity of content is regarded as an index of the richness of mental furniture and the freedom and versatility to make use of it in going beyond the three most obvious and conventional content categorizations (animal, human, and anatomy) to include more varied and original content specifications.

6. *Total number of Z minus simple W.* The ability to see relationships between things and to organize them into meaningful gestalts may well be the best brief definition of useful intelligence there is. The more relations and interconnections one sees, the richer and more energized one's thoughts and perceptions are likely to be. Complexity of organization is thus seen as a central aspect of cognitive richness.

RPFS Scoring Procedures

Scores of 3 (good), 2 (medium), and 1 (poor) are assigned to each of the 14 scale components on the basis of scoring standards listed in the next sections. Thus, it is possible to obtain scores ranging from a maximum of 42 to a minimum of 14 on the overall scale. These overall scores may conveniently be categorized as follows:

Score	Category
42	Fully functioning, no impairment
40 through 41	Mildly impaired functioning
36 through 39	Moderately impaired functioning
30 through 35	Severely impaired functioning
29 through 21	Very severely impaired functioning
20 and below	Incapable of functioning outside of hospital or hospital-like setting

Single scores at any one point in time show where an individual stands relative to other individuals. However, with a test-retest format—for example, before and after therapy—the scale can also be used to show where an individual stands relative to himself. This can be done on three bases. First, one can compare change on the basis of category shifts—from scoring in the very severe category before therapy to scoring in the severe category after therapy. Second, one can compare change on the basis of scores[2]—from scoring 36 at pre-therapy to 38 at post-therapy, a positive change which takes place intra-categorically, in this case within the moderately inpaired category. Finally, to pick up more subtle changes, one can use an even less stringent system based on raw change scores. To do this, compare the raw scores on each component at test with those at retest and assign a simple plus, minus, or zero to each component, depending upon whether the raw scores change in a favorable direction, remain the same, or change in an unfavorable direction. The final raw change score is then the algebraic sum of the changes on all 14 components.

Finally, in addition to the three levels of scoring for the overall scale, one also can derive subscale scores. On the structure subscale, the obtainable range goes from 24 to 8; on the function subscale, the obtainable range runs from 18 to 6.

[2]This was the procedure followed in the present research and, for most purposes, it seems by far the best one because scale scores are finer, more precise, and more clearly meaningful than either category shifts or raw change score shifts.

Table 3
RPFS Scoring Standards

Standards for Assessing Structure Scores

Components	Good 3 points	Medium 2 points	Poor 1 point
1. P	7 or more	5 or 6	4 or less
2. Bizarre	Rating of 0	Rating of 1	Rating of 2
*3. F+%	80% or more	60% to 79%	Below 60%
**4. B+%	80% or more	60% to 79%	Below 60%
5. Pure C, Y, T, V	none	one	2 or more
6. Disturbed M	none	2 or more minus, OR 2 or more in isolated body parts	1 or more Mb, FMb, Mfm, or BD OR 2 or more minus and 2 or more in isolated body parts
7. Affective ratio AND	R to last 3 cards between 25% and 49%, no more than 2 one-response cards and no rejects	Below standard for affective ratio, OR approach type, with no rejects	Below standard for affective ratio AND approach type, or 1 or more rejects
Approach type	No DW; W at least 5; Dd no more than 15%; and no single card responded to only with Dd		
8. Preoccupation AND Primary space	No content preoccupation. No more than 1 primary space response	Moderate content preoccupation OR 2 or more primary space responses	Moderate content preoccupation AND 2 primary space responses OR severe preoccupation, or 3 or more primary space responses

*Clients with no pure F responses receive a rating of 1 (poor).
**Similarly, clients with no B responses receive a rating of 1 (poor).

Standards for Assessing Function Scores

Components	Good 3 points	Medium 2 points	Poor 1 point
1. M	4 or more	2 or 3	one or none
2. C, CF, FC	4 or more	2 or 3	one or none
3. B%	Over 25%	15% to 25%	less than 15%
4. R	30 to 59	20 to 29 OR 60 to 75	Under 20 OR over 75
5. Z–Simple W	10 or more	5 to 9	4 or less
*6. Content Categories	7 or more	5 or 6	4 or less

*It should be noted that H and Hd count as *one* content category, not two. Similarly, A and Ad count as *one* content category, not two. It should also be noted that only primary categories count and not secondary categories, e.g., a response scored WM + H, R1 would be credited only for the category H, not for the category R1.

Appendix

Scoring Standards for Bizarreness and Preoccupation

General Standards

Extreme standards are to be used in both cases—bizarre means frankly psychotic, and preoccupied means really obsessed with a repetitive theme, so that other content begins to be excluded.

Special Application

In cases which are borderline with regard to bizarreness and preoccupation, the scorer should use these two categories to make his overall clinical judgment count, penalizing records which seem to him to obtain total scores higher than they deserve and treating gently records which seem to him to be scoring lower than they deserve.

Card Rejections

Rejects automatically count as bizarre with one point subtracted for one reject and two points subtracted for two or more rejects.

THE TEST RELATIONSHIP: ADMINISTRATION, SCORING, AND RELIABILITY

In examining the components of the RPFS and the scoring standards for it, it may have occurred to the test-sophisticated reader that, in this system, clients are very heavily penalized for what they do not say. Regardless of its content, a very short record cannot get a perfect score, and a very short, sparse record with card rejections is likely to get a very low score indeed. Using the ordinary method of Rorschach administration, this would be an extremely hazardous procedure because, given a sparse record, one cannot know whether the client produced so little because he could not produce more or because he did not try to produce more—and, if not, then why not.

In the present research, an attempt was made to settle this dilemma by instructing every client at the outset to give at least two responses per card and reminding him of this requirement every time he failed to meet it until he had given at least twenty responses. Clients who protested their inability to comply were firmly encouraged if lack of confidence seemed to be the obstacle and firmly challenged if unwillingness seemed to be the obstacle. No client was allowed simply to reject a card or to skim through the cards with a single, superficial response to each without making either what appeared to the examiner to be a sincere and sustained effort or a clear, conscious, considered, and admittedly voluntary refusal to do so. The only exceptions were cases where a client showed extreme anxiety in response to a particular card; even in such cases, the exception was made only with respect to that particular card.

As a result, a reasonable degree of confidence can be placed in the assumption that sparse records in the present research reflect genuine inability resulting from inner impoverishment, blocking, or confusion of a serious magnitude, or genuine refusal resulting from severely pathological anxieties. The scale was deliberately designed with this method of administration in mind and should not be used without it. It is regarded as an essential method if one is to use the scale at all and a preferable method even if one is not using the scale because it greatly improves the technical adequacy of inkblot data. Inadequate records cannot be eliminated, but an examiner can and should make reasonably certain that they reflect inadequately functioning personalities and not inadequate efforts by either clients or testers which result in uninterpretable data. In addition to improving the quantity, quality, and interpretability of the data, this method of administration has the added technical advantage of reducing the variability of R and insuring that such variability as remains is meaningful enough to be worth the problems it entails, problems which are very clearly spelled out by Fiske and Baughman (1953), among others.

Moreover, handled correctly, it is a genuinely therapeutic method of administration, which leaves the client feeling that he has been taken seriously, has had a real encounter, and has not been found wanting. These therapeutic effects can be achieved as easily and as honestly with clients who produce inadequate records as with those who produce adequate records. All that is required is sincere approval for sincere effort and genuine respect for and faith in each client's potential, whether he is currently able to realize it or not.

To those who feel that the method seems harsh and demanding, particularly for inadequate clients, it should be pointed out that the alternative is actually much harsher. Usually, it involves tacit acquiescence in the client's

unrealistic and painful evaluation of himself as a creature too grossly inadequate to meet reasonable external demands or too monstrous to permit exposure of thoughts and feelings which would provoke abhorrence or wrath in
the onlooker. One cannot force such people to perform, produce, or reveal
themselves, and one should convey this fact clearly, making sure the client
knows that you have neither the power nor the desire to compel him against
his will, but making equally sure that he knows that you know that the
choice is his—and that it *is* a choice: he *can* produce and share, later if not
now, in some other situation if not in this one, with some other human being
if not with you. He should also be made aware of the fact that he has had a
real opportunity to produce and share and that he will have other such
opportunities.

In sum, the style of administration recommended does not force the
client to do anything, but it does force the tester who agrees to use it to
accept responsibility for obtaining the best data possible and for making the
process of obtaining that data as therapeutic for the client as possible. Ideally,
the tester should leave the encounter satisfied with the worth of his data, and
the client should leave it with an enhanced sense of his own worth.

The point of view with regard to testing elaborated above is diametrically
opposed to a prevalent one which sees the tester's role as that of a neutral
observer who must attempt to turn himself into a blank screen so as to avoid
biasing the test results. In the present research, it was assumed that it is
neither possible nor desirable for testers to function as blank screens, just as it
is neither possible nor desirable for therapists to do so. The assumption here
was that the best protection against bias is to give research subjects a genuine
stake in telling the truth as they see it by designing research which is relevant
to what they regard as significant questions, by making this clear to them,
and by soliciting their voluntary participation in a mutual search for honest
answers. In the author's experience, when this is done, most research subjects
"tell it like it is" with force and clarity, even correcting the tester when
necessary; when it is not done, subjects tend to respond to examiner cues,
real or fantasied, regardless of any and all attempts to eliminate them.

The contention here is that the infinite malleability and endless suggesti-
bility manifested by research subjects in many contemporary studies is not a
general human characteristic but a specific reaction to a specific situation, a
situation in which the subject has no knowledge about or interest in the basic
research questions and no independent motivation to give honest and
thoughtful answers. In such a situation, the only motivation a subject is likely
to have is that supplied by the examiner. It is hardly surprising then that he
tends to produce whatever he thinks the examiner wants.

In more general terms, the point here is that much research bias results
from the common practice of dehumanizing subjects by treating them like
objects, black boxes to be manipulated so as somehow to extract information

from them. From this perspective, it seems obvious that the problem will not be solved by dehumanizing testers and investigators along with their subjects but by rehumanizing the research process and all of its participants, an ideal that was earnestly striven towards in the present study. The fact that every client who completed therapy agreed to a post-therapy testing appointment, and every client showed up for his appointment at the scheduled time, may be some indication that this ideal was at least partially realized. This seems particularly likely in view of the fact that many of these clients were very poor people who, in addition to spending carfare, often had to miss work or hire a babysitter in order to keep their testing appointments. In this context, it should also be noted that clients who rated their therapeutic experience as unsuccessful were just as faithful in returning to report on it as were those who rated it successful.

The independent stake of these clients in the research was the major protection against bias but it was not the only one. Another important protection was the fact that the tester made it a rule never to reread a client's pre-therapy material before the post-therapy testing session. Since it was impossible to remember the client's initial responses on complex tests like the Rorschach in any detail, it was impossible to know whether he was doing better, worse, or the same on the retest until after it was completed.

As a further precaution, all scoring which involved a subjective element was done by blind raters, and independent reliabilities were established for each such scoring system. In *most cases*, a single blind rater scored all of the responses and a second blind rater independently rescored a random sample of them. With the RPFS, an even more stringent procedure was followed. Because it was the crucial system in this research, and because it was a new and untried system derived from inkblot data which has been notorious for the unreliability with which it has been scored in the past, two blind raters independently scored every record in the study. In addition, the whole RPFS scoring system was constructed so as to eliminate meaningless unreliability by focusing on significant ranges (for example, F+ from 60% to 80%) rather than on single numbers (for example, F+ percentages of 66 as opposed to 67), wherever possible.

NON-RORSCHACH MEASURES OF IMPAIRMENT AND IMPROVEMENT

All of the major hypotheses to be tested in this study have to do either with client impairment or with client improvement, and the RPFS is the main instrument from which both of these central measures are derived. How secure a foundation does the RPFS provide? How good a measure of impairment and improvement is it? Theoretical adequacy as described in the preceding chapter is a necessary but hardly a sufficient basis for answering such questions. The fact that something should work is no guarantee that it does work. Evidence that the RPFS does, in fact, work, that it does reliably and meaningfully distinguish between different degrees of psychological impairment and improvement, can only come from empirical tests demonstrating significant relationships between RPFS scores and a variety of other criterion measures. The purpose of this section is to describe and discuss those other criterion measures.

With regard to impairment, three independent measures were used: one subjective measure, therapists' judgments; and two objective behavioral measures, hospitalization and productivity. Because traditional diagnostic categories provide an unreliable index of severity of impairment (e.g., Zubin, 1967), therapists' judgments were assessed by means of a simple four-point rating scale which each therapist was asked to fill out for each of his clients at pre-therapy. To maximize comparability, the four points on this severity of impairment scale were made to correspond to the four major divisions of the RPFS, as follows:

(1) very severe, e.g., psychotic, psychotic character, or borderline psychotic;

(2) severe, e.g., character disorder or neurotic character, addiction, perversion;

(3) moderate, e.g., neurotic, any type;

(4) mild, e.g., maladjustment, situational reaction in an otherwise healthy person.

Hospitalization was defined as having been an inpatient in a mental hospital or on a psychiatric ward of a general hospital for any period of time at any point in the past. This was, of course, a strictly nominal measure, with all clients being classified into either the hospitalization history or the no-hospitalization history category. The other behavioral measure of severity of impairment, productivity, was also nominal, but it differed with regard to the time span covered in that it was a strictly present-oriented measure. Productive clients were those who were either working or attending school at the start of treatment; nonproductive clients were those who were doing neither.

Thus, it was hypothesized that if the RPFS was an adequate measure of impairment, it should be able to discriminate between clients who were rated more severely and less severely disturbed by their therapists, between clients with a past history of hospitalization and those without such a history, and between currently productive and nonproductive clients. It was assumed that any single measure which related significantly to all three of these indices of impairment was likely to be a meaningful measure indeed.

With regard to assessing the adequacy of the RPFS as a measure of improvement, the same standard was set. RPFS change scores were expected to relate significantly to three independent measures of outcome—in this case, therapists' judgments, clients' judgments, and behavioral change. This optimistic triple prediction was made despite the fact that previous studies (e.g., Cartwright, Kirtner, and Fiske, 1963; Cartwright and Roth, 1957; Fiske, Cartwright, and Kirtner, 1964; Kogan, Hunt, and Barteline, 1953; May and Tuma, 1964; Rogers 1954) have shown that independent measures of outcome tend to correlate poorly or not at all with one another. The assumption here was that previous measures failed to correlate with one another for the same reason that the descriptions of several blind men feeling different parts of an elephant would fail to correlate with one another. Tail, trunk, and flanks are all legitimate parts of an elephant, but none, by itself, includes enough of the beast to overlap with other parts, let alone to provide an adequate picture of him as a whole. Because the RPFS was designed to be a representation of the outcome elephant in its totality, it seemed reasonable to expect enough overlapping to produce at least modest correlations between it and the various parts represented by other reliable and presumably valid measures of outcome.

Therapists' judgments of outcome were obtained by asking each therapist to rate his client on a six-point global outcome rating scale at post-therapy. A six-point scale was devised for this purpose because it was felt that this was the maximum number of meaningful distinctions that participants in a treatment situation could reasonably be expected to make. In addition, it was felt essential to include two options which have generally been overlooked by the devisers of rating scales in this area, the first having to do with the possibility of a mixed outcome in which gains in one area (say, structure) are offset by losses in another (for example, function), and the second having to do with what might be referred to as a failure in spades, that is, not the mere absence of improvement but the actual presence of deterioration. Much recent research (e.g., Bergin, 1963; Truax and Carkhuff, 1964) indicates that the latter is, alas, more than a theoretical possibility; the persistent divergence of different outcome measures may well be an indication that the former is also a real phenomenon. The RPFS was designed to make it possible for both of those outcomes to register if they should occur, and it seemed reasonable to create outcome rating scales for treatment participants that allowed for the same range of possibilities. In obtaining participants' outcome ratings, it was also important to make sure that they were ratings of *relative* improvement to insure comparability with the RPFS and fairness to severely disturbed clients. Accordingly, instructions on the therapists' outcome rating form read as follows:

> In making these ratings of the outcome of your case, please do *not* try to compare your client with other clients or with some abstract norm representing optimal mental health. Instead, compare him as he is now with

the way he was at the beginning of therapy. In other words, it is amount of change, not absolute degree of health which we are trying to assess.

Global Rating. In general, this client has shown:
(1) a great deal of positive change;
(2) a fair amount of positive change;
(3) a small amount of positive change;
(4) positive change in some areas, negative in others;
(5) no significant change;
(6) a deterioration.

Clients were asked to rate outcome over the same six-point range, but the phraseology was adapted to meet their situation as follows:

We are trying to learn more about helping people so that we can do as good a job as possible. You can help us by giving your opinion of the results of your therapy. Please read all six of the statements below and check the one that best describes the way you feel now as compared to the way you felt when you first came here. Neither your therapist nor any other person who knows you will be allowed to see your answers. Please be absolutely frank and give your honest opinion.

I feel:
(1) very much better
(2) pretty much better
(3) a little better
(4) better in some ways, worse in others
(5) about the same
(6) worse than before.

The third independent measure of outcome, the behavioral one, was again a simple nominal measure of an objective difference. Clients were rated as improved if they had not been working or attending school at pre-therapy but were doing either or both of those things at post-therapy.

If the RPFS meets all six of the tests of its adequacy described above, it will be of obvious benefit in assessing the need for treatment and the results of treatment. In addition, it was hoped that the RPFS might provide some clues about optimal directions for treatment in particular cases, clues which might ultimately help to improve the percentage and degree of success in therapy. As a beginning step in this direction, an attempt was made to explore the relations between treatment goals and severity of impairment.

THE ISSUE OF TREATMENT GOALS

Much has been written on the aims of treatment, but whether these involve some approach to human perfection (e.g., Freud, 1963; Rogers, 1963) or something more modest and limited (e.g., Alexander, 1961; Colby, 1951; McNair and Lorr, 1964), it is always the therapist's goals that the writers seem to have in mind. When clients' goals are considered at all, they are usually given a less lofty name, such as "expectations," "motivation for treatment," or "defensiveness," the last designation being most common when what the client thinks he needs conflicts with what his therapist thinks he needs. In the present study, it was assumed that clients as well as therapists have what may legitimately be described as treatment goals and that client goals are at least as valid as therapist's goals—probably more so, albeit often less articulate.

It was further assumed that treatment goals tend to be selected on one of two major bases and to fall into one of two major categories. The two major bases for the selection of treatment goals are as follows: (1) goals can be chosen on the basis of a person's general values and particular psychotherapeutic orientation, in which case they tend to be constant for all clients in all situations; or (2) goals can be chosen on the basis of an assessment of the particular needs and deficits of particular clients, which tend to vary from case to case. The hypothesis in this study was that therapists' goals are usually chosen on the first basis, hereafter referred to as the general orientation basis, and clients' goals tend to be chosen on the second basis, hereafter referred to as the specific deficit basis.

Regardless of the basis of the choice, there are two major types of goals: those which correspond to man's unique, inner-oriented psychological characteristics, and these which correspond to his common, externally oriented social characteristics—or, in terms of the RPFS, to the two major divisions of the scale, structural soundness and functional richness. In this research, each client and each therapist was asked to specify his goals for each case by selecting one of these two major treatment goals as his primary aim. Primacy was emphasized because it was felt that the two goals were not mutually exclusive and that both clients and therapists might reasonably want both. Thus, the point of the choice was not to force the exclusion of either alternative but to encourage the establishment of a clear treatment focus and to gather information on the relative importance of different aims for the two participants in the treatment situation. For therapists, the choice was phrased as follows:

Primary treatment goal: (Select only one.)
(a) ego strengthening, improved contact with reality, more adequate defenses and emotional control;
(b) deep level exploration, improved contact with self, greater emotional freedom and expressivity.

For clients, the same essential choice was offered, phrased in somewhat different terms. They were asked to:

Please read both statements below and place a check next to the one which best describes the main thing you hope to get out of treatment.

(a) I hope to get rid of unpleasant symptoms and to be more in control of myself.

(b) I hope to understand myself better and to be more in touch with my own feelings.

As a check on the meaningfulness of clients' choices, each client was asked to specify whether it was hard to decide which statement to check. If he answered yes, he was asked to indicate the reason for the difficulty by choosing among the four possibilities below:

I really want both of those things._____
I don't really want either of those things. _____
I'm not sure what I want._____
I know what I want but I don't know what those two statements mean.

_____

Therapists' comprehension of the choices was assumed and not tested, but a check was made on the stability of therapists' goals by asking them, at post-therapy, whether the goal they had chosen at pre-therapy remained constant or underwent some change as the case progressed.

In order to test the assumption that clients' treatment goals tend to be related to their specific needs and deficits, whereas therapists' goals tend to be selected on a general orientation basis, it was hypothesized that clients' goals would be significantly related to the severity of initial impairment, with more severely impaired clients recognizing their need for control and strengthening and choosing that as their primary goal, and less severely impaired clients feeling secure enough in their relation to reality to reach out for more freedom and expressivity and choosing that as their primary goal. Conversely, it was hypothesized that therapists' goals would not be significantly related to severity of initial impairment but would instead be randomly distributed along the continuum of impairment formed by the RPFS scores of the forty-five clients in this research sample.

If the data prove meaningful, and these hypotheses are borne out, it will not prove that the customer is always right, but it will strongly suggest that he is not inevitably wrong either. It will also suggest that factors other than resistiveness enter into his feelings about the direction that treatment should take. If this turns out to be the case, it will indicate that therapists might do well to pay more respectful heed to conflicting client aims than most of us have been inclined to do. Perhaps many of our "resistive" clients are rightfully resisting therapeutic goals and procedures which they intuitively recognize as inappropriate to their particular needs.

CHAPTER **6**

clients and therapists

CLIENT PROGNOSTIC MEASURES AND IMPROVEMENT

Assuming that the RPFS meets all of the tests of its adequacy spelled out in the last chapter, it should pave the way for a meaningful test of the major hypothesis of this study: that individual psychotherapy, under appropriate conditions, can be an effective method of helping not only those classical clients traditionally served by this method but also those nonclassical clients who have rightfully become the main focus of community mental health endeavours. To make this test, the next requirement was a reasonably precise and complete definition of the term nonclassical client and a set of quantitative measures appropriate to that definition.

This task was a relatively simple one because there is widespread agreement, even among therapists of sharply differing orientations, about the characteristics that divide classical or "good" clients from nonclassical or "bad" ones and because a vast amount of research has already been done on these characteristics resulting in a series of reliable and objective measures of what are generally referred to as client prognostic factors. Strupp (1962) describes the consensus, details the characteristics relevant to it, and expresses the common professional attitude toward it[1] quite neatly in the following statement:

> It is becoming increasingly clear that therapists have fairly specific (and valid) notions about the kinds of attributes a "good" patient should

[1] Complacent acceptance of therapeutic exclusiveness and even a species of pride in it is common but by no means universal among professional therapists. The late David Rapaport, for example, described the exclusiveness phenomenon in these haunting and painfully pointed terms in 1960: "Therapies or therapists ... end up by establishing their own McCarran Act" (page 115).

possess as well as about those attributes which make a patient unsuitable for the more usual forms of investigative, insight-producing psychotherapy. Patients considered good prognostic risks are described as young, attractive, well-educated, members of the upper middle class, possessing a high degree of ego-strength, some anxiety which impels them to seek help, no seriously disabling neurotic symptoms, relative absence of deep characterological distortions and strong secondary gains, a willingness to talk about their difficulties, an ability to communicate well, some skill in the social-vocational area, and a value system relatively congruent with that of the therapists. Such patients also tend to remain in therapy, profit from it, and evoke the therapists' best efforts (pp. 470–71).

Even from a cursory examination of the above paragraph, it is apparent that the two factors stressed throughout this volume, social class and severity of impairment, play the major role in separating what most therapists regard as good and bad patients or, in the terms preferred here, between classical and nonclassical clients. In addition, however, a number of other attributes are mentioned which seem related to these two major factors but not essential or invariant components of either one of them. Among these latter attributes, three general subsidiary factors can be distinguished: amenability to treatment in terms of internal dynamics, general attitudes congruent with therapists' values, and initial in-therapy behavior compatible with therapists' preferences.

Using these five factors as a basis for definition, an appropriate measure was selected for each of them. The measures selected all provided a range of scores or ratings. In each case, previous research had shown that low client scores were significantly related to failure in psychotherapy, or to therapists' apprehensions of failure and consequent client rejection. For purposes of this research, then, a nonclassical client was defined as a person who received low scores on any one of these five measures.

The underlying assumption here was that previous research with these instruments did not measure the treatment potential of nonclassical clients but the treatment limitations of typical therapists operating within the climate of typical treatment institutions. Because the therapists in this study were thought to be an atypical group operating within an atypical climate (see chapter 2), it was hypothesized that they would not manifest the typical therapeutic limitations and that without them, categorical client limitations would tend to evaporate.

In other words, the contention here was that success in psychotherapy is primarily a function of therapist variables, with client variables assuming major importance only in the absence of appropriate therapeutic conditions. Accordingly, in this research, the same measures were used but very different outcome predictions were made. It was hypothesized that the majority of clients in this research would show improvement on the RPFS as a result of therapy and that clients who received low scores on each of these five prognostic measures would show just as much improvement as clients who achieved high scores on them.

Factor one, social class, was measured by means of the Hollingshead and Redlich Two Factor Index of Social Position (Hollingshead and Redlich, 1958), a composite, weighted score utilizing occupation and education and resulting in five class levels, ranging from class I, the highest, to class V, the lowest. Adhering to the line drawn by previous research with this instrument, clients in classes I, II, and III were placed in the high prognostic group, and clients in classes IV and V were placed in the low prognostic group, a line which, roughly speaking, falls between unemployed and/or blue collar workers with only a grade school or a high school education and white collar workers with at least some college training. The specific hypothesis here was that in this study, unlike those that have preceded it (e.g., Auld and Myers, 1954; Grey, 1966; Imber, Nash, and Stone, 1955; Sullivan, Miller, and Smelser, 1958; Winder and Hersko, 1955), lower class clients would respond as well as higher class ones.

Factor two, severity of psychological impairment, was assessed via therapists' judgments. Clients rated as mildly or moderately disturbed by their therapists were placed in the high prognostic group, and clients rated as severely or very severely disturbed were placed in the low prognostic group. Once again, the hypothesis was that despite previous findings to the contrary (e.g., Barron, 1956; Cappon, 1964; Fairweather and Simon, 1963; Garfield and Affleck, 1961; Goldman and Mendelsohn, 1969; Heilbrunn, 1963; Hunt, Ewing, La Forge and Gilbert, 1959; Katz, Lorr and Rubinstein, 1958; Knapp, Levin, McCarter, Wermer, and Zetzel, 1960; Lohrenz, Hunter, and Schwartzman, 1966; Lorr and McNair, 1964; Luborsky, 1959; Miles, Barrabe, and Finesinger, 1951), severely and very severely disturbed clients would, in this study, show as much improvement as their less distressed brothers.

Factor three, amenability to treatment, was measured by Klopfer's Rorschach Prognostic Rating Scale (Klopfer, Ainsworth, Klopfer, and Holt, 1954), a measure which has predicted therapeutic outcome with a high degree of success previously (e.g., Cartwright, 1958; Endicott and Endicott, 1964; Johnson, 1953; Mindess, 1953; Sheehan, Frederick, Rosevear, and Spiegelman, 1954. See also Butler and Fiske, 1955, page 338). This scale can best be described as an attempt to measure ego strength, amount and type of emotional responsiveness, and degree of motivating anxiety, internal psychological characteristics which are obviously related to but not identical with severity of impairment (e.g., Adams, Cooper, and Carrera, 1963).

Using this popular scale, one can sort clients into one of six groups, ranging from group I, which Klopfer describes as "a very promising case that just needs a little help," to group VI, which he describes as indicating "a hopeless case." In the present research, clients whose scores placed them into Klopfer's groups I, II, and III were classified as high prognostic cases, and clients whose scores placed them into Klopfer's groups IV, V, and VI were classified as low prognostic cases, a division which separates clients Klopfer describes as having a better than 50–50 chance of improvement in treatment and clients he describes as having only a 50–50 chance or less. The prediction here, of course, was that these odds would not apply and that a majority of clients on both sides of the dividing line would improve as a result of therapy.

Factor four, general client attitudes, was assessed by means of the ten-item Authoritarianism Scale which Gallagher, Sharaf, and Levinson (1965) have found to be related to client acceptability to therapists. The Authoritarianism Scale, according to Gallagher *et al.*, measures "a cluster of social attitudes and modes of cognitive-emotional functioning which includes the following: a strong preference for dominance-submission in social relationships; anti-intraception—that is, an aversion to understanding the self as a personality; stereotyped moral attitudes which see life in terms of simplistic good and evil; and a tendency to externalize bad traits, projecting them onto alien groups, away from oneself and one's own social group" (1965, pages 301 and 302).

Needless to say, Gallagher *et al.* consider this cluster of attitudes and modes to be a negative one, and they go on to suggest that people with high scores on the Authoritarianism Scale (43 to 70) are poor treatment risks and that people with low scores (16 to 42) are good ones.[2] In the present research, the same score demarcation lines were used for dividing clients into high and low prognostic groups, but in keeping with the basic premise of this study with regard to the treatability of all those who need and want help, it was hypothesized that there would be no difference in outcome between the two groups. The assumption here was that positive attributes like democratic values, an awareness of psychological influences, flexibility and openness to experience are, under favorable circumstances, happy results of treatment, not necessary prerequisites for it.

Factor five, initial in-therapy behavior, was assessed using the Rice Voice Quality Rating System, a measure of what might be thought of as psychological sophistication and openness which is unusual insofar as it is not a paper and pencil test at all but a categorization system applied to recorded samples of a subject's voice, such as those derivable from therapy tapes. The system focuses on noncontent aspects of speech and involves classifying each

---

[2] Lorr, Katz, and Rubinstein (1958), and McNair, Lorr, and Callahan (1963), reached a similar conclusion, using a different form of the F Scale; they found that clients with high F scores were more likely to drop out of therapy.

sample into one of four categories which Rice (Rice and Wagstaff, 1967, page 558) defines as follows:

1) Emotional. Responses placed in this first subclass may take a number of different forms, but in general there is energy overflow rather than control. The voice breaks, trembles or chokes. The general impression is one of disruption of the usual voice patterns with varying degrees of effort at control.

2) Focused. These responses are characterized by a good deal of energy, but not by a wide pitch fluctuation. There are irregularities in the stress of syllables, and stresses are not usually accompanied by much pitch rise. There are marked irregularities of tempo. Impressionistically, the total effect is one of pondering, of energy turned inward in an exploring fashion.

3) Externalizing. These responses are characterized by comparatively high energy and by a wide pitch range in the sense defined by Trager (1958). There is an unusually regular stress pattern with the heavy stresses accompanied by a rise in pitch. This stress pattern, together with the presence of terminal contours that rise or fall in expected places, gives an effect of cadence or preformed pattern. The total effect is one of energy turned outward, a "talking at" quality.

4) Limited. Responses placed here are characterized by low energy, a narrow pitch range, and an even tempo. The stress pattern is typical for English, but the stresses themselves are relatively weak. The voice is thinned from below. The general impression one gets is that of limited involvement, of distance from what is being expressed.

Using this ingenious system, Rice and her co-workers have found that clients who produce three or more responses categorizable as Focused in an early interview tend to achieve favorable therapeutic outcomes, whereas those who produce no such responses or only one or two of them tend to be unsuccessful. In the present research, it was assumed that while the categorization system is a valid and interesting one, the results achieved with it to date tell us more about the limitations of usual therapists than they do about those of clients who enter treatment with little or no Focusing Ability. Accordingly, the same demarcation lines were used to divide clients in this sample into high and low prognostic groups, but once again, the opposite prediction was made: high prognostic clients on this measure will do no better than low prognostic ones.

CLIENT DESCRIPTIVE CHARACTERISTICS AND IMPROVEMENT

If all of these negative hypotheses are borne out, it will indicate that lower class, severely disturbed, and psychologically unsophisticated clients are not the therapeutic untouchables they are often regarded as being, but it will not, in and of itself, convince the skeptic that client factors are generally less relevant than therapist factors. After all, such a skeptic might argue, clients in this sample are a heterogeneous lot of people who differ widely on a number of basic descriptive characteristics which are not tapped by the above-described prognostic measures. Moreover, as was noted in chapter 3, some of these clients received drug and/or activities therapy in addition to individual psychotherapy. Perhaps improvement in psychotherapy is related to some of these other client variables, or perhaps it is really a function of concurrent treatment rather than primarily a result of therapist variables.

To meet this objection, an exploration was undertaken of the relationship between therapeutic outcome and six additional client factors which various observers have suggested might have prognostic significance. Accordingly it was hypothesized that there would be no difference in outcome between clients who were receiving concurrent treatment and those who were not, between clients who had had prior outpatient psychotherapy and those who had not, between clients with a history of hospitalization and those without such a history, between initially productive and nonproductive clients, between clients of the same race as their therapists (white clients) and clients of a different race (black clients), and between younger clients (ages 16-35) and older ones (36 and over).

All in all, a total of eleven measures of client factors were used, and in each case, it was predicted that the positive relationships between high prognostic scores or attributes and degree of improvement found by previous researchers or noted by previous observers would not manifest themselves in the present study. The assumption here was that previous research findings and clinical observations reflected the biases and limitations of typical therapists in typical treatment settings rather than being a function of the inherent defects of nonclassical clients. If this proves to be the case, then prognostic measures for therapists would seem more to the point than prognostic measures for clients. In other words, if therapists in this sample do prove successful with nonclassical clients, then it will be especially important to try to understand what characteristics make it possible for them to achieve these results. With such an understanding, it ultimately should be possible to make positive results usual rather than unusual in the treatment of nonclassical clients. In the next subsection, an attempt will be made to specify a number of potentially relevant therapist variables as a basis for testing their relationship with psychotherapeutic improvement.

THERAPIST QUALITIES AND IMPROVEMENT

In the 1950s, studies of psychotherapy generally involved attempts to ascertain the global worthwhileness of treatment by determining the percentage of cases considered improved as a result of therapy. These studies triggered hot arguments between opponents and proponents of psychotherapy (e.g., De Charms, Levy, and Wertheimer, 1954; Eysenck, 1952, 1964; Luborsky, 1954; Meehl, 1955; Rosenzweig, 1954; Sanford, 1953; Strupp, 1963), but the controversy masked a basic agreement: both sides recognized that all of the studies considered contained methodological shortcomings so serious that they failed to provide any valid evidence as to the efficacy of psychotherapy. The main trouble with these studies was that in addition to lacking an adequate criterion of improvement, they made the unwarranted assumption that therapy was a homogeneous variable, a constant, regardless of who sat in the therapist's chair.

Evidence amassed in the sixties (e.g., Kiesler, 1966; Truax and Carkhuff, 1964) indicates that this is a totally erroneous assumption and that therapy varies dramatically depending on the practitioner. Group factors like professional affiliation, orientation, and technique do not seem to account for this variance. What seems to matter are the individual human qualities of the therapist, which vary as much within groups as they do between them. In this study, five such human qualities were hypothesized to be related to successful therapeutic work, and it was predicted that significant differences in outcome would be associated with them.

The importance of these hypotheses is twofold. First, and most immediately, they are important because they provide necessary research controls by allowing comparisons based on differential predictions for cases where these qualities are present, or present in sufficient degree, and cases where they are not. Second, they are important because, ultimately, they may help to provide a genuinely meritocratic basis for selecting, training, and evaluating therapists and potential therapists. At present, such decisions are largely matters of expert judgment, an expert being anyone who has been working in the field long enough to have acquired the power to make such decisions. Unfortunately, power is no guarantee of wisdom or skill and mistakes can be quite costly, to therapists and would-be therapists as well as to clients and those close to them.

Given this situation, plus some recent progress in research on therapist factors, it is understandable that some researchers are eager to press forward not only with further research but also with sweeping practical applications of the research that has already been done. The danger here is that premature reliance on inadequately validated measures will simply take us out of the frying pan and into the fire, replacing one set of arbitrary criteria with another less capricious but equally arbitrary set. Certainly, it is important to select therapists who can do the job, particularly with nonclassical clients, but it is equally important to refrain from screening out suitable candidates who do not happen to conform to irrelevant standards.

To insure that the standards we ultimately impose are truly relevant and not just a new form of thought control, it would seem reasonable to require the following as a minimal test of adequacy before any presumed measure of a relevant therapist factor is put to widespread practical use. First, the measure should make some theoretical sense; second, it should correlate with at least one other measure of the same thing; and third, it should work in more than one test with more than one type of therapist and more than one type of client. Despite the progress in this area in the last decade, none of the measures developed thus far have met all three of these tests of adequacy. Thus, their validity is still an open question, and one is entitled to make any hypotheses about them one pleases.

In the present study, in addition to hypothesizing that five measures of therapist characteristics would be relevant to therapeutic outcome, it was hypothesized that five others would prove irrelevant. Measures which have worked successfully in past studies were included in the negative as well as the positive hypothesis group, and some new measures and variables were added to both. All of them are described and discussed below.

POSITIVE THERAPIST FACTOR HYPOTHESES

Positive hypothesis one was that experienced therapists would prove more successful than inexperienced ones. This prediction was made despite the fact that a number of studies in recent years (e.g., Carkhuff, 1966; Carkhuff and Truax, 1965; Feifel and Eells, 1963) have failed to provide any support for the notion that veteran clinicians are superior to novices. It was made because a close look at the way in which experience was defined in many such studies leaves considerable room for doubt about how broadly one is justified in generalizing from them. For one thing, the difference between experienced and inexperienced clinicians has often been quite minimal—first- as opposed to second-year trainees, for example—and even when the difference was superficially greater, say, one year or less versus five years or more, the meaningfulness of the distinction has usually been open to question on more substantive grounds.

Time, after all, is not a causal agent in and of itself; it is a medium in which events take place, and the number of potentially beneficial events or learning experiences that actually do take place in any specified time span may vary quite widely. One clinician, for example, may treat as many as twenty or thirty clients in a single year, while another sees only one or two. Such a gross difference in experience would be totally obscured by an exclusive focus on elapsed time per se. To avoid such obscurity, it is necessary to control for number of clients seen as well as for number of years spent in the field. In addition, the type of clients seen should also be taken into account because experience with one type of client population is not necessarily relevant to therapeutic work with a different population.

In the present study, experience was defined so as to take account of all of these factors (see chapter 3 for specifics), in hopes of providing a fairer test of the value of experience than had heretofore been made. Such a test seemed important not because it was deemed important or even desirable to protect the status of the old, let alone to restrict, demean, or exact subservience of the young, but simply because one likes to feel that one can learn and improve as a result of one's experience and that, consequently, one will be a better therapist later than he was earlier. Actually, the best test of whether one is moving along a path or running on a treadmill would probably be a longitudinal study in which the same therapists were retested at different points in their career and compared with themselves rather than with others. In the context of the present research, this was not feasible, and it was necessary to settle for the cruder comparison described above and to attempt to mitigate its crudeness by defining the variable as tightly as possible.

Hypothesis two has to do with a therapist factor which has seldom been tested before but was referred to repeatedly in the first chapter of this book: democratic as opposed to authoritarian values. Usually, when this variable is included in psychotherapy studies at all, it is the client's authoritarianism that is under scrutiny and not the therapist's, the typical prediction being that less authoritarian clients will fare better than more authoritarian ones. In the present study, it was hypothesized that the degree of authoritarianism initially manifested by clients would have no effect on outcome but that the degree of authoritarianism manifested by therapists would have a marked effect, with less authoritarian therapists achieving significantly better results.

Measuring the depth and genuineness of a therapist's commitment to democracy is, however, no easy task. Measures useful with other populations (Adorno, Frenkel-Brunswik, Levinson, and Sanford, 1950; Gallagher, Sharaf, and Levinson, 1965; Rokeach, 1960) seemed inappropriate for subjects from a test-sophisticated group in which virtually everyone considers himself to be a liberal. The trick was to devise a measure which might begin to discriminate between individuals with a truly egalitarian outlook and individuals who simply pay lip service to egalitarian values because that is the conventional, socially desirable thing to do in their circles. With this aim in mind, a new version of the F scale was drawn up and inserted into the therapist's Self-Description Form, which is included in its entirety in Appendix B. For convenience, the relevant section is reproduced below.

> Question 9. Your position on therapeutic issues: Please indicate the extent to which you either agree or disagree with each of the following statements by placing one of the following marks next to each.

+3 agree strongly   -3 disagree strongly
+2 agree moderately   -2 disagree moderately
+1 agree slightly   -1 disagree slightly

_____ a) Successful completion of personal treatment should be a mandatory requirement for all therapists.

_____ b) Ideally, close supervision of individual therapy should be provided for all therapists on all or most of their cases at all stages in their careers.

_____ c) There are some cases which should not be treated by non-medical therapists without psychiatric supervision.

_____ d) Heads of treatment facilities for the mentally ill should generally be medically trained.

_____ e) If they had had a successful treatment experience, most political radicals of both the right and the left would change their views on society and its ills.

_____ f) Patients can profitably decide many things in inpatient settings with patient government systems but decisions about discharges and passes should be made only by the professional staff.

_____ g) Nonpsychotic adults convicted of offenses like prostitution and homosexuality need help whether they know it or not and therefore the courts should make outpatient treatment mandatory for them.

_____ h) Involvement of the poor in programs planned for their welfare is essential, but, because they are mainly oriented to immediate gratification, it is unrealistic to give them top level decision-making powers in planning such programs because long range goals would inevitably suffer.

_____ i) Most people who are very concerned about possible threats to civil liberties involved in large scale community mental health programs are either naive or reactionary.

_____ j) To co-ordinate service and facilitate effective mental health programs on a community-wide basis, any properly qualified professional should have access to any information about a patient in the hands of any other properly qualified professional without either having to obtain the patients' consent.

A reading of the above items *in this context* should make their rationale self-evident and, sadly, obsolete; this is a trick that will not work twice. It did, however, appear to work the first time. Therapists in the study seemed too caught up in the specific clinical content of the items to pay much attention to their more general philosophical and political implications, and, of course, they were not told that this was a version of the classic authoritarianism test which would be scored and interpreted in the same manner as the original. Even assuming that some of the therapists were aware or partially aware of the underlying liberal-illiberal continuum, however, it is unlikely that liberal answers given reflected the sheer social desirability of such answers because the scale was deliberately designed to make liberal answers conflict with conventional clinical wisdom, thus equalizing the pull of social desirability in both directions. This strategy worked well enough to produce an adequate range of scores and the a priori cutting point of 30 was used to divide the group into high prognostic (low scoring) and low prognostic (high scoring) individuals on this measure.

Hypotheses three and four both have to do with the effect of empathic understanding on psychotherapeutic outcome. Empathy was deemed worthy of special emphasis because all schools of psychotherapy aimed at the internal modification of its recipients agree on its importance (e.g., Federn, 1962; Fiedler, 1950a, 1950b; Greenson, 1960; Kohut, 1959; Rogers, 1956; Raines, 1956; Schafer, 1959), because clients also seem to regard it as a crucial therapist variable (e.g., Heine, 1950, 1953), and because it is the one factor which has consistently shown a significant positive relationship to outcome in empirical studies (e.g., Barret-Lennard, 1962; Cartwright and Lerner, 1963; Truax, Wargo, Frank, Imber, Battle, Hoehn-Saric, Nash, and Stone, 1966; Truax and Carkhuff, 1965; Truax, 1963; Van der Veen, 1967).

Despite these promising indications, both the generality and the validity of previous findings are open to question on two major counts. First, controlled studies relating empathy to outcome have tended to involve a quite restricted range of therapists (mainly those of the client-centered persuasion) and a quite restricted range of clients (mainly middle class neurotics). Second, the measures of empathy used in these various studies have differed from study to study, and each study has used only one measure. Problems exist with regard to the validity of each type of measure, and the relation, if any, between different types of measures is an open question.

In the present study, it was assumed that empathy is a complex variable with at least two major aspects: background empathy and foreground empathy. Background empathy involves one's overall grasp of another human being's general feeling about himself as an integrated totality, his relatively stable, overall emotional experience of himself. Foreground empathy involves one's moment-to-moment grasp of the immediate feeling state of another human being, his transient, ever-shifting emotional state. Since one's general feeling about oneself is largely an outgrowth of past experience and one's immediate feeling state is largely a reaction to present experience, background empathy is necessarily more past-oriented and foreground empathy more present-oriented.

Looking at the role of empathy in psychotherapy with this conception in mind, it can be seen that, while all schools of psychotherapy aimed at the internal modification of its recipients agree on the importance of empathy, different schools have tended to emphasize different aspects of the phenomenon. In particular, psychoanalysis has tended to stress background empathy in both the theory and the practice of therapy, while client-centered people have tended to stress foreground empathy in both their theory and their practice.

Similarly, different measures of empathy have tended to tap one aspect of empathy more than another. For example, the Cartwright-type predictive measure, in which therapists are asked to answer personally relevant questions as they think their clients would, is chiefly a measure of background empathy; the Truax-type concurrent measure, in which clinical judges rate responses to clients on therapy tapes, is chiefly a measure of foreground empathy. In the present research, it was assumed that maximal and maximally effective therapeutic empathy involves simultaneously high degrees of empathy for both foreground and background emotional experience. Thus, it involves empathically grasping the immediate feeling state of another *and* the overall emotional context in which he experiences that feeling state.

Another way of saying this is to suggest that a high degree of foreground empathy will allow one fluidly to grasp and respond to the common human essence in another's immediate flow of feeling, and that a high degree of background empathy will allow one to grasp and respond to the unique personal quality, tone, and resonance which these universal emotions have for a particular person with a particular history in a particular situation at a particular time. Thus, when both aspects of empathy are high and highly integrated, the empathic response will have immediacy and depth and will reflect both the universal and the unique aspects of its recipients' experience.

In line with this conception of empathy, two measures were utilized, a predictive and a concurrent one. It was hypothesized that each would bear a positive relationship to outcome and that the two would correlate with one another to at least a modest degree. It was also hypothesized that therapists with high prognostic scores on both measures would achieve better results than therapists with high prognostic scores on only one. The Truax Accurate Empathy Scale (Truax, 1961) was used unaltered to measure concurrent empathy in order to test its effectiveness with the heterogeneous group of clients and therapists in the present study. However, the Cartwright scale (Cartwright and Lerner, 1963) of predictive empathy had to be greatly altered to make it applicable to this sample, and so a new measure was devised.

In the predictive empathy measure developed for this study, each therapist was asked to predict his client's self-ratings as either true or false on a scale composed of forty self-descriptive items. These items differed for each client and were derived from his response to a modified, extended, and reworded version of the Butler and Haigh Q-sort. This special Q-sort consisted of 120 self-descriptive statements, each one printed separately on a small card. These 120 items were divided into two decks, a positive deck containing 60 positive self-descriptive statements and a negative deck containing 60 negative self-descriptive items. Administration was a four-stage procedure in which the client was first presented with the positive deck and told that each card in it said something that was good, or at least something that some people felt was good about themselves. He was asked to read every statement in the deck and to pick out the ten good things he felt were most true about himself. When he finished, he was asked to go back over the remaining fifty cards and to pick out the ten good things he felt were least true about himself. Next, he was handed the negative deck and told that each card said something that was bad, or at least something that some people felt was bad about themselves. He was again asked to read each card and to pick out the ten bad or sad things he felt were most true of himself. Finally, he was asked to reread the remaining fifty cards and to pick out the ten bad or sad things he felt were least true about himself. Thus, the final scale consisted of forty items selected by the client out of a pool of 120 items, and although item content varied from client to client, formal properties of the scale always remained constant with twenty true items (ten positives and ten negatives) and twenty false ones (ten positives and ten negatives).

This procedure has a number of advantages in both clinical and research terms. Clinically, it tends to provide a satisfying and therapeutic experience for the client because (1) it allows him to present his positive as well as his negative feelings about himself and to start and finish with the positives; (2) it makes it easy and pleasurable to think about and to present to another his picture of himself because it provides a high degree of structure plus a high degree of choice; and (3) it tends to foster the client's sense of himself as an autonomous agent with choice and control over the material he presents, an active collaborator rather than a passive recipient submitting to a mysterious procedure designed to expose him and uncover his faults or force him into some ill-fitting prefabricated "box." Most important as a basis for these positive effects is the fact that the client chooses his items out of a large pool and is encouraged to discard those he considers irrelevant and those which, relevant or no, are difficult for him to apply to himself because he does not know if they are true or false about himself, or feels they are neither or both.

In research terms, the procedure and the items themselves were designed to reduce middle class bias and to insure their applicability to an extremely wide range of clients. Because both instructions and item wording are much simpler than in the Kelley Role Repetoire Test, from which the items in the original Cartwright measure were derived, and also simpler than in the original Butler and Haigh Q-sort, from which many of the items in this series were derived, the test can be taken even by psychotically confused and/or semi-literate lower class clients and, with the procedural alteration of reading the items aloud to the client, by illiterate and/or retarded clients.

This procedure is also a fairer test of therapists' empathy than most others of its type for two reasons: (1) since all the items may reasonably be assumed to be meaningful for the client because he chose them, therapists are not penalized for being wrong about matters that are not relevant for their clients; and (2) since all are clear items in the true-false directional sense, the therapist is not penalized for being "wrong" about items the client himself is unsure about. Thus, it seems fairer on this test to weight all errors equally than it does on other similar tests. Perhaps it might be legitimate to describe this feature of the test as a sort of clinical approach to an equal interval scale.

One further research advantage is that by combining the client's first and fourth sorts (positive characteristics he possesses and negative characteristics he is free of), one gets a picture of the client's positive self-image; by combining the client's second and third sorts (positive characteristics he lacks and negative characteristics he has), one gets a picture of his negative self-image. Thus, in addition to testing the therapist's overall empathy for his client, one can also derive separate measurements on his empathy for his client's positive and negative self-images. Since therapists were also asked to rate themselves on the items their clients selected, it should be possible to explore and test the effects of actual similarity on assumed similarity and dissimilarity, and in so doing, to lay to rest one of Cronbach's (1955) criticisms of predictive empathy measures.[3]

The fifth and last positive hypothesis was that therapists' initial expectations of success or failure for each case would have a significant effect on outcome, with positive expectations being related to positive results and negative expectations to negative results. Previous research suggesting the likelihood of such effects has already been cited (see chapter 1). Because negative expectations with regard to the ability of nonclassical clients to profit from psychotherapy are so widespread, a demonstration of reverse effects in the

---

[3]Cronbach's other two major objections seem equally surmountable. With regard to stereotype accuracy, a frequency count of the number of times clients who selected an item rated it true, compared to the number of times they rated it false, indicated that there were too few stereotypic client answers for any therapist to get very far by predicting on that basis. With regard to scale elevation, in strict terms, that is eliminated by the use of a nominal rather than an ordinal scale. Looking at this problem more broadly, however, one might reasonably view the fixed ratio of true to false items as reintroducing an analogous trap but one that can easily be sprung by telling the therapists at the outset that twenty items are always true and twenty false. That procedure was not followed in the present study, however. Therapists were simply told to mark the items true or false as they thought their clients would have done.

present context seemed particularly desirable. Accordingly, expectations were assessed by asking each therapist to check one of the five options listed as part of his overall description of each of his clients at pre-therapy. Cases for which therapists checked options a or b were grouped together as high prognosis cases and those for which therapists checked options c, d or e were combined to form the low prognosis group with regard to therapist expectations.

Question 10. Therapists estimate of prognosis:

_____a) Very good; I feel pretty certain that I can help this client.
_____b) Good; I feel that I can probably help this client.
_____c) Fair; I feel the odds are 50/50.
_____d) Guarded; there's an outside chance but I feel the odds are against it.
_____e) Very guarded; I feel that this client will probably drop out or otherwise frustrate my attempt to help him but I plan to try anyway.

NEGATIVE THERAPIST FACTOR HYPOTHESES

If all five of the positive hypotheses described above are borne out, it will indicate that the ideal therapist is an experienced person with strongly democratic values, a high degree of empathic understanding, and an optimistic view of his client's treatment potential. In addition to including some elements which other researchers and clinicians might leave out, this definition omits a number of factors which others have considered significant. For example, many clinicians regard the therapist's own experience as a client as the single most important element in his training, arguing that a therapist will not be able to help others effectively unless and until he has had a successful treatment experience of his own. In some circles, this belief is so strongly held that clinical candidates are not merely encouraged but required to undergo treatment, and their potential as therapists is evaluated on the basis of their performance as clients. If this viewpoint is correct, then it should follow that the more successful a therapist's own personal treatment has been, the more positive will be the effects he produces on his clients—or at least, this is how the hypothesis might be stated by a believer who was inclined to subject his belief to an empirical test. Alas, believers have not been so inclined; a search of the literature in this area revealed numerous authoritative pronouncements and no hard data at all.

In the present study, this viewpoint was presumed to be incorrect, and it was hypothesized that therapists who had had no treatment and therapists who were less than enthusiastic about the treatment they had had would be just as successful with their clients as those who, on the therapist's Self-

Description Form, rated at least one course of personal treatment as "maximally successful." Such an outcome was felt to be particularly likely in the present study where therapists were dealing primarily with nonclassical clients because unqualified enthusiasm for one's own treatment was viewed as a crude and indirect, but potentially useful, estimate of professional orthodoxy. The underlying assumption here was that because the orthodox clinical establishment does not have a record to be proud of with regard to the poor and the severely disturbed, too close an adherence to or too great an enthusiasm for orthodoxy would probably not be an asset in dealing with nonclassical clients. Indirect measures of professional orthodoxy were felt to be useful for much the same reason that an indirect measure of authoritarianism was considered necessary. Currently, professional unorthodoxy is about as fashionable an expressed viewpoint as is liberalism and democracy, but with the former as with the latter, what is professed and what is practiced can be two quite different things. As might be expected, when asked directly (see Question 3 on the therapist's Self-Description Form) no therapist in the present study described himself as an orthodox practitioner of anything, except for one woman who listed her orientation as "Experiential" and explained this as meaning she believed in being strictly herself.

Lest the above be misinterpreted as a polemic against treatment for therapists, it should probably be emphasized that this is not the point at all. Rather, the point is that treatment ought to be optional, not mandatory, for therapists as well as for other human beings, and that some degree of restlessness or dissatisfaction with one's helpers, one's mentors, and/or oneself should not be used to disqualify anyone as a therapist or potential therapist. The assumption here is that in addition to the characteristics spelled out in the preceding section, therapists need only a *modest* degree of psychological stability plus a marked awareness of the strengths, weaknesses, possibilities, and limitations present in themselves and others, an awareness that some people manage to achieve without therapy and others fail to achieve with it. Therapists do not need to be psychological supermen, nor should they be docile, subservient, and uncritical with regard to any orthodoxy or authority, even one of their own choosing.

Three more negative and contrary hypotheses flow, at least in part, from this view of the good therapist as a very human human being and a somewhat skeptical and critical one at that. These hypotheses have to do with therapists' initial subjective reactions to their clients. A number of observers in this field have suggested that positive therapist reactions to clients are essential and that negative reactions are anathema if successful treatment is to take place. Unfortunately, many clients, particularly many severely disturbed clients, are so angry and suspicious, so sunk into stereotyped ruts, or so lost in labyrinths of confusion that only a saint could respond with instant unconditional positive regard or genuine warmth. Ordinary human beings are not likely to find such clients particularly likeable, interesting, or comprehensible at the outset, and the contention in this research is that they do not need to, as long as they have some basic respect for them as human beings and can see some possibility of ultimately developing more positive feelings as a result of sustained mutual work together.

Accordingly, it was hypothesized that therapeutic outcome would be unaffected by the degree of (1) liking, (2) interest, or (3) emotional understanding which therapists felt they had for their clients at pre-therapy. Therapists' reactions to their clients were assessed via item 11 on the Therapist's Description of Client Form which reads as follows:

> Please estimate your subjective gut-level reaction to this client in terms of the following:
>
> a) Degree of liking he invokes in you.
>   High _____ Medium _____ Low _____
> b) Degree of interest he arouses in you.
>   High _____ Medium _____ Low _____
> c) Degree of emotional transparency he has for you, e.g., degree to which you feel you can accurately sense what he is feeling.
>   High _____ Medium _____ Low _____

To test these hypotheses, therapists who checked high on each measure were placed in one group and therapists who checked either medium or low were placed in the other.

The final negative hypothesis in the therapist factor series has to do with the effects of therapist type, in terms of something called the Whitehorn-Betz A-B Scale (e.g., Betz, 1962; Whitehorn and Betz, 1960), on therapeutic outcome. For readers unfamiliar with this instrument who may be hoping for a clear description of the meaning of the typology derived from it, the best that can be done is to provide some initiation into the higher ignorance shared by those of us who are familiar with it. Briefly, the Whitehorn-Betz scale is an empirical device for classifying therapists as either A's or B's, according to the answers they give to a variable series of items drawn from the Strong Vocational Interest Blank for Men.

The Strong Vocational Interest Blank is a test which determines whether a subject's interest patterns are similar to those expressed by members of a variety of occupational groupings. Essentially, type A therapists are those whose interests turn out to be similar to those expressed by lawyers and dissimilar to those expressed by math and physical science teachers, whereas type B therapists are those who manifest a reverse pattern. That much is clear, and little else. The personality traits which presumably underlie these divergent interest patterns are a mystery, and the relevance of those mysterious traits to psychotherapy is even more mysterious.

Nonetheless, it is a fact that various versions of the Whitehorn-Betz Scale have repeatedly and significantly distinguished between more and less successful therapists working with various sorts of clients. For example, A therapists seem to do better with schizophrenics, although, paradoxically, they seem to prefer nonschizophrenics; B therapists seem to do better with nonschizophrenics, although they too seem to have the reverse preference (e.g., Betz, 1963a, 1963b; Kemp, 1966). Of course, a number of post hoc explanations have been offered for these puzzling findings, but they tend to be rather far-fetched. For instance, it has been suggested that A therapists are more empathic and less authoritarian than B's. Perhaps, but what that has to do with the interests of lawyers and math-physical science teachers is still unclear. In addition, this suggestion raises the question of why A therapists are not good with everybody and B therapists not bad with everybody—a hard question to answer unless one wants to argue that democracy and understanding are of value for psychotics but not for other people.

In summary, what we have here is a measure which seems to work, although it does not add very much to our comprehension of what is involved in successful psychotherapy. Such a state of affairs is not unduly troubling to researchers for whom prediction is an end in itself, but it is frustrating for those of us who aim at understanding and see prediction as useful mainly insofar as it provides a means to that end.[4]

Accordingly, in this study, it was hypothesized that the A-B distinction would fail to relate to therapeutic outcome, partly out of sheer bias against atheoretical measures and partly because, although some previous researchers with this instrument have neglected to specify the sex of their therapists, it seems probable that males have predominated in most other samples and there are slightly more females than males in this one. To classify therapists as either A's or B's for this test, it was necessary to decide which of the numerous versions of the scale to use, a decision which was resolved in favor of the McNair, Callahan and Lorr form (1962) because these authors provided the clearest methodological rationale for the items included.

The actual items in this version of the scale are 13 in number, listed in verbatim form below, complete with official instructions, so that readers who like puzzles may amuse themselves by trying to figure out which answers would be given by which sorts of people—and why and what it has to do with psychotherapy anyway.

---

[4] Whitehorn and Betz themselves *are* concerned about understanding, as well as about prediction, and they have made significant contributions in both areas. The trouble is that their understanding is not really derived from and does not really fit their predictive measure and vice versa.

Whitehorn-Betz A-B Scale
McNair, Callahan and Lorr 13 Item Version

Part I. Occupations. Indicate for each occupation listed below whether you would like that kind of work or not. Don't worry about whether you would be good at the job or about your possible lack of training in it. Forget about how much money you can make in it, or whether you can get ahead in it. Think only about whether you would like the work that has to be done in the job.

      Mark on the answer sheet in the column labeled "L" if you like that kind of work.

      Mark in the column labeled "I" if you are indifferent (*that is, don't care one way or another*)

      Mark in the column labeled "D" if you don't like that kind of work.

Work fast. Put down the first thing that comes to mind. Answer every one.

	L	I	D
17. Building Contractor			
19. Carpenter			
59. Marine Engineer			
60. Mechanical Engineer			
87. Ship Officer			
94. Toolmaker			

Part II. School Subjects. Show as you did in Part I your interest in these school subjects, even though you may not have studied them.

	L	I	D
121. Manual Training			
122. Mechanical Drawing			

Part III. Amusements. Show in the same way as you did before in Parts I and II whether or not you like these ways of having fun. Work rapidly. Do not think over various possibilities. Record your first feeling of liking, indifference or disliking.

	L	I	D
151. Drilling in a company			
185. Making a radio set			

Part IV. Activities. Show in the same way as you did before how you feel about these activities.

	L	I	D
189. Cabinetmaking			
218. Looking at shop windows			

Part VIII. If the item below describes you, mark in the first column ("Yes"); if the item does *not* describe you mark in the third column ("No"); and if you are not sure mark in the second column ("?").

	Yes	?	No
368. Have mechanical ingenuity.			

CHAPTER 7

time factors, dropouts, and summary

TIME FACTORS IN TREATMENT

Freud, the father of psychotherapy, tried to help his clients achieve a total recall of the past in hopes of effecting a total and permanent transformation of the present and future. He tried to do this by playing an essentially passive role and providing his clients with a blank screen on which to project their buried fears and fantasies. Not surprisingly, he found that treatment, so defined and so conducted, was an interminable process. In the forties and fifties, dissatisfaction with such goals and such techniques became widespread among psychoanalysts (e.g., Alexander, 1961; Colby, 1951), as well as among other sorts of therapists. As goals and techniques changed, ideas about time factors in treatment began to change also, but more slowly.

Today, most therapists, regardless of orientation, are active participants in a treatment process which focuses on the past only insofar as it clearly and significantly affects the present. They do not expect to transform people or to guarantee them a permanent future prophylaxis. Yet, many therapists still cling to the view that effective therapy is always a long, slow process, requiring years rather than months, and many researchers still insist that long term follow-ups are a necessity if therapeutic results are to be adequately evaluated.

In the present research, it was hypothesized that treatment outcome would not be related to treatment length as measured by either the number of months or the number of sessions involved. Moreover, a demonstration of *current* positive effects was regarded as a sufficient test of the utility of psychotherapy. With regard to the first point, there is already a good deal of research evidence (e.g., Errera, McKee, Smith, and Gruber, 1967; Lorr, McNair, Michaux, and Riskin, 1962; Stieper and Wiener, 1959) suggesting the absence of any simple linear association between degree of improvement and duration of treatment; there is even some ingenious work suggesting that relatively brief treatment with a deadline set from the outset may be especially beneficial in some cases (e.g., Shlien, 1957; Shlien, Mosak, and Dreikurs, 1962).

As is so often the case, however, most of these studies deal only or mainly with mildly or moderately disturbed middle and upper class clients. Hence, their relevance to nonclassical clients is an open question, particularly since most therapists seem convinced that the more severely disturbed a client is, the longer it takes to bring about any significant changes in him. The recent increase in the frequency of very brief intervention attempts with severely disturbed and/or lower class clients brought about by the community mental health movement are of little help in refuting this pessimistic conviction. Most community mental health workers tend to deal with such clients only under special circumstances (e.g., crisis therapy) or to use criteria of improvement which most therapists would reject. They would reject them because, while most therapists no longer nurse illusions about effecting total transformations, they rarely settle for minimal maintenance or a return to a previously unsatisfactory status quo, yet most community mental health efforts with nonclassical set their sights no higher than that.[1]

In the present research, all clients who completed therapy were severely disturbed according to their initial RPFS scores (the range was from 23.5 to 35). The criterion of improvement used, a significant gain in pre- to posttherapy RPFS scores, was stringent enough to make possible a quite specific and meaningful test of the relation between treatment length and treatment outcome with non-classical clients. To provide further evidence on this point, it was also hypothesized that there would be no relation between initial severity of impairment, as measured by the RPFS, and treatment length, as

---

[1] Potential social and political implications of the goals of many community mental health practitioners are depressing to say the least. Consider, for example, the following quotation from a recent issue of the *Community Mental Health Journal*: "Moreover, rehabilitation of the patient in the neighborhood where he will ultimately live as an independent agent overcomes a major shortcoming of hospital treatment, namely, the creation of an ideal or unrealistic hospital milieu which may make adjustment to the extramural community rather difficult" (Weinman, Sanders, Kleiner, and Wilson, 1970, p. 15). The big question here, of course, has to do with just how far we want to go in accepting the conditions in the client's community of origin and rejecting deviations from them as too "ideal" or "unrealistic"—a very big question indeed, considering the fact that conditions imposed on the communities many hospitalized clients come from are such that living with vermin and being treated like them is par for the course. Hopefully, the gentlemen who wrote the sentence quoted above do not really mean to suggest that we wouldn't want such people to get used to anything better, but a little more clarity on such points would be reassuring.

measured by either the number of months or the number of sessions involved. Thus, if all of these hypotheses are borne out, it will suggest that psychotherapy may be a reasonably practical as well as a reasonably effective component for community mental health programs aimed at the urban poor.

Reasonable practicality is, however, a very vague phrase, and before hypotheses about time factors in treatment could be meaningfully tested, it was necessary to define it with greater precision. Accordingly, in the present study it was assumed that six months or less, and 25 sessions or fewer, was a practical amount of time and that, in general, clients treated for longer periods were unlikely to achieve greater benefits. To test this assumption, cases falling within that range were defined as short-treatment cases, and cases falling outside it were defined as long-treatment cases, the hypothesis being that there would be no difference in either impairment or improvement between them, except possibly at the extremes.

Extremes refer to very short cases, defined as less than two months or ten sessions, and to very long cases, defined as more than twelve months or 75 sessions. Although no limitations with regard to treatment length were imposed upon therapists or clients in the present study, familiarity with the working methods of most therapists in the study made it seem unlikely that there would be many extreme cases. However, it was decided that if a substantial number of cases did fall outside the two to twelve month or 10 to 75 session range, another hypothesis would be tested, namely, that both extremes are counterproductive. Extremely brief treatment was hypothesized to be counterproductive for the obvious reason that instantaneous change is unlikely; treatment participants seeking it are likely to be either frustrated or fooled. Extremely long treatment was hypothesized to be equally counterproductive for the less obvious reason that the danger of stimulating excessive dependency while disappointing excessive hopes is great and likely to outweigh whatever gains are made. Belief in the reasonableness of the second hypothesis was buttressed by an observation made in other settings that in prolonged therapies treatment often seems to function as a substitute rather than as a preparation for a satisfying life. To prevent such distortions of the function of treatment, it seems advisable to terminate most cases after no more than a year, reassuring clients who are loath to leave that they can always re-enter treatment at a later date if they so desire.

Indeed, there are many indications that such re-entries are extremely common anyway, regardless of whether treatment is long or short and quite independent of its success or failure. Critics who consider such re-entries as automatic failures do so because they assume that successful therapy is a once and for all, make-or-break experience, which ought to provide permanent invulnerability. Such an assumption flies in the face of all that has been learned in the past twenty years about the importance of the contemporary milieu, physical as well as social, in maintaining or undermining adequate levels of human psychological functioning (e.g., Solomon, Kubzansky, Leiderman, Mendelson, Trumbull, and Wexler, 1961; Carson, 1969; Fiske and Maddi, 1961; Goffman, 1961). It seems painfully inappropriate for nonclassical clients who belong to the least powerful and least protected segment of our society and are subsequently subjected to the most extreme degrees of stress and deprivation. The best answer to such unrealistic and unwittingly reactionary critics is contained in an old saying: He who does not lose his mind under certain conditions has no mind to lose.

In the present study, it was assumed that all nonclassical clients had minds to lose and that helping them regain control of their minds would not guarantee immunity to future environmental assaults but would make it easier for them to work with their fellows to counter and perhaps ultimately to prevent such assaults and their humanly destructive consequences. That, after all, is what primary prevention is all about, and that is why it is needed in addition to, but not instead of, psychotherapy.

DROPOUTS FROM TREATMENT

Dropouts are clients who make a unilateral decision to leave treatment before they have accomplished their aims and before their therapists have given up hope of helping them to do so. Usually, they make their exit after less than ten sessions, occasionally after as many as fifteen or twenty. Professionals commonly regard them as a subspecies of therapeutic failure, and consistent with a general tendency to lay all blame for therapeutic failures at clients' doors, they are seen as possessing a variety of fatal flaws which account for their uncooperativeness. Researchers have been zealous in attempting to uncover these fatal flaws and to construct screening devices which will prevent them from getting into treatment in the first place.

Fortunately for the reputation of dropouts, some unusual research by Lewis Brandt (Brandt, 1964; Riess and Brandt, 1965) has made it rather clear that there is something very suspect about this whole approach. What made Brandt's research unusual was that instead of assuming that dropouts were untreatable people, self-exiled into some permanent outer darkness, he decided to check on what actually happened to a sample of them. By this wonderful expedient, he discovered that a substantial proportion of them had simply entered treatment elsewhere, raising the equally wonderful spectre that, at least with this client group, the bad clients in one study may be the good ones in another.

In the present research, it was assumed that dropouts were neither particularly good nor particularly bad clients and that their therapists were probably not consistently unique either. The latter assumption seemed reasonable in light of a phenomenon observed frequently at the Blank Park Center in the period preceding the formal initiation of the study: many dropouts not only re-entered treatment, they also asked to be reassigned to the same therapist. In view of the frequently expressed conviction that therapeutic time spent with dropouts is therapeutic time wasted, it is also interesting to note that, in many of these cases, returning dropouts seemed to have derived benefit from their earlier contact and perhaps even from their abrupt termination of it and the no-treatment period that ensued.

Thus, it seemed reasonable to assume that dropouts are a fairly mixed group, containing some people who have rejected treatment, some who are only seeking a more compatible therapist, and others who have already found one but need some time to think the matter over. To test this assumption, it was predicted that there would be no significant differences between dropouts and other clients and few, if any, differences in their therapists.

More specifically, the null hypothesis was tested with eleven client factors, ten therapist factors, and one case factor, a total of twenty-two tests in all. The client and therapist factors are, of course, the same ones utilized in the study as a whole, factors which are described in previous chapters and listed once again in the summary at the end of this chapter. The added case factor is a derivative of the previously described goals measure and involved classifying cases according to whether clients and therapists had chosen the same or different goals at pre-therapy.

SUMMARY OF HYPOTHESES

This chapter is the concluding one in this section, and in winding it up, it seems useful to present a summary to help the reader who has been focusing on the trees in the last several chapters to look at the forest as a whole once again. To this end, all of the hypotheses described and discussed in previous chapters are summarized in outline form below.

I. Hypotheses having to do with the adequacy and utility of the Rorschach Psychological Functioning Scale.

   A. The RPFS will prove a reliable measure of both impairment and improvement as determined by:
      1. adequate interscorer reliabilities on total scores;
      2. adequate interscorer reliabilities on subscores;
      3. adequate interscorer reliabilities on component scores.

   B. The RPFS will prove a meaningful measure of the adequacy of psychological functioning as determined by:
      1. a significant relationship with therapists' judgments of severity of impairment;

2. a significant relationship with behavioral data on client hospitalization history;
3. a significant relationship with behavioral data on client productivity, defined as the ability to hold a job or stay in school;
4. a significant relationship with therapeutic goals selected by clients but not by their therapists.

C. The RPFS will prove a sensitive measure of change as a result of therapy or other hypothesized change-producing agents as determined by:
1. a significant relationship with therapists' judgments of outcome;
2. a significant relationship with clients' judgments of outcome;
3. a significant relationship with behavioral change, as measured by entry or re-entry into school or employment;
4. some ability to predict and/or explain divergent judgments of outcome by clients and therapists.

D. RPFS total scores will be more adequate in more tests of impairment and improvement than either structure or function scores alone.

II. Hypotheses having to do with improvement in psychotherapy.

A. The majority of clients in this study will show improvement as a result of therapy as judged by:
1. RPFS change scores;
2. therapists' outcome ratings;
3. clients' outcome ratings.

III. Hypotheses having to do with the relation of client factors, therapist factors, and time factors to improvement.

A. Hypotheses with regard to client factors.
1. There will be no positive difference in degree of therapeutic improvement achieved by clients who are high and clients who are low on the following client prognostic measures:
   a. the Hollingshead and Redlich Two Factor Social Class Index;
   b. severity of psychological impairment at pre-therapy as measured by therapists' ratings;
   c. the Klopfer Rorschach Prognostic Rating Scale;
   d. the Rice Client Voice Quality Rating System;
   e. the F Scale measure of authoritarianism.
2. There will be no positive difference in degree of therapeutic improvement manifested by clients who differ with regard to the following descriptive characteristics:
   a. concurrent treatment;

b. prior outpatient psychotherapy;
c. prior hospitalization;
d. initial productivity;
e. race;
f. age.

B. Hypotheses with regard to therapist factors.
1. There will be a positive difference in degree of therapeutic improvement produced by therapists who are high and therapists who are low on the following therapist prognostic factors:
a. amount and type of therapeutic experience;
b. nonauthoritarianism or degree of commitment to democratic values as measured by a special version of the F Scale;
c. degree of therapeutic empathy as measured by a special predictive empathy test at pre- and/or post-therapy;
d. degree of therapeutic empathy as measured by the Truax concurrent empathy scale at pre- and/or at post-therapy;
e. subjective expectation of success for each case.
2. There will be no positive difference in degree of therapeutic improvement produced by therapists who are high and therapists who are low on the following therapist prognostic measures:
a. therapist type as measured by the Whitehorn-Betz A-B Scale;
b. therapist's initial self-rated liking for each client;
c. therapist's initial self-rated interest in each client;
d. therapist's initial self-rated understanding for each client;
e. therapist's own history as a client and feelings about it.

C. Hypotheses with regard to time factors.
1. There will be no difference in degree of initial RPFS impairment between long and short treatment cases as measured by:
a. number of months of treatment;
b. number of sessions involved.
2. There will be no difference in degree of final RPFS improvement between long and short treatment cases as measured by:
a. number of months for each case;
b. number of sessions for each case.

IV. Hypotheses having to do with dropouts from treatment.

A. There will be no difference between terminators and remainers on the following client factors:
1. history of hospitalization;
2. social class;
3. Klopfer RPFS scores;

   4. age;
   5. prior outpatient psychotherapy;
   6. therapists' ratings of severity of impairment;
   7. initial productivity;
   8. authoritarianism;
   9. Rice client voice quality;
  10. race;
  11. concurrent treatment.

B. There will be no difference between terminators and remainers on the following therapist factors:
   1. Whitehorn-Betz type;
   2. experience;
   3. predictive empathy;
   4. concurrent empathy;
   5. democratic values;
   6. personal treatment history;
   7. liking for client;
   8. interest in client;
   9. understanding of client;
  10. expectations for client.

C. There will be no difference between terminators and remainers on the following case factor:
   1. client and therapist goal discordance.

SUMMARY OF MEASURES AND PROCEDURES

Data to test these hypotheses were obtained by testing each client and each therapist in the study at pre-therapy and at post-therapy and by collecting tapes of early, intermediate, and late therapy sessions for each case. The test battery for clients consisted of a special Q-sort self-description, a version of the F Scale, a Rorschach, a TAT, and a client goal selection form at pre-therapy, which was replaced by a client outcome form at post-therapy. Data collected from therapists included a therapist's self-description form, a therapists' description of client form, an empathy test, a therapy session attendance form, and a therapist's outcome rating form. Forms created for this research provide the basis for a number of tests and are reproduced in full in Appendix B. All tests and forms were administered by a single administrator, and all subjective scoring was done by blind raters with independent reliabilities established anew for each.

    In analyzing results, data was treated ordinally when feasible and nominally when necessary. Nominal cutting points were established on an a priori basis and consisted either of a specific point or the group median. Levels of significance were also assigned in advance with .05 considered significant and .10 considered as a trend toward significance. Except with regard to dropouts, all tests were one-tailed because all hypotheses were directional. Directional hypotheses were of two types: (1) positive hypotheses in which the prediction is of the A-will-be-greater-than-B sort; and (2) negative hypotheses, where the literature suggests a directional hypothesis of the A-will-be-greater-than-B sort, and the specific prediction here is that A will not be greater than B. Hypotheses in relation to dropouts were the only nondirectional ones in this study, and all tests of these hypotheses were two-tailed.

part III:

research results and implications

adequacy of the rpfs

The purpose of this chapter is to redescribe the clients in this research in terms of the RPFS scores they obtained at the start of therapy and at the end of it, and to report the results of tests aimed at assessing the meaningfulness of these scores as indices of impairment and improvement. To accomplish that purpose, we shall first present data on the reliability of the measure and then go on to consider its validity, first as an index of impairment, and second as an index of improvement. Finally, in the last subsection, we will consider the human meaning of various specific types of improvement, with a view to understanding the value of such changes for the individual clients involved, for their therapists, and for society as a whole.

DATA, SCORING, AND RELIABILITY

To be a meaningful measure of impairment, improvement, or anything else, a test score must first of all be something that two or more properly trained judges can independently agree upon, if not perfectly in every instance, then at least closely in most instances. Such agreement is called interscorer reliability and is a necessary but not a sufficient condition of meaningfulness or validity. Without it, a test score is no more than an arbitrary mark on a piece of paper, varying each time it is applied and quite without reference to variations in the person it is supposed to be describing. With such agreement or consistency, a test score is more than an arbitrary mark; it is a piece of information, but one that may or may not have the specific meaning its proponents think it has. That is why validity must be demonstrated apart from reliability but can only be demonstrated after reliability has been established.

To establish reliability and pave the way for tests of validity, it is necessary to have a sufficient sample of cases to rule out chance agreement and to insure that the scores assigned to the cases by each scorer are not biased by information about the clients from sources other than the test in question itself. Absence of potentially biasing information about the clients is important for a trustworthy evaluation of interscorer reliability because scorers are human beings and, human beings being what they are, scorers who think they are supposed to find a particular thing in a particular case sometimes find just that, whether it is there or not. Deliberate cheating is not the main danger here. Research scorers who are deliberately dishonest are as rare as they are disgraceful, but research scorers are as capable of unwittingly fooling themselves as are the rest of us—and that, of course, is very capable indeed.

In life generally, self-deception is very hard to prevent; in research, it is relatively easy. Indeed, research might reasonably be defined as the science of preventing self-deception. The traditional research method of preventing scorer self-deception of the sort described above is the use of so-called blind scorers, scorers who have had no contact with the clients and have no potentially biasing information about them or about the research hypotheses they are supposed to help demonstrate. Such blind scorers then apply their skills to the records drawn from a large enough sample of clients to facilitate statistical tests of the precise degree of agreement between them and the precise odds that such a degree of agreement might have been obtained by chance.

In this study, the sample of clients consisted of the forty-five individuals who entered psychotherapy with our fifteen therapists between 1966 and 1968. Thirty of these clients had completed treatment, twelve had dropped out, and three were still in treatment at the point when data collection ceased in January 1970. Thus, the RPFS scoring system was applied to a total of 75 Rorschach protocols, 45 pre-therapy records, and 30 post-therapy records. All scoring was done by two independent blind scorers, both of whom were experienced clinicians with solid backgrounds in therapy as well as in testing.[1]

Usually, when blind scoring is desired in a therapy study, records are coded and randomized so that scorers cannot tell which records were produced by the same person and which are pre- and which are post-therapy records, a practice which tends to make the scoring task a rather boring and mechanical one. In the present study, a different procedure was used, in hopes of making the work more meaningful and interesting for the scorers while still protecting the study from bias. To this end, both scorers were told that they would be dealing with a number of pairs of records drawn from the same clients at different points in time. They were also told that their scoring would be used to test the hypothesis that individual psychotherapy is an

---

[1] Dr. Margery Baittle and Mrs. Karol Kane Weinstein of Chicago, Illinois.

effective method of helping nonclassical as well as classical clients. Blinding was accomplished by telling both raters that the records were drawn from a number of control as well as experimental groups and that, as a result, only some clients were expected to show improvement over time; others were expected to stay the same or to deteriorate. It was pointed out that since they had no way of knowing how many clients were in each group, or which were which, they could best help the study along by evaluating each pair of records as honestly and fairly as possible, trying to remain equally sensitive to all three potential outcomes for each case.

Fifteen completed cases were then selected at random, and the thirty resultant protocols were presented in pairs to the scorers with the date of each testing session clearly marked on each protocol. As a check on the effectiveness of this procedure for handling the problem of scorer bias, only one rater (K.W.) was allowed to score the remaining cases in this fashion. For the other scorer (M.B.), the thirty records of the remaining fifteen completed cases were coded and randomized and interspersed with the fifteen protocols from the uncompleted cases so that it was impossible to tell which was which or when any of them were obtained.

Results indicate that the procedure devised for this study worked at least as well as and perhaps better than the traditional one. M.B. scored exactly the same number of cases improved and unimproved under both the paired and the unpaired condition. Degree of improvement was also closely comparable but degree of nonimprovement was more varied, with the magnitude of deterioration tending to be greater under the paired condition. Thus, it seems clear that the use of the paired scoring procedure did not bias the scorers in favor of the research hypothesis and, in addition to making the task more gratifying for the scorers, it probably served to increase the validity of difference scores by reducing intracase variability in the scoring standards applied by each rater.

Reliability of RPFS scoring was assessed using the Spearman-Brown formula. To make the tests as stringent as possible, all these rank difference correlations were corrected for ties, a procedure which tends to lower obtained correlations with this statistic. As can be seen from Table 4, final obtained correlations range from .65 to .96, indicating that the RPFS can be reliably scored by experienced clinicians. While correlations on all scores are acceptable, it is clear that pre- and post-therapy total scores are generally more reliable than difference scores and that function scores are generally more reliable than structure scores. These positive results are even more encouraging in light of the fact that the aforementioned experimentation with scoring conditions had an adverse effect on interscorer reliability, which was particularly marked with regard to difference scores. As would be expected, M.B. and K.W. agreed more closely when both scored under the same condition than they did when they scored under different conditions (when K.W. was scoring in pairs and M.B. was working with single records).

Table 4
RPFS Reliability: Total Scores, Change Scores, and Subscores

Score	n	Spearman	Spearman-Brown
RPFS Pre-therapy Total Scores	45	.759	.862
RPFS Post-therapy Total Scores	30	.772	.871
RPFS Total Difference Scores	30	.484	.652
RPFS Pre-therapy Structure Scores	45	.563	.720
RPFS Post-therapy Structure Scores	30	.703	.825
RPFS Structure Difference Scores	30	.697	.821
RPFS Pre-therapy Function Scores	45	.938	.968
RPFS Post-therapy Function Scores	30	.830	.907
RPFS Function Difference Scores	30	.703	.825

A component by component analysis of the fourteen elements which enter into these overall RPFS scores also contributes to optimism with regard to the reliability of the instrument, as can be seen from Table 5. Pearson product moment correlations are highly and consistently significant for all but two components and even these two show a positive trend at either pre-therapy or post-therapy. Pearson r was used to test component reliability because neither Spearman correlations nor contingency coefficients were applicable in this instance. Spearman r_s was inapplicable because the range of scores per component was only one to three (see RPFS scoring manual in chapter 5), and contingency coefficients were inapplicable because there was no basis for a fourfold table. Thus, although nonparametric statistics are generally preferable when dealing with Rorschach data of this type, it seemed reasonable to use a parametric device in this one case, particularly since it did not serve to bias results in the direction of the hypothesis. In fact, because we are frequently dealing with noncomparable distributions here and because this tends to reduce r, the correlations reported are probably somewhat deflated.

In sum, despite its complexity and its heavy reliance on clinical judgment, RPFS reliability is quite satisfactory and could probably be made even better in future tests by clarifying the manual instructions for the two components which produced the greatest amount of rater divergence and by having all scorers work with paired records all the time. Having found a satisfactory degree of agreement, it was decided to use the mean of the two raters for each case as the datum in all subsequent analyses. The reliability of this mean is given by the Spearman-Brown values in the preceding table.

Table 5
Reliability of RPFS Components

Components	Pre-therapy			Post-therapy		
STRUCTURE	r	r^2	P	r	r^2	P
P	.714	.509	.0005	.773	.597	.0005
Bizarre	.225	.050	.10	.010	.000	n.s.
F+	.449	.210	.005	.668	.447	.0005
B+	.159	.025	n.s.	.250	.062	.10
Pure Affect	.601	.361	.0005	.567	.321	.005
Dist M	.403	.162	.005	.660	.435	.0005
Aff and App	.802	.643	.0005	.690	.476	.0005
Preoc and Prim	.391	.152	.01	.430	.185	.025
FUNCTION						
M	.825	.680	.0005	.687	.472	.0005
C	.791	.625	.0005	.583	.340	.005
B%	.591	.349	.0005	.606	.367	.0005
R	.912	.831	.0005	.939	.883	.0005
CC	.843	.710	.0005	.765	.585	.0005
Z-W	.663	.439	.0005	.694	.481	.0005
	n = 45	df = 43		n = 30	df = 28	

THE RPFS AS A MEASURE OF IMPAIRMENT

Pre-therapy RPFS scores of the 45 clients in the study ranged from 22.5 to 38.5, with a median of 32. In terms of a priori scale categories, this means that the level of psychological functioning of these entering clients ranged from very severely impaired to moderately impaired and that the typical client was functioning at the low end of the severely impaired range. Severity of disturbance in this sample is even more striking when one looks at Table 6 and notes that there are only three clients in the moderately impaired category and none at all in the mildly impaired and the unimpaired categories. Thus, if RPFS scores prove trustworthy, this is a seriously disturbed group indeed, excluding, at the low end, only those incapable of functioning outside of a hospital or hospital-like setting and those right on the border of this line.

Evidence from the three additional measures of impairment described in chapter 5 reinforces this conclusion. As can be seen from Table 7, two-thirds of these clients were rated severely or very severely disturbed by their therapists, more than half of them were currently unproductive, and more than one-third of them had been hospitalized one or more times in the past.

Table 6
RPFS Total Scores at Pre-Therapy
n = 45

Category	Potential Range	Actual Range	n
Fully functioning; no impairment	42	–	0
Mildly impaired functioning	40–41.5	–	0
Moderately impaired functioning	36–39.5	36–38.5	3
Severely impaired functioning	30–35.5	30–35	29
Very severely impaired functioning	14–29.5	22.5–29.5	13
Incapable of functioning outside of hospital or hospital-like setting	14–20	–	0

Table 7
Non-Rorschach Measures of Impairment at Pre-Therapy
n = 45

Impairment Classification	Therapists Judgments		Hospitalization History		Current Productivity	
Low impairment	Mildly or moderately disturbed	15	No hospitalization history	28	Working or attending school	20
High impairment	Severely or very severely disturbed	30	Previous hospitalization(s)	17	Not working or attending school*	25

*Only two of these 25 unproductive clients were mothers with pre-teenage children at home.

The Mann-Whitney U statistic was used to test the relationship of RPFS scores to these three independent measures of impairment. In each case, the prediction was that clients in the low impairment category would have significantly higher RPFS scores and that clients in the high impairment category would have significantly lower RPFS scores. Results illustrated in Table 8 indicate that this is indeed the case: RPFS scores are strongly related to all three measures. These results are particularly impressive when one considers that we are dealing with a restricted range of RPFS scores and that, as a consequence, the discriminations required are very fine ones. Thus, it seems reasonable to conclude that the RPFS is a sensitive and valid measure of impairment.

Anecdotal evidence repeatedly underlined this conclusion, most strongly so in those few cases where the RPFS diverged sharply from other measures of impairment. For example, one of the clients in the initial entering group, who was placed at the low end of the very severely impaired range by both raters, was a young man who had no previous history of hospitalization, was productively employed, and was rated by his very experienced therapist, at

Table 8
Relation of RPFS Pre-Therapy Total Scores to Three
Independent Measures of Impairment
n = 45

RPFS Scores and:	U	U'	Z	Corrected Z	P
Therapists' Ratings	129	321	-2.311	-2.3177	.01
Hospitalization History	117	359	-2.832	-2.8410	.005
Productivity Status	114.5	385.5	-3.095	-3.1017	.001

the outset, as only moderately disturbed. After a few weeks of therapy, however, this therapist changed his mind to the extent of hospitalizing the client when he revealed a carefully worked-out plan for a multiple murder and rape involving, among other things, fratricide, matricide, and incest.

THE RPFS AS A MEASURE OF IMPROVEMENT

RPFS change scores of the 30 clients who completed therapy in time to be included in this study ranged from +6.5 to -6.5 with a median of +1.5.[2] Changes were in a positive direction for 23 of these 30 clients and in a negative direction for four of them. The remaining three clients showed no change, achieving the same total score at pre-therapy and at post-therapy. Thus, according to the RPFS, more than three-quarters of the clients in this sample showed a gain in psychological functioning following psychotherapy. Therapists were even more optimistic in their assessment of outcome. As can be seen in Table 9, they rated no client as deteriorated and only one client as unimproved. Clients were less uniformly enthusiastic than therapists; none of them felt that they had deteriorated but ten of them did feel that they were better in some ways and worse in others, or the same. The remaining 20 clients, two-thirds of the group, felt they had profited from the experience.

From these preliminary results, it is clear that a majority of the clients in this study improved after therapy, according to three separate measures of

[2]In evaluating the meaningfulness of even fairly small pre-post changes, three facts should be borne in mind: (1) the RPFS scoring system was constructed so as to make each point represent a theoretically significant difference and not just a numerical one; (2) the two responses per card instructions at both pre- and post-therapy greatly reduces the danger of differences due to fluctuations in productivity at different points in time; and (3) all difference scores reported reflect the average of two independent ratings and, as a result, a client whose change score is, for example, +1 was seen as having improved to that degree by both raters or as having improved by as much as 2 points by at least one rater. Thus, while it is still possible that very small numerical improvements in any single case may represent chance fluctuations, it is quite unlikely that findings for the group as a whole can be explained away on such a basis.

Table 9
Client and Therapist Outcome Ratings
n = 30

Outcome Ratings		Number of Cases Receiving Each Rating	
Ratings	Scores	Therapists	Clients
Marked positive change	+3	7	11
Moderate positive change	+2	14	6
Slight positive change	+1	8	3
No change	0	1	1
Positive & negative change	0	0	9
Negative change	–	0	0

outcome, but it is not clear whether clients with high RPFS change scores were the same ones rated most improved on the other two measures and whether clients with low RPFS change scores were the same ones rated least improved on the other two measures. To test these relationships, client and therapist ratings were divided into a high improvement group (scores of +3 or +2) and a low improvement group (scores of +1 or 0) and the Mann-Whitney U test was used to determine the ability of RPFS change scores to discriminate between the two groups.

Results, illustrated in Table 10, are unequivocally positive. RPFS change scores are significantly related to both clients' and therapists' outcome ratings, and in addition, they successfully discriminate between clients who showed a clear behavioral improvement and those who did not: clients who were not working or attending school at pre-therapy but were doing either or both of those things at post-therapy had significantly higher RPFS change scores than other clients. Thus, in addition to providing a meaningful measure of impairment, the RPFS also seems to offer a highly satisfactory way of assessing treatment outcome.

Table 10
Relation of RPFS Change Scores to Three
Independent Measures of Outcome
n = 30

RPFS Scores and:	U	U'	Z	Corrected Z	P
Therapists' Ratings	58	131	−1.651	−1.661	.05
Clients' Ratings	70.5	150.5	−1.674	−1.683	.05
Behavioral Change (Productivity)	44.5	131.5	−2.040	−2.052	.025

To ascertain the contribution of each of the two RPFS subscores to these positive results and to compare subscore results with total score results, all

Mann-Whitney U tests performed with total scores were repeated for structure alone and for function alone. Results shown in Table 11 indicate that the
contribution of each subscore to the overall validity of the instrument is
about equal (structure alone discriminates significantly about as often as
function alone, albeit in different areas) and that, on the whole, the two
subscores are markedly more potent when combined to form a total score
than either one is alone.

Table 11
Contribution of RPFS Subscores to Positive Results
for Impairment and Improvement

	Mann-Whitney U Probabilities		
RPFS Impairment and:	Structure	Function	Total RPFS
Therapist's Ratings of Disturbance	.4641	.0040	.0102
Hospitalization History	.1894	.0040	.0023
Productivity Status	.0143	.0084	.0010
RPFS Improvement and:			
Therapists' Ratings of Outcome	.0918	.3192	.0485
Clients' Ratings of Outcome	.1379	.0764	.0465
Behavioral Outcome (Productivity)	.0197	.4168	.0202

Positive as these results are, it should be noted that the RPFS is a relatively expensive way of assessing outcome, requiring a fair investment of time
by testers and scorers with solid clinical backgrounds, well-trained in the use
of projective techniques. Thus, it seems reasonable to ask whether it is good
enough to be worth the trouble. As a preliminary answer to that question, it
might be pointed out that in addition to the theoretical advantages suggested
in chapter 4, the RPFS is less subject to gross bias than are the assessments of
either participant in the treatment situation even without blind scoring (e.g.,
Amble and Moore, 1966) and more consistently applicable than any single
behavioral measure.

Moreover, as shown in Table 12, the RPFS not only correlates with three
other measures of outcome, it correlates better with more of them than any
of the others. To achieve comparability for these tests of relative correlative
power, the RPFS was converted into a nominal measure by dividing change
scores at the median and using contingency coefficients throughout. This, of
course, reduced the potency of the RPFS and added the handicap of an
arbitrary dividing line, but even under these adverse circumstances, it still
related better to client and therapist assessments than they did to each other,
and it was the only measure which also tended to relate to behavioral
outcome.

In addition to its superior correlative power, the RPFS also has
explanatory power, helping to clarify some of the reasons why other measures

Table 12
Comparison of Outcome Measures I: Relative Correlative Power

Outcome Measures	Phi	P
RPFS Scores and Therapist ratings	.466	.025
RPFS Scores and Client Ratings	.413	.05
RPFS Scores and Behavioral Change	.308	.10
Therapist Ratings and RPFS Scores	.466	.025
Therapist Ratings and Client Ratings	.308	.10
Therapist Ratings and Behavioral Change	.065	n.s.
Client Ratings and RPFS Scores	.413	.05
Client Ratings and Therapist Ratings	.308	.10
Client Ratings and Behavioral Change	.070	n.s.
Behavioral Change and RPFS Scores	.308	.10
Behavioral Change and Therapist Ratings	.065	n.s.
Behavioral Change and Client Ratings	.070	n.s.
	df = 1	

of outcome tend to correlate poorly or not at all with each other. By glancing back at Table 11, the reader can see that clients in this study were most likely to rate therapy as successful if it resulted in an improvement in those characteristics reflected in function subscores, whereas therapists' ratings and behavioral outcome corresponded more closely to changes in structural soundness. And, as indicated in Table 13, further analysis involving a comparison of the differential effects of two additional factors on outcome measures suggests that client evaluations are more likely to be influenced by even very slight negative changes in either subscore than are any of the other measures, including RPFS total change scores, a finding that is consistent with clients' preference for the "better in some ways, worse in others" rating category. Table 13 also shows that clients' evaluations of treatment outcome are influenced to a significant extent by initial agreement or disagreement between client and therapist with regard to goal selection, whereas other measures, including the RPFS, appear to be independent of this factor. Thus, evidence indicates that the RPFS correlates with all relevant measures because it is sensitive to all relevant types of change and yet not unduly sensitive to any one type or to any extraneous or semi-extraneous factors.

Table 13
Comparison of Outcome Measures II: Differential Effects of Two Factors

Negative Subscore Change and:	Phi	P	Goal Discordance and:	Phi	P
Client Outcome	−.395	.05	Client Outcome	−.509	.01
Therapist Outcome	.028	n.s.	Therapist Outcome	−.144	n.s.
RPFS Outcome	−.339	.10	RPFS Outcome	−.176	n.s.
Behavioral Outcome	.040	n.s.	Behavioral Outcome	.064	n.s.

Finally, it should be noted that the sensitivity of RPFS impairment discriminations is also relevant to its success as a measure of improvement and to its applicability to very severely disturbed clients. More specifically, the RPFS appears to have a low enough base and a fine enough calibration to make it as fair a test of relative improvement for the very severely disturbed as it is for their more fortunate brothers. Further research with very different sorts of samples is, of course, necessary to determine whether the ceiling of the test is high enough to permit comparably fine discrimination at the other end of the continuum.

All things considered, the RPFS seems to provide a highly satisfactory way of assessing improvement as well as impairment for clients like the ones in this sample. However, RPFS improvement scores are change scores and a number of authors (e.g., Fiske, Cartwright, and Kirtner, 1964; Fiske, Hunt, Luborsky, Orne, Parloff, Reiser, and Tuma, 1970) have raised serious questions about the validity of change scores, suggesting that when the reliability of a measure is less than perfect, difference scores derived from it are likely to be unduly affected by the subjects' initial starting points, with those initially low on the measure tending to show a spurious pre- to post-test gain, and those initially high on it tending to show a spurious pre- to post-test loss.

For reasons too complex and technical to be detailed here, it seemed unlikely, to the present author, at least, that the RPFS change scores reported here were appreciably influenced by this phenomenon. As an added precaution, however, RPFS difference scores were corrected for this possibility, using the formula offered by Tucker, Damarin, and Messick (1966), and all of the relevant Mann-Whitney U tests were recomputed, using these corrected change scores. Corrected change scores ranged form +7 to +18 with a median of 14.25; as can be seen by comparing the results shown in Table 14 with those in Table 10, the relationship of those corrected scores to other measures of outcome was somewhat weaker than that of the uncorrected scores, albeit still strongly significant in two out of three cases. Thus, regardless of one's position on the desirability of using corrected or uncorrected change scores, the RPFS appears to provide a valid measure of both improvement

Table 14
Relation of RPFS Corrected Change Scores to Three
Independent Measures of Outcome
n = 30

RPFS Scores and:	U	U'	Z	Corrected Z	P
Therapists' Ratings	71	118	−1.064	−1.070	n.s.
Clients' Ratings	70	151	−1.695	−1.706	.05
Behavioral Change (Productivity)	47.5	128.5	−1.899	−1.911	.05

and impairment, with a number of significant advantages over other methods of making these crucial assessments.

Encouraging as these results are, it is important to remember that no single study can fully establish the validity of any measure and that this is especially true when the sample involved is a relatively small one as it is in the present study. Careful replication and cross-validation is essential before the RPFS can be used with any degree of confidence as a measure of either impairment or improvement in the absence of additional confirming data from other, more traditional measures like the ones included in this study. Because RPFS scoring requires a very high degree of skill, sensitivity, and judgment, plus thorough prior training in the basic Rorschach technique, even a successful replication by one group of researchers will not insure equivalent results the next time if the scorers are not comparable in ability.

Assuming, however, that replication is successful and that demonstrably adequate scorers are used each time, it is also important to point out that the positive features of RPFS assessments outlined above need not be limited to the evaluation of psychotherapy. The same system can be used with equal justice to evaluate the success of any sort of treatment or intervention aimed at improving the psychological functioning of its recipients. This is fortunate because, as pointed out in previous chapters, the need for sound program and personnel evaluation is not limited to psychotherapeutic endeavours but is endemic to the mental health field, particularly during the present period of rapid change and restless experimentation.

In fact, the results of psychotherapy demonstrated in this study are good enough so that in addition to calling for replication, it seems reasonable to begin to shift the burden of proof to other types of treatment, asking that equivalent results be demonstrated for them before they are touted as substitutes for psychotherapy. Of course, when the other methods of treatment to be evaluated promise to reach greater numbers of troubled people in less time and at less cost, they do not need to produce results as good merely to justify their existence, but they do need to demonstrate some positive effects if they are to claim a permanent place in the treatment armamentarium. Ineffective techniques are not a bargain at any price.

Speaking of prices, the cost of RPFS assessments need not be prohibitive, even for large-scale programs. Obviously, the RPFS is not adaptable to mass testing; it is an intrinsically individualized method, but all that is required to transform it into a practical device for large-scale program evaluation is proper scientific sampling of the population the program claims to reach. Despite the current popularity of attempts to deal with the problem of evaluation by collecting and centralizing cheaply obtainable information on every person who comes into contact with an intervention system, the ominous anticivil-libertarian potential of such total data files makes an evaluation system which virtually requires sampling vastly to be preferred. Only in this way can confidentiality be truly safeguarded. As long as total systems exist, it is naive or dishonest to claim, as some have done, that there is no danger that unscrupulous or misguided persons will ever find ways to use them. Happily, the RPFS seems to have the potential to help make scientific evaluation of positive psychological change a reality without producing a "Big Brother" atmosphere or jeopardizing basic human rights.

SCORE CHANGES AND THEIR HUMAN MEANING

RPFS results reported thus far appear to have done a good job of telling us how much objective improvement took place in our client sample as a whole, but they cannot tell us how much subjective value to place on specific types of improvement in specific cases. Subjective value is, of course, a matter each of us must decide for ourselves, but some clarification of the sorts of issues involved may be in order. One major consideration has to do with the value one places on amount of improvement per se, an intrinsically relative standard, as opposed to the attainment of ideal end states, an intrinsically absolute one.

Some examples may be helpful here, and to make the issue emerge as clearly as possible, it seems best to focus first on the three clients who showed the maximum amount of improvement manifested in this study. As it happens, these were three very severely impaired Black women, each of whom attained an RPFS change score of +6.5: a Mrs. Smith who went from a pre-therapy score of 29.5 to a post-therapy score of 36; a Miss Jones who went from 26 to 32.5; and a Mrs. Home whose scores parallel those of Miss Jones. These cases raise the issue of relative versus absolute values very clearly because, despite their very substantial gains, none of them ended up anywhere near the ideal end state represented, in this research, by the maximum possible RPFS score of 42.

Mrs. Smith was a woman in her late forties with four grown children and a tenth-grade education. Three years before she entered treatment, she had divorced her second husband, a jazz musician working as a day laborer, on grounds of incompatibility, and for financial reasons, had moved in with her widowed mother and the lighter-skinned older sister her mother had always favored. One year before, her youngest son had left the home, and six months earlier, she had managed to qualify, by examination, for training for a fairly high level white collar job, despite being considerably older and having considerably less formal education than the other applicants.

Externally, she had adjusted well to her new living situation and to the training program, avoiding friction at home by keeping largely to herself and learning her prospective job duties quickly and well enough to earn high praise from her supervisors and colleagues. Internally, however, she was increasingly tormented, feeling that when her children came to visit they were really visiting her mother and sister, and that her supervisors and colleagues only pretended to admire her and were really laughing at her behind her back.

As these feelings intensified, she found it harder and harder to leave her room and began missing days and then whole weeks of work, withdrawing more and more from family interaction, eventually appearing only for meals, and that on an increasingly erratic basis. Three months before entering treatment, she dropped out of the training program altogether because she heard voices telling her to do so; three weeks before that, she developed the delusion that her food was being poisoned. She came to the center as a voluntary self-referral because she perceived, with obvious correctness, that she was losing her mind.[3]

Her state of mind and sense of self at that time is well summarized by her first response to her initial Rorschach: "Like looking down on a spider whose web has collapsed. All the fine lines are gone; it's just a mass—spider is trapped inside, cut off." And indeed, she was cut off, from the objective reality outside herself, as represented by an initial structure score of 16 (the optimum here for full contact is 24), and from the subjective reality inside herself, as represented by an initial function score of 13.5 (the optimum here for full self-access is 18).

Nine months and 23 sessions later, she still had not realized her full psychosocial potential, but her structure score was five points higher and she was back at work, this time pleasing herself as well as others. In addition, her function score had improved by 1.5 points and she was back in contact with her ex-husband, a contact both of them found satisfying enough and different enough from their previous encounters to merit remarriage. The spider was still present on her post-therapy Rorschach, but its web was in better shape and it was joined by "a jet plane taking off."

Example two, Miss Jones, was a very pretty, taciturn teenager who came to the center because "my mother nagged me into it." Her mother, she thought, was nagging her because she played the TV and phonograph all night and "disturbed people." Asked who the people were, she said it was really only her mother; her father and older brothers were "indifferent" because they were sound sleepers. Asked what she was doing up all night, she said she didn't like to sleep because she disliked dreaming while asleep. She found it

[3]Contrary to much popular and some professional opinion, accurate perceptions of this sort are not at all uncommon in psychotics and incipient psychotics. Actually, it is about as hard to be crazy and not know it as it is to drive on a flat tire without noticing it and for much the same reason—because it is uncomfortable as all hell and prevents you from getting where you want to go. Acknowledging craziness to others is, of course, another matter, particularly when those others seem to have a stake in assuming the victim's ignorance of his own condition.

more interesting to dream while awake, something she did frequently, lying in bed during the day while her mother, father, and brothers were at work. As an example of a waking dream, she described looking down on her own body, which was being whirled out into space while she watched dispassionately until it disappeared from sight, sometimes in a quiet fade-out and sometimes with the help of a distant explosion.

Questioning elicited the fact that she had recently dropped out of high school "because I was tired of it," had made no effort to look for work, and had stopped seeing all of her old friends. She said that her parents had accepted her I-was-tired-of-it explanation without comment, seemed relieved that she no longer stayed out late at night with her friends, and had asked no questions about her future plans. Her therapist did not ask either. When he gently told her that he thought she might be pregnant, she laughed and said, "Yes, that's what the doctor said." Her former boyfriend, however, had said, "No, that's impossible," and there was no point in contradicting people, was there?

On the RPFS, Miss Jones was initially in about the same shape as Mrs. Smith in terms of structure (initial subscore of 15.5) but was considerably more cut off from her own energies, feelings, and fantasies (initial function subscore of 10.5), a rather ominous finding in an adolescent who should have been at the height of her subjective vitality. She herself was rather uninterested in exploration in the latter area, however, and was mainly concerned about "getting rid of unpleasant symptoms and being more in control of herself," her unequivocal choice on the goal selection form. Her therapist tried to work on both problems, but his major emphasis was different from hers. Four months and 32 sessions later, and two months before her baby was due, she thanked him for his help but said she thought she had gotten as much as she needed for the present and wanted to terminate. He tried to discourage her from leaving, fearing a post-partum psychosis, but since she was steadfast in her decision, he had no choice but to accept it.

Her post-therapy Rorschach showed a gain in structure of 4 points and a gain in function of 2.5 points; as it turned out, she was correct about that being sufficient for her immediate purposes. She called, two months later, sounding very uncrazy indeed, to advise that she had a very lively daughter whom she thought was exceptionally pretty. She also reported that she was feeling fine and looking forward to bringing her daughter home—not to her parents' house but to the home of a female relative with whom she had spent the last month of her confinement. She added that she had had no contact with the baby's father, had no desire for any, and that, although her parents had finally recovered from their trance, at least to the extent of offering financial support, she had already lined up a job and planned to begin work in a month or two. She sounded tired and a bit anxious, but her predominant feeling seemed to be one of pride in her own autonomy and in the child she had produced. Not an ideal outcome, perhaps, but not bad for a little girl who initially saw herself (on her pre-therapy Rorschach) as "a rat with a dress on, a dancing kind of rat."

The last of the three examples in this high scoring, or at least, high improving category, Johnnie Home, was a childless married woman in her mid-thirties, referred by a general practitioner after repeated examinations and tests had revealed no physical basis for her numerous physical complaints. These included, among other things, feelings of intense heat in the center of her body, followed by feelings of extreme coldness and "deadness"; invariant nausea and frequent vomiting on eating her first meal of the day, whenever and whatever that was; and a sense, at times amounting to a literal conviction, that her forehead was swelling and doubling in size. In addition, Johnnie suffered from acute anxiety attacks, bordering upon and sometimes erupting into outright panic, a state she was particularly liable to experience whenever her menstrual period started and whenever the topic of death came up.

Johnnie had suffered with one or another of these symptoms, on and off, for as long as she could remember, but they had only begun to appear simultaneously and with steadily growing intensity and frequency in the last few years, following the final breakup of a longstanding affair she had had with a church soloist 20 years her senior, a shy and gentle man with whom she had always taken the sexual initiative and who had suffered severe pangs of conscience about their relationship. At the point when Johnnie entered treatment, she and her first and only husband had reunited for about the fifth time in their stormy fifteen-year marriage but were living together on a rather distant and formal basis. She was feeling especially frightened and depressed about herself because her symptoms had finally forced her to give up the factory job she had managed to hold onto for the last ten years.

Johnnie was my client, and, initially, her case seemed more puzzling than the others because her symptoms did not fully jibe, in timing, severity, or substance, with their apparent precipitant, the loss of her lover. This would probably have continued to puzzle me for an indefinite and quite possibly disastrous period of time had I not had the distinct advantage of having been her tester as well as her therapist,[4] an experience which enabled me to see her in a whole new light. Her response to the Rorschach was particularly striking and enlightening. Briefly, she produced an essentially monomaniacal record in which she saw, over and over again, the disembodied and bizarrely elaborated

---

[4]I did not, of course, score her record; that was done by the same scorers who did all of the other records, and in the same manner.

genitals of a female corpse (the skeleton of a vagina; the shadow of the skeleton of the vagina; vagina and uterus, dead, with the flesh decaying; and so forth). Occasionally, a related secondary theme showed up, albeit in less blatant and more disguised form: a perception of a giant phallus, seen in contexts and with elaborations suggestive of a deity. Interspersed with these two related preoccupations were essentially formless and contentless responses expressive of overwhelming anxiety and guilt, a sense of something massive, dark, and threatening which Johnnie struggled to name and eventually called "a stain."

What this suggested was a desire for sexual contact with a tabooed male figure who was seen as larger than life, literally as well as symbolically, and a fear that such contact would result in her death. Johnnie appeared to fear death not only as a punishment for what seemed to her an unspeakable transgression but also for a more concrete and specific reason: because her fantasy lover was a giant and she was not. Thus, she imagined herself being literally broken apart, as expressed by her assignment of a skeleton to boneless organs.

The obvious assumption about the identity of the sexually taboo and God-like lover was that he was Johnnie's father and that the above material was a kind of psychotic version of the Oedipus complex. What was less obvious was why Johnnie's experience of what is, after all, a common, if not a universal, stage was such a peculiarly and lastingly traumatic one. The hypothesis that suggested itself was that Johnnie's father had been a terrifying and violent man, in fact as well as fantasy, and that incestuous contact with him had also been more of a fact than a fantasy.

In light of this hypothesis, Johnnie's affair with the saintly singer appeared as an attempt to satisfy her pathological wish for intercourse with a God-like male figure and to master her pathological fear of such intercourse by acting out the sexually aggressive role rather than the sexually passive one forced upon her in childhood. From this standpoint, it made sense that the affair with the singer was vital to her shaky psychological equilibrium and that, when it ended, her wishes and fears were once again expressed through somatic symptoms and psychotic fantasy about their original object.

Confirmation of these hypotheses was not long in coming, from multiple sources, and while a working-through of the original childhood trauma and its aftermath did not produce an unscarred, fully functioning personality, it did result in the correction of some significantly distorted notions, with a consequent disappearance of symptoms that enabled her to return to work. It also resulted in a release of emotional energy, redirected toward the present, which facilitated a new, deeper, and more satisfying relationship with her husband, an unsaintly but likeably human man, whose own history was as traumatic as hers but in a way that made him the opposite of her fears and a perfect compliment for her. Both types of gain were reflected in her final improvement score, an increase of 2.5 points on the structure subscale and of 4 points on the function subscale, adding up to a total gain of 6.5 points achieved in a period of 6 months and involving 25 sessions.

In summarizing the cases of these 3 clients, it seems fair and accurate to say that their improvement was humanly real as well as statistically significant and meant a great deal to them and to their therapists.[5] What it means to an outside observer, however, depends upon his own personal value system. If reduction in human suffering and increase in human joy is of primary value, then these cases are success stories. On the other hand, if the attainment of an ideal or norm is of primary value, then these three ladies didn't make it; vulnerable, hurt, and limited at the start of therapy, they were vulnerable, hurt, and limited at the end of it, only less so.

Thus, one who holds to absolute standards might conclude that if this is the best that can be done with such people, then the time devoted to helping them would be better spent in working with clients who are closer to the ideal to begin with and are therefore more likely to reach it. On the other hand, one who holds to relative standards might, with equal justification, conclude that if this much relief can be attained by and for those who need it most, then much of the therapeutic time currently spent helping those whose suffering and deprivation is minimal should be reallocated to the care of clients like the ones in this study.

The issue here, as I see it, is whether one cares about human beings insofar as they help one to reach an ideal in this field, or whether one cares about ideals in this field insofar as they help one to reach human beings. Again, each person does have an inalienable right to choose for himself, but it would be refreshing to call the respective choices by their right names. The choice, I think, is between therapeutic humanism and therapeutic elitism. Insofar as this book is a polemical essay as well as a research report, it is a polemic against mental health elitism and, particularly, against elitism that lacks the courage of its own convictions and masquerades as something else, most commonly called "necessity," "realism," or "inevitability."

There is, however, a third common value stance, and people who take it, pragmatists, are likely to be somewhat impatient with this whole discussion. A pragmatist, in the sense in which the word is intended here, might say that material payoff is what really counts and that I have erred in failing to lay sufficient emphasis on the real value of therapy demonstrated by these results: that these three clients were not contributing materially to our society by working or learning at the start of treatment and were doing so or

[5] All three clients rated themselves very much better (ratings of +3); two of their therapists agreed, and the third thought that his client was pretty much better (rating of +2).

planning to do so at the end of it. Such a critic might also stress the likelihood that without therapy these three clients would have ended up in state hospitals, a drain on the resources of the community—an outcome that seems likely because, although none of them had been hospitalized before, all three of them were already scoring in a range in which hospitalization rates were very high,[6] and all three of them appeared to be recent arrivals to this unlucky range who were still deteriorating when they entered therapy.

Readers whose sensibilities are offended by the seeming callousness of the pragmatic approach might want to note that its implications are really gentler than those inherent in the elitist approach and quite compatible with those of the humanist approach—but, alas, only up to a point. Humanism and pragmatism can generally walk hand in hand when it comes to large gains like those achieved by the three cases summarized above; they tend to part company when it comes to small gains and/or certain types of mixed outcomes like those in the example presented below.

Mr. Good, a man in his early fifties, was the kind of Black man that conservatives are wont to point to with pride as living proof that our society is not really so harsh a place for the poor and the discriminated against, providing that they work hard and believe in the American dream. Mr. Good had done both of those things with a vengeance all his life. The son of an illiterate, hungry-poor Southern sharecropper, he had graduated from high school a star athlete, honor student, and elected officer of his senior class. He had gone on to become the first Black apprentice in a particular skilled trade, the first Black noncommissioned officer in a particular army unit, and more recently, the first Black foreman in a particular factory.

Married to a decorative but rather helpless Black woman of middle class origins, he was a faithful husband who fathered three children and never shirked or even tried to share his responsibilities as family bread-winner, disciplinarian, inspirational leader, chauffeur, and handyman. In addition, he was active in his community and an officer in various social, charitable, and self-help organizations which, while not radical enough to suit his sons or young radicals generally, were still highly respected by most of his peers. Although his style of dress was rather conservative, he was always impeccably groomed—even to the point of changing his clothes from the skin up every evening before he left the factory—and was tall and handsome enough to be regarded generally as a fine figure of a man.

All in all, he was a paragon—of strain and exhaustion. Carrying a heavy burden to begin with, his reward, for each of his victories, had been the

---

[6] Thirteen of the 45 entering clients scored below 30 on the RPFS, and 8 of them had been hospitalized one or more times in the past. Thirty-two entering clients scored 30 or better on the RPFS, and only 9 of them had ever been hospitalized. See Table 8 for the statistical significance of the relationship between RPFS scores and hospitalization.

addition of new and heavier weights to his pack. Not surprisingly, he had finally developed a terrific backache. The physician he consulted just prior to entering therapy had found him in splendid shape for a man of his years and had not only dismissed his complaint but had prevailed upon him to devote what little spare time he had left to helping to coach a team of local youngsters who had been in trouble with the law. Good for the community no doubt, but anathema to him.

As it turned out, he had always disliked contact sports and physical activity generally and had begun playing in high school in hopes of getting a college scholarship which never materialized. He had caught on to the fact that this was a false hope in his junior year and had wanted to quit and devote his after-school time to the study of math, one of the few things he really liked. By then, however, he was the best hope of his segregated high school football team, and a stern but fatherly lecture from his Black coach about his responsibility to the Black community and their need for a victory ended his tenuous hope of eventually becoming a bookkeeper or even a CPA via self-study and night school courses.

For similar reasons, he was unable to refuse the honor of being chosen, this time by an interracial committee, to crack the color bar in his particular industry and had, in fact, learned his lesson well enough to refrain from even expressing his reluctance. By the time he got to the army, he had learned his place so well that he did not even tell himself how much he dreaded leading bigoted white soldiers into combat—after all, his white commanding officer was so proud of having promoted him, and it was a step forward for the race, wasn't it?

His whole life had consisted of such steps and probably would have continued to do so, especially since he was, in his fifties, more tired than ever before but so self-alienated that he could only speak in pious platitudes. The nonverbal message he conveyed was, however, quite different for those willing to hear it. When he began complaining of backaches, one of his sons heard and responded by convincing him to come to the center. When he did, he produced a Rorschach that was conventional and business-like in terms of content, except that he saw animals being dissected with unusual frequency and gave unusually detailed and graphic descriptions of the dissection process.

Initially, this seemed a simple reflection of the underlying anger one would expect in so frustrated a man. As testing progressed, this explanation began to seem insufficient, mainly because his descriptions were more reminiscent of delicate surgery than of crude mayhem, with transformation, not torture, as the underlying aim. Despite all the detail, the nature of the transformation itself was unclear and tended to remain so. What was clear was that all of the animals who underwent the process were referred to as "he" at first, but not after dissection. At that point, and apparently without Mr.

Good's conscious awareness, the "he's" became "its" and, later, "she's." Unconsciously, it seems, Mr. Good was imagining what it would be like to be transformed into a woman.

To see this as evidence of latent homosexuality would be, I think, to miss the point, just as an exclusive emphasis on the element of hostility in these responses misses the point. Mr. Good did not really want to fight men, still less to fornicate with them; he wanted rest, relief, and relaxation, and his standards for manhood were so severe that he could not imagine being free to indulge such simple pleasures with a clear conscience unless he were a woman.

An improbable interpretation? Perhaps, but imagine, if you will, this harrassed and burdened man lying in bed in the morning, facing another endless day of joyless duties, unable to reject them without suffering an intolerable loss of self-esteem, and no longer sustained in his marathon by the physical vigour of youth or the hope that further "successes" would win him any honorable relief this side of the grave. Imagine him lying there, awake and aching, and contemplating his wife, peacefully asleep beside him, with no need to leave the house all day and little to do in it, what with the children grown and gone, except to tidy up a bit and fix his supper. A free day and a free conscience—isn't she, after all, a good wife and mother, in society's eyes and in his own? Of course she is, of course, of course—and what luxury to be a lady.

That, at any rate, was my understanding of the underlying pressures and unconscious associations that contributed to the shaping of some of Mr. Good's less conventional Rorschach responses. Be that as it may, most of his responses were extremely conventional, proper, and oriented toward the external world in a highly realistic way, so much so as to earn him a structure score only two points short of perfection on this subscale (22 points out of a possible 24). On the other hand, his "healthy" responses had an impersonal, unenlivened quality that resulted in his achieving a function score that was below the mean of even this severely disturbed sample of clients (13 points out of a possible 18). This curtailment of subjective vitality was reflected in the joylessness of his life, but that did not stop him from performing his duties adequately in conventional terms or from achieving the highest overall pre-therapy RPFS score (35) of any client in this group.

Seven months and twenty-five sessions later, his overall score had increased by only .5 or one-half of one point; yet, both he and his therapist were well pleased with the results of their work together and felt that a considerable change had taken place. Inspection of his post-therapy subscores indicated that this perception was more than a shared delusion. At the end of therapy, his function subscore had increased by 2.5 points, but his overall score gain was slight because his structure subscore slipped by 2 points, declining to the nonspectacular but nondangerous level of 20. Thus, he had gained a considerable measure of the freedom and relief he sought but had paid a price for it, losing some of the discipline that had enabled him to be such a superconscientious citizen.

Looking at the matter strictly in terms of his own welfare, it would have been preferable if he had been able to gain increased freedom without losing any of his capacity for discipline, only learning to put it to use for his own purposes rather than for those of others. That, however, was not how it turned out, and Mr. Good did not mind. He did not, of course, know his RPFS scores or subscores, but he did notice that he was somewhat less accurate and organized at work and in committee meetings, and he did see that as the price of his new found freedom, but he felt it was a price well worth paying. In fact, he decided to resign from some of his organizational responsibilities and began to think seriously about something he had never considered before—the possibility of early retirement.

All in all, therapy was of subjective benefit to Mr. Good and seemed likely to be of some for his wife also. She began to give some indications that she didn't really care for her stereotypic role either and that, encouraged by his changes, she might try to make some too, for her own pleasure as well as for his. From a purely pragmatic point of view, however, Mr. Good's therapy was of no objective benefit to society in general, or for the particular state that underwrote its cost. After all, Mr. Good's material productivity was not increased but decreased by his treatment. Moreover, the preventive argument does not seem tenable here because Mr. Good cannot really be described as having been in any great or immediate danger of a breakdown requiring hospitalization at state expense. His pre-therapy total score was too adequate for that. A long-range breakdown would, of course, have been possible but, all things considered, not very probable.

Thus, unlike the other cases presented in this subsection, Mr. Good is not a winner from a pragmatic outsider's point of view. His treatment may fairly be described as more-or-less successful only in humanistic terms. Since those are the terms of this book, he does count as at least a minor success here, taking his place on the same side of the ledger with the three women previously described and with nineteen other clients whose improvement scores covered the range between his low of +.5 and their high of +6.5.

results using the rpfs

As detailed in the preceding chapter, 23 of the 30 clients who completed treatment in time for inclusion in this study showed gains in psychological functioning on the RPFS following psychotherapy, gains which ranged from +.5 to +6.5 on the basis of raw difference scores. In this chapter, an attempt will be made to examine the relationship between degree of RPFS improvement and a variety of client and therapist factors in hopes of explaining these highly satisfactory results with a supposedly unsatisfactory group of clients and, in the process, casting doubt on some widely held notions about so-called bad clients and offering support for some less widely held notions about good therapists.[1]

CLIENT FACTORS AND IMPROVEMENT

Bad clients were defined as individuals who were lower class and/or severely disturbed with dynamics that make them ostensibly unamenable to therapy and with attitudes and behaviors which therapists have traditionally regarded as therapeutically counterproductive. Social class was assessed by means of the Hollingshead and Redlich Two Factor Index; severity of disturbance was measured by therapists' ratings; amenability to treatment was assessed via Klopfer Prognostic Scale scores; attitudes were measured by the F (Authoritarianism) Scale and initial in-therapy behavior by the Rice Voice Quality Rating System.

The initial, entering group of 45 clients contained a large percentage of bad clients in the sense defined above and, as can be seen from Table 15, the final group of 30 clients who completed therapy is still heavily saturated with

---

[1] Readers interested in the relationship between client and therapist factors and non-RPFS measures of improvement will find relevant material in Appendix C.

Table 15
Initial Client Prognostic Characteristics
for the 30 Completed Cases

Sample Description	Social Class	Severity of Disturbance	Klopfer Prognosis*	Authori- tarianism	Rice Voice Quality†
Number of High Prognosis Cases	12	12	15	15	4
Number of Low Prognosis Cases	18	18	15	15	22
X̄ Scores on Ordinal Measures	45.60	–	1.08	41.36	–
Potential Range of Scores	11 to 77	–	+17 to –12	10 to 70	–
Actual Range of Scores	11 to 73	–	+6 to –8	21 to 64	–

*Scoring was done by Drs. Arthur Van Cara and Larry Pacoe, two clinicians sympathetic to the Klopfer method; they agreed on prognostic categorization in 70% of the cases.

†Voice quality ratings were made by two of Dr. Rice's former students, Drs. Jack Vognsen and Neal Warren; they agreed in 75% of the cases rated. Sample size is 26 rather than 30 here because no usable pre-therapy tapes were obtained on 4 cases due to recording difficulties.

such people. At least half of the final sample fell into the low prognostic category on each of these five prognostic measures. Five clients were low on all five variables, and only two were high on all five. Thus, in conventional terms, this sample contained 2 good clients, 23 bad ones, and 5 God-awful ones.[2]

Further consideration of the distribution of these factors with a focus on patterns of interrelations between them serves to underline some of the harsher realities of contemporary society, realities of the "them that has shall get, Them that's not shall lose" variety.[3] Most striking is the fact that 72 percent of the lower class clients in this sample were rated as severely or very severely disturbed by their therapists, whereas only 41 percent of the higher class clients were rated as being that troubled and hurt.

This finding is consistent with the results of epidemiological research summarized in chapters 1 and 2 and is an especially sobering finding in the

[2] For readers who may be curious about the prognostic score cards of the four clients described in the preceding chapter, we might briefly note that Mrs. Smith got favorable scores on only two out of the five prognostic measures, Miss Jones and Mr. Good on only one out of five, and Mrs. Home on none. Thus, if these prognostic measures had been used in the way they often are, to help screen out unsuitable candidates for therapy, all four of these clients would have been rejected. More specifically, all four of them would have been rejected on grounds of social class and Klopfer prognosis—three of them because of therapists' ratings of severity of impairment and Rice Voice Quality Ratings, and two of them on grounds of authoritarianism.

[3] The words are from a song written by Billie Holiday.

context of the present study where therapists' ratings are very difficult to dismiss as mere reflections of bias on the part of middle class professionals against lower class individuals. In this study, there is good reason to believe that the therapists were relatively free of such biases (see chapter 2), and in addition, their ratings correlated significantly with other, more objective measures of impairment, suffering, and wasted human potential (see chapter 8).

Lower class individuals also tend to end up on the wrong side of the tracks with regard to the other three prognostic measures used in this study: 61 percent of them are rated poor in amenability to treatment on the Klopfer measure; 55 percent of them fall into the poor prognostic category because they score high on the test of authoritarian attitudes; and 87 percent of them fail to manifest the focusing ability that Rice and others feel is most conducive to productive self-exploration in a therapeutic context. Comparable figures for their more socioeconomically fortunate fellow clients are lower in each instance, being, respectively 33 percent, 41 percent, and 80 percent.

These percentages serve to underscore the fact that differences in occupational and educational status, and in the rewards contingent upon them, tend to be associated with differences in personality, attitudes, and behavior, but they do not, in and of themselves, help to explain the reasons for the differences. My own view is that the circumstances of life for lower class individuals in our society are such that they more frequently and more intensely operate to tear down ego strength and emotional responsiveness and to foster and reward acceptance of arbitrary authority, punishing instances of egalitarian self-assertion more forcefully with members of this group than with members of other groups.

Looking at the findings from this standpoint, it is not surprising that a relatively high percentage of lower class individuals might tend to have shaky egos, to over- or under-control their emotions, and to see the world of human relations largely in terms of dominance-submission. Given this state of affairs, it is also to be expected that such people would rarely enter therapy with the sort of trust and confidence in themselves and others that would facilitate thoughtful, open, nondefensive, and nonhysterical self-exploration of the sort reflected in responses scoreable as Focused in the Rice Voice Quality Rating System.

If the study were to end at this point, findings like these could, of course, be used to argue that lower class clients really do lack the capacity to benefit from psychotherapy because of the association of unfortunate personality, attitudinal, and behavioral attributes with social class. However, there would be no inevitability about such a conclusion, even if we were not going to go on and put an alternative hypothesis to the test. This is so because the same findings can just as easily and reasonably be intrepreted as indicating that lower class individuals have simply lacked adequate opportunities and appropriate conditions for developing and sustaining certain positive capacities and attributes and that both psychotherapy and social change can and should work to provide such opportunities and conditions.

Evidence relevant to the question of which of those views is correct will be presented very shortly, but first it is necessary to take a quick look at the way these 30 clients stack up on other, more general descriptive characteristics. Thus, the final sample contained 20 women and 10 men, and as can be seen from Table 16, it included a preponderance of Black clients, all of whom were in treatment with white therapists, a substantial number of people who were unproductive, and a fair sprinkling of older clients. Most of these individuals had had some previous treatment on either an outpatient or an inpatient basis, and one-third of them were receiving some form of supplementary treatment, involving either drug or activities therapy.[4]

Table 16
General Descriptive Client Characteristics
for the 30 Completed Cases

Age*		Race		Initial Productivity		Prior Hospital- ization		Prior Therapy		Concur- rent Treat- ment	
16 to 35	21	White	13	Productive	15	No	21	Yes	15	Yes	10
Over 35	9	Black	17	Unproductive	15	Yes	9	No	15	No	20

*$\bar{x}$ = 31.8; Range = 16 to 57.

In all, eleven measures of client characteristics are involved: 5 specific prognostic measures, and 6 additional descriptive characteristics assumed by some to have prognostic significance. The assumption in this study was that none of these measures would work as they have in the past because therapeutic improvement is basically a function of therapist characteristics, with client characteristics assuming major influence only in the absence of appropriate therapeutic conditions. Accordingly, it was predicted that low prognostic clients would show just as much improvement following psychotherapy as high prognostic clients and that other client characteristics would also prove unrelated to treatment outcome.

To test these hypotheses, clients were rank-ordered on the basis of their RPFS improvement scores, and Mann-Whitney U tests were run for each of

---

[4] Again, for those interested, the four clients whose case histories were summarized in the preceding chapter were all Black and all in treatment with white therapists; 3 of them were initially unproductive, two of them were "older," none of them had had any previous treatment, and only one of them received supplementary treatment. The supplementary treatment in that one case consisted of a two-week supply of Librium (a common tranquilizer) along with instructions to take one a day on an "as needed" basis.

the eleven specified client factors. Results, illustrated in Tables 17 and 18, are consistent with the predictions of this study, offering no support for conventional assumptions about the untreatability of nonclassical clients. On the basis of raw gain scores, low prognostic clients, particularly lower class and severely disturbed ones, actually seem to do better than high prognostic clients. On the basis of the more conservative corrected gain scores, they still do at least as well. The single, partial exception is Rice Voice Quality, which shows a trend towards significance with corrected change scores but not with raw change scores.

Other client characteristics also show no relation to outcome or a relationship opposite to that which would be predicted on the basis of conventional assumptions. Older clients do as well as younger ones, ex-hospital inmates do as well as those who have never required inpatient care, and initially unproductive clients do as well as or better than productive ones. So, too, with race and racial similarity: there are no significant differences in outcome between Black and white clients or between same race and cross-racial client-therapist pairs. Clients who have had prior outpatient psychotherapy also do no better and no worse than those without such experience, and clients receiving psychotherapy alone do just as well as those receiving psychotherapy plus drug or activities treatment. Thus, it appears that under appropriate conditions, individual psychotherapy can be an effective method of helping nonclassical as well as classical clients.

Table 17
Relationship Between RPFS Raw Change
Scores and Client Factors

Client Prognostic Factors	U	U′	n or Z[†]	Corrected Z	P
Social Class	60.5	155.5	12 × 18	–	.025*
Therapists' Ratings of Severity	71	145	12 × 18	–	.10*
Klopfer Scale	94	131	15 × 15	–	n.s.
Authoritarianism	109.5	115.5	15 × 15	–	n.s.
Rice Voice Quality	36.5	51.5	.5330	.5363	n.s.
Client Descriptive Factors	U	U′	n or Z	Corrected Z	P
Age	81.5	107.5	.5883	.5914	n.s.
Race	97.5	123.5	13 × 17	–	n.s.
Initial Productivity	64.5	160.5	15 × 15	–	.05*
Prior Hospitalization	85.5	103.5	.4073	.4094	n.s.
Prior Psychotherapy	106.5	118.5	15 × 15	–	n.s.
Concurrent Treatment	86.5	113.5	10 × 20	–	n.s.

*Significant in the direction contrary to previous findings with this measure: here, low prognostic clients do better than high prognostic clients.

[†]Z tables were used when either n_1 or n_2 was greater than 20. Auble's (1953) tables for the Mann-Whitney U statistic were used when both n_1 and n_2 were 20 or less.

Table 18
Relationship Between RPFS Corrected
Change Scores and Client Factors

Client Prognostic Factors	U	U'	Z or n	Corrected Z	P
Social Class	84	132	12 × 18	–	n.s.
Therapist's Ratings of Severity	100	116	12 × 18	–	n.s.
Klopfer Scale	99.5	125.5	15 × 15	–	n.s.
Authoritarianism	84	141	15 × 15	–	n.s.
Rice Voice Quality	25	63	−1.350	−1.359	.10

Client Descriptive Factors	U	U'	Z or n	Corrected Z	P
Age	93.5	95.5	−0.045	−0.046	n.s.
Race	102.5	118.5	13 × 17	–	n.s.
Initial Productivity	96.5	128.5	15 × 15	–	n.s.
Prior Hospitalization	74.5	114.5	−0.905	−0.911	n.s.
Prior Psychotherapy	109.5	115.5	15 × 15	–	n.s.
Concurrent Treatment	99	101	10 × 20	–	n.s.

Of course, in the strictly technical sense, nonsignificant results alone can never be cited as unequivocal proof of the truth of negative hypotheses, but such results certainly do serve to cast serious doubt on contrary assumptions, especially in the context of positive findings with regard to improvement for the group as a whole. Thus, it seems fair to conclude that results of the study thus far strongly suggest that bad clients suffer mainly from a bad press and that the obstacles to helping them are neither inherent nor immutable. Perhaps the only really untreatable clients are adult outpatients who will not make a voluntary therapeutic contract because they really have no wish to be treated. At least, that is the assumption that seems most compatible with these findings, and for reasons suggested in previous chapters and spelled out more fully in later ones, it is a vastly preferable assumption on social, political, and ethical grounds.

THERAPIST FACTORS AND IMPROVEMENT

Fourteen of the 15 therapists who participated in the study had completed at least one case in time for inclusion in the final sample.[5] Each of these therapists was rated as either high or low on 10 therapist factors, 5 of which were predicted to be related to improvement and 5 of which were predicted to be unrelated to improvement. These 10 factors may conveniently be divided into two major groupings: general factors which remain constant for all

[5] Six therapists contributed 3 completed cases each, 4 therapists contributed 2 each, and the remaining 4 therapists contributed 1 each.

cases treated by a particular therapist, and case-specific factors which had to be measured anew for each therapist in relation to each of his clients. Thus, numbers in the vertical columns in each section of Table 19, which describes the therapist sample, add up to either 14, the number of therapists, or to 30, the number of cases.

In terms of general factors, the sample was evenly divided between experienced and inexperienced therapists and between Whitehorn-Betz type A and type B therapists. With regard to nonauthoritarianism or democratic values, the 5 therapists who scored below the a priori cutting point of 30 were placed in the high prognostic category, and the 9 therapists who scored at or above that point were placed in the low prognostic category. Therapists were divided according to their self-evaluations of their own experience as clients by placing all therapists who rated at least one course of personal treatment as "maximally successful" in the high prognostic category and therapists who rated their own experience as "moderately" or "minimally" successful in the low prognostic category. Five of the inexperienced therapists had not yet been in treatment, and consistent with the hypothesis that successful experience as a client is not a consistently necessary prerequisite for effective work as a therapist, they were grouped with the lows, making a total of 10 low prognostic and 4 high prognostic therapists on this variable.

With regard to case-specific factors such as the initial, self-rated subjective reactions of therapists to their clients, it is clear from Table 19 that, on the whole, this was a highly motivated and optimistic but not a saintly group of therapists. More specifically, therapeutic interest in and optimism about clients was initially high in better than two-thirds of the cases, but liking and a sense of emotional understanding for clients was high, at the outset, in less than half of the cases. With regard to empathy, each therapist was rated on two measures for each of his clients at both pre- and post-therapy, and cases were divided at the median each time by placing therapists who scored above the median in the high prognostic category and therapists who scored at or below the median in the low prognostic category.

The relationship of each of these ten therapist factors to therapeutic improvement was assessed using, once again, the Mann-Whitney U test. In the results shown in Tables 20 and 21, the single most striking relationship is that between democratic values or nonauthoritarianism on the part of the therapist and client improvement as measured by raw change scores, a relationship which is significant at the .005 level. This relationship is still basically positive but much less strongly so using corrected change scores; the reason for the drop in strength of association seems noteworthy. Corrected change scores operate to reduce or cancel out differences between more and less severely disturbed clients, and close inspection of the data indicates that this weakens the relationship because, while democratic values on the part of the

Table 19
Therapist Prognostic Factors

General Factors	Experience as Therapist	Non-Authoritarianism*	Experience as Client	Whitehorn–Betz Type
Number of High Prognosis Cases	7	5	4	7
Number of Low Prognosis Cases	7	9	10	7

Case Specific Factors: Subjective Reactions	Initial Liking	Initial Understanding	Initial Interest	Initial Expectations
Number of High Prognosis Cases	14	10	22	22
Number of Low Prognosis Cases	16	20	8	8

Case Specific Factors: Two Types of Empathy	Predictive Empathy**		Concurrent Empathy[†]	
	Pre-therapy	Post-therapy	Pre-therapy	Post-therapy
Number of High Prognosis Cases	14	13	9	10
Number of Low Prognosis Cases	15	16	16	11
$\bar{X}$ Scores	15.24	12.96	3.34	3.76
Potential Range of Scores	0 to 40 (Low scores = high empathy)		1 to 9 (High scores = high empathy)	
Actual Range of Scores	5 to 21	7 to 21	1 to 7	2 to 8

*Possible range of scores = 10 to 70; actual range = 11 to 44; and group $\bar{X}$ = 29.
**Sample size is 29 rather than 30 here because one of the clients was my own, and since I administered the tests, I saw her answers and was therefore unable to make a valid test of my own predictive empathy.
*Problems with the tape recording equipment resulted in a number of inaudible tapes, reducing n to 25 at pre-therapy and 21 at post-therapy. Scoring of these tapes was done by Dr. Truax's own staff at the Arkansas Institute. All tapes were scored by 3 independent raters and reliability coefficients ranged from .73 to .89.

therapist are of some importance for clients generally, they seem to be of really vital importance mainly for the most severely disturbed ones.

These indications are particularly interesting in light of the fact that such grossly disturbed clients are the very ones most likely to be the recipients of exactly the opposite sort of treatment. Benevolent authoritarianism is frequently recommended for them on the grounds that they are too confused or needy to handle a more egalitarian type of relationship. Fortunately, most of therapists in this study did not subscribe to that common viewpoint but clung instead to a basic respect for even the most confused and needy clients' capacity to make choices and take responsibility for their own behavior, and this appears to be the crucial reason for the unusually good results achieved with such clients in the present study.

Positive as these results are, they are obviously only a beginning. In addition to needing more ingenious and permanently repeatable tests of therapists' values,[6] we also need to learn more about the concrete specifics of how these values are manifested and communicated in the therapeutic relationship and about the possible interaction or facilitating effects of democratic values on other aspects of the therapeutic relationship.

The most obvious possibility here is that democratic values create an ambience which helps clients avail themselves of their own resources, but it may also be that such values make it easier for very confused and needy people to avail themselves of other good things the therapist has to offer, such as warmth, support, acceptance, protection, understanding, and clarification. For example, it may be that a democratic ambience facilitates the acceptance of external aid by removing the price tag that so often accompanies it—a forfeiture of what little sense of or hope for autonomy the client has left. Such a forfeiture can be especially humiliating and terrifying for someone who already feels vulnerable, threatened, and overwhelmed. Thus, if it is seen to be a necessary prerequisite of help acceptance, it may be experienced as an impossibly high price to pay, no matter how badly the client needs the goods it will buy.

Another possible line of connection between democratic values and other factors relevant to improvement may have to do with the relationship between respect and self-esteem. Self-esteem is generally regarded as a necessary basis for adequate psychological functioning, and good therapy is generally expected to foster it, but exactly how it does this is far from clear. My own hunch is that while love, warmth, and acceptance from others may provide sufficient or nearly sufficient conditions for the fostering of self-esteem in very small children, respect from others is an equally important source of

---

[6] Unobtrusive measures of the type recommended by Webb, Campbell, Schwartz, and Sechrest (1966) will probably be necessary here, but the task of finding or devising unobtrusive measures relevant to this factor will be extremely difficult.

self-esteem for older children and an essential one for all adults, no matter how regressed or primitivized they appear. Democratic values on the part of a therapist necessarily imply a very healthy degree of respect for his clients, and thus, such values may have a very potent and beneficial effect on their self-esteem, an effect which fosters the display and development of real competence.

Such an effect might well be greatest for grossly disturbed people because, if the preceding analysis is correct, respect may be what they need most and get least in their nontherapeutic relationships. For a theoretical basis for this line of speculation, Robert White provides an ideal source with his concept of competence motivation, a concept which he has described and defended with clarity, eloquence, and force in several publications (e.g., White, 1961; 1963). Robert White's many excellences notwithstanding, in the present context, all of this is, of course, sheer speculation. Results of this study indicate that democracy helps; they do not indicate precisely how and why it does so.

Nonetheless, I would like to offer one further speculation before concluding this discussion. The difference between a democratic ambience and a grossly permissive one may prove to be as crucial as that between a democratic and an authoritarian one. Indeed, certain extreme forms of permissiveness actually seem more closely related to authoritarianism than they do to democracy because the domination of one person by another is still central to the relationship. It is central in an authoritarian relationship because the stronger party dominates the weaker one, and central in a limitlessly permissive one because the weaker party is allowed to dominate the stronger one.

My own understanding of a democratic relationship is one in which democracy is a reality for both parties. As a result, each is free to set his own limits and, if necessary, to defend them until they are respected. Thus, therapists who allow their clients to call all the shots do not seem to me to be much more democratic than therapists who call all the shots themselves. Apropos of this point, informal observation of the therapists in this study suggested that they were generally quite good at protecting their own autonomy as well as that of their clients. As the reader may recall, the items in the special F Scale used to classify therapists as more and less democratic contained items relevant to professional autonomy as well as to client autonomy.

So much for the discussion of positive results with one positive hypothesis. Results for the other four therapist factors predicted to be positively related to improvement produced the first real disappointments of this study. Therapists' experience,[7] predictive empathy, concurrent empathy, and ex-

---

[7]There were some teasing hints of differences between experienced and inexperienced therapists with regard to extreme outcomes, both positive and negative, suggest-

pectations[8] all failed to discriminate significantly between more and less improved cases, or even to manifest a positive trend in this direction.

Table 20
Relationships Between RPFS Raw Change
Scores and Therapist Factors

Therapist Factors Predicted to be Related to Improvement	U	U′	n or Z	Corrected Z	P
Experience	88.5	136.5	15 × 15	–	n.s.
Non-Authoritarianism	35.5	173.5	11 × 19	–	.005
Predictive Empathy:					
At Pre-therapy	88	122	14 × 15	–	n.s.
At Post-therapy	86	122	13 × 16	–	n.s.
Concurrent Empathy:					
At Pre-therapy	62	82	9 × 16	–	n.s.
At Post-therapy	49	61	10 × 11	–	n.s.
Expectations	63.5	112.5	–1.1489	–1.1559	n.s.

Therapist Factors Predicted to be Un-related to Improvement	U	U′	n or Z	Corrected Z	P
Initial Liking	93	131	14 × 16	–	n.s.
Initial Understanding	91	109	10 × 20	–	n.s.
Initial Interest	86	90	.0937	.0943	n.s.
Evaluation of own Experience as Client	44.5	131.5	2.0401	2.0524	.05*
Whitehorn–Betz Category	55.5	169.5	15 × 15	–	.01**

*Significant in the opposite direction: therapists who rated their own experience as clients as "maximally successful" worked *less* effectively with the people they treated in this study.

**Type B therapists achieved better therapeutic results than type A therapists.

DISCUSSION OF POSITIVE HYPOTHESES THAT FAILED

Results with empathy were especially disappointing in light of a virtual consensus on the importance of this variable and the uniformity of positive results from previous research relating it to outcome. Two possible explanations suggest themselves. One is that empathy is less important for nontraditional clients than it is for traditional ones. The other is that current measures of empathy are too crude and superficial to reflect accurately the phenomenon—and are probably biased as well.

In the absence of any compelling evidence either way, the reader is, of course, free to choose for himself between these alternatives; but for me, the

---

ing the possibility that experienced therapists may tend to have more impact on their clients than inexperienced ones, for better or for worse, but the data was not adequate to make a valid test of this post hoc hypothesis.

[8] Expectations did, however, discriminate significantly between terminators and remainers, as shown in the following chapter.

Table 21
Relationships Between RPFS Corrected Change
Scores and Therapist Factors

Therapist Factors Predicted to be Related to Improvement	U	U'	Z or n	Corrected Z	P
Experience	107.5	117.5	15 × 15	−	n.s.
Nonauthoritarianism	65.5	143.5	11 × 19	−	.10*
Predictive Empathy:					
At Pre-therapy	103	107	14 × 15	−	n.s.
At Post-therapy	103.5	104.5	13 × 16	−	n.s.
Concurrent Empathy:					
At Pre-therapy	53.5	90.5	9 × 16	−	n.s.
At Post-therapy	51	59	10 × 11	−	n.s.
Expectations	83	93	−0.234	−0.236	n.s.

Therapist Factors Predicted to be Un-related to Improvement	U	U'	Z or n	Corrected Z	P
Initial Liking	106.5	117.5	14 × 16	−	n.s.
Initial Understanding	100	100	10 × 20	−	n.s.
Initial Interest	78.5	97.5	−0.446	−0.448	n.s.
Evaluation of own Experience as Client	53.5	122.5	−1.618	−1.628	.10**
Whitehorn–Betz Category	80.5	144.5	15 × 15	−	n.s.

*Misses the .05 level by only .5.

**Positive trend in the opposite direction: therapists who rated their own experience as clients as "maximally successful" worked *less* effectively with the people they treated in this study. This trend just misses being significant at the .05 level.

likelihood seems great that the fault lies with the measures and not with the variable. Fifteen years of experience as a sort of jack-of-all trades, trouble-shooter, and trouble-maker in relation to nonclassical clients has left me with a strong subjective conviction that empathy is, if anything, more rather than less important in working with the down-and-outers who comprise this group. More objective evidence for assigning a major share of blame to measurement errors and misconceptions, my own included, may be derived from that fact that the two measures of empathy used in this study totally failed to correlate with one another (Spearman rs = .23 at pre-therapy, and .06 at post-therapy) and discriminated no better in combination than either one did singly (Mann-Whitney U still unequivocally nonsignificant).

Readers conversant with the literature in this area are also aware that there is no dearth of technical criticism of current measures of empathy (Cronbach, 1955), nor of implied clinical criticism expressed through attempts to define the phenomenon in more complex terms (Schafer, 1959). Fortunately, most technical objections raised seem answerable; unfortunately, most propounders of complex theoretical definitions offer few clues as to how their formulations might be tested.

For whatever they are worth, my own hunches are as follows. First, with regard to the predictive measure of empathy devised for this study, it may have been vitiated by the fact that therapists were not advised that their clients had been given a forced choice, so that 20 items were always true and 20 false. In addition, it seems possible, in retrospect, that the predictive form of empathy may be an important therapeutic tool for therapists who have a particular style of handling experience and relating to others, and a relatively unimportant and undeveloped capacity in other therapists with a different but equally effective style of handling experience and relating to others.

Second, with regard to the Truax measure of concurrent empathy, my guess is that it is biased in favor of client-centered and other therapists who consistently express their empathy in a particular manner that is more often appropriate for mildly and moderately disturbed clients than for severely and very severely disturbed ones. More specifically, the Truax measure seems geared to the direct, immediate, and explicit clarification of clients' feelings by therapists, whereas with many very frightened and miserable clients, the truly empathic response often seems to involve saying or doing something that implicitly serves to lessen their negative feelings, at least for the moment. Eventually, everyone needs to come to terms with his feelings, experiencing and sharing them as fully as possible; but if one's feelings are truly and overwhelmingly terrifying and destructive of a fragile grasp of self and surroundings, having them continuously highlighted by even the best-intentioned of therapists can be a devastating experience.

If measurement errors and biases like these are eliminated from current measures, it may yet be possible to produce a valid measure of empathy. That, at any rate, is the sort of faith one clings to if one believes that everything that truly exists is truly measurable but that false approximations are falsely measureable; the trick is to reject the latter without ceasing to struggle for the former.

Alas, experience and expectations also struck out. Here, it is harder to find fault with the measures. Perhaps all of these variables are simply irrelevant, and individual democratic values alone are sufficient to create potent therapeutic effects. However, if one accepts that interpretation, one might then be forced to assume that the poor outcomes achieved with nonclassical clients in previous studies indicate an absence of democratic values among those other therapists. Perhaps therapists in the present study are a unique group of democratic mavericks, and we clinicians in general are really a pretty authoritarian bunch. Or, perhaps democratic values are more widespread but simply fail to manifest themselves in relation to nonclassical clients in usual settings. If so, there must be something about the general climate in usual settings which militates against such manifestations and something about the milieu at the center where this research was done which did not.

A milieu-plus-personality explanation seems preferable to a personality explanation alone when one considers the fact that inexperienced therapists did as well as experienced ones in this study. While a reasonably good case can be made for the relative uniqueness of our experienced therapists, it is hard to make any case at all for the uniqueness of the inexperienced ones. Experienced therapists who had chosen to remain in this setting over a long period of time may well have been self-selected for nonauthoritarianism, but the inexperienced newcomers were either unselected or selected on other bases. Social-work field-work students were simply assigned to the center by their respective universities, and psychology internship applicants were chosen by the center on the basis of academic records and recommendations and, when possible, on impressions from screening interviews which focused on factors other than authoritarianism.

Thus, what seems to have happened here is that a fairly typical group of inexperienced therapists was introduced into a milieu dominated by a fairly atypical group of experienced therapists who manifested a highly democratic set of attitudes in relation to a nonclassical client population, with liberating results for all concerned. Perhaps that, after all, is the major function of experience: not to enable one to outdo the work of others but to facilitate it by providing a favorable climate for the constructive expression of positive attitudes. If so, then experience may be a relevant factor, but in a different sense than is usually assumed and requiring a different measurement strategy than that employed here.

With regard to expectations, it may be that a distinction needs to be drawn between general expectations for categories of persons and specific expectations for particular individuals. With such a distinction, one could then explore the relationship between these two aspects of expectations, a relationship that may be crucial under certain circumstances. In this study, for instance, most of the therapists held positive expectations with regard to the treatment potential of nonclassical clients in general but some of them had doubts about the treatment potential of a few specific clients within the nonclassical group. Perhaps this general and presumably permanent positive stance was potent enough to overcome any specific and presumably temporary negative ones.

This is, of course, sheer speculation at this point but the possible ramifications of such an analysis are intriguing. Consider, for example, the possible differential effects of a therapist, employer, or teacher whose attitude toward his client, employee, or student is some variant of "Blacks in general are no good but you look like an exception, 'a white nigger.' " Contrast that with, "Blacks in general are fine but I'm not sure about you at this point."

RESULTS OF NEGATIVE HYPOTHESES

But enough speculation, for the moment, and back to results, this time in relation to the five negative hypotheses about therapist factors. As predicted, therapists' initial, subjective feelings of liking, interest, and understanding for their clients proved unrelated to outcome (see Tables 20 and 21 again). Therapists' unqualified enthusiasm for their own experience as clients not only failed to improve their performance, it actually seemed to hinder it. Therapists who rated their own treatment as maximally successful achieved significantly poorer outcomes with these clients than did therapists who evaluated their own experience more moderately and therapists who lacked such experience altogether.

Taken as a whole, these results strongly reinforce suggestions offered earlier that the good therapist is more honest than he is saintly and tends to be a somewhat critical and unorthodox person who evaluates his own experience and his reaction to others according to the way it is and not according to some notion of the way it ought to be. Thus, the picture of the good therapist that emerges from this research is that of a highly democratic person who is keenly aware of his negative as well as his positive feelings, a person who respects the validity and autonomy of his own experience and that of others and is thus capable of "telling it like it is." My own inclination is to assume that a high degree of sensitivity and tact is also required to make the process of telling it like it is a truly constructive and therapeutic one, but until better measures of empathy are devised, the reader should take that assumption with as many grains of salt as his taste requires. This research provides no support for it whatsoever.

It does, however, provide support for the importance of a therapist factor that this researcher tried to dismiss as irrelevant. My fulminations notwithstanding, the Whitehorn-Betz A-B distinction scores again, at least with raw change scores (take one last look at Tables 20 and 21). Type B therapists achieved significantly better results with this group of severely disturbed nonclassical clients. At this point, I do not know what that means except that I had better put aside my prejudices and take a new look at the Whitehorn-Betz A-B typology. That, however, will take some time and some more research; first, I have to finish writing this book. Enough said.

10

time factors,
treatment goals,
and dropouts

TIME FACTORS IN TREATMENT

Results of the study thus far indicate that psychotherapy can be an effective method of helping nontraditional clients but leave open the question of whether it is a practical one. Data summarized in Table 22 suggest a positive answer. On the average, the good results reported in preceding chapters were achieved in less than 9 months and required less than 30 hours of face-to-face contact between client and therapist.

If we assume that for every 3 hours of contact time, the average therapist spent one additional hour thinking about each case, discussing it with others, and handling records and phone calls on it, the total average time per case is still only about 40 hours, or, approximately one week. Assuming an average professional salary of $10,000 to $15,000 per year, this means that the cost per client was somewhere between $200 and $300, neither an insignificant nor an exorbitant price, particularly compared with the cost of other social services.[1] Even more to the point might be a thorough cost-benefit analysis of other community mental health methods in relation to psychotherapy, but that is a matter for further research. For the present, it is enough to note that a substantial proportion of supposedly difficult or even untreatable clients improved significantly in what looks like a quite reasonable amount of time and for a not too horrendous cost.

These results indicate that the public got its money's worth (the center was a tax-supported institution which offered services to clients at no charge

---

[1] Some authors have suggested that we cut costs still further by hiring non-professionals as therapists, a suggestion that is dealt with in chapter 11.

Table 22
Time Factors in Treatment: Completed Cases

Treatment Length			
Number of Sessions		Number of Months	
Short therapy ≤ 25 sessions	Long therapy ≥ 26 sessions	Short therapy ≤ 6 months	Long therapy ≥ 7 months
n = 15	n = 15	n = 13	n = 17
x̄ = 18.0	x̄ = 41.5	x̄ = 5.0	x̄ = 11.4
Range = 10-25	Range = 26-72	Range = 3-6	Range = 7-26
All Cases		All Cases	
n = 30		n = 30	
x̄ = 29.8		x̄ = 8.6	
Range = 10-72		Range = 3-26	

to them), but they leave open the possibility that particular clients were short-changed, especially when one looks back at Table 22 and notes that the range of time factors in treatment was considerable: some clients received seven or eight times as much therapeutic time as others. Perhaps benefits were distributed unequally, with long cases improving more than short ones; or perhaps more seriously impaired clients required a greater expenditure of time to achieve the same benefits. Results summarized in Table 23 indicate that this is not the case. As predicted, Mann-Whitney U tests show no significant relationship between either improvement or impairment and treatment length, whether measured in terms of number of sessions or number of months and regardless of whether raw or corrected RPFS change scores are used.

Table 23
Relation of Time Factors to RPFS
Improvement and Impairment

Treatment Length and Improvement	U	U'	n	P
Length in sessions and raw change scores	105	120	15 × 15	n.s.
Length in sessions and corrected change scores	93.5	131.5	15 × 15	n.s.
Length in months and raw change scores	89.5	131.5	17 × 13	n.s.
Length in months and corrected change scores	101.5	119.5	17 × 13	n.s.
Treatment Length and Impairment	U	U'	n	P
Length in sessions and initial RPFS impairment	97	128	15 × 15	n.s.
Length in months and initial RPFS impairment	82.5	138.5	13 × 17	n.s.

Thus, this study, like many others before it (Avnet, 1965; Lorr, McNair, Michaux, and Riskin, 1962; Muench, 1965) documents the lack of any simple linear relationship between treatment length and outcome and indicates in addition that, under appropriate conditions, rate of improvement is no slower in more severely impaired clients than it is in less severely impaired ones. Yet, contradictory results do turn up occasionally in the literature (e.g., Bailey, Warshaw, Eichler, 1959; Lindsay, 1965; Wispe, and Parloff, 1965) and belief in a positive relationship between duration and outcome remains widespread, facts which in themselves call for an explanation. To explore this issue, the relationships between treatment length and the three other measures of treatment outcome used in this study were also examined. Results shown in Table 24 seem to pinpoint the source of confusion. Clients' ratings and behavioral ratings, like RPFS ratings, are independent of treatment length, but therapists' ratings are not.[2] In other words, the more time a therapist spends with his client, the more he is likely to feel he has helped him, but no independent measure is likely to confirm his judgment.

Table 24
Relations Between Treatment Length and Three
Additional Measures of Outcome

Length in Sessions &:	Phi	P	Length in Months &:	Phi	P
Therapists' Ratings	.218	.10	Therapists' Ratings	.455	.01
Clients' Ratings	.202	n.s.	Clients' Ratings	.086	n.s.
Behavioral Ratings	.094	n.s.	Behavioral Ratings	.081	n.s.

Additional hypotheses with regard to extreme lengths being counterproductive were not testable due to lack of data. All cases fell within the 10 to 75 session range, no case took less than 2 months, and only 5 cases took more than 12 months. Thus, we can only speculate about possible adverse effects of extremely short or extremely long therapy with a group of clients like those in the present study. And, we have no compelling explanation for the temporal variance within the present sample. Perhaps the longer cases really needed more time to achieve the same results as the shorter ones for some obscure reason unrelated to impairment. On the other hand, it seems equally possible that some of the longer cases might have been treated in less time without any reduction in benefit. If so, therapy may be even more practical a component for community mental health programs than these already encouraging results suggest.

---

[2] Fiske, Cartwright, and Kirtner (1964) and Nichols and Beck (1960) have also documented a positive relationship between length of treatment and therapists' evaluations of outcome but found no comparable evidence for such a relationship on the basis of other measures.

Before concluding this section on this highly optimistic note, one sobering point needs to be emphasized. All of the measures of improvement in this study were relative measures, in which clients were judged by the distance they had moved from their initial starting point and not in terms of whether they had actually reached some ideal end point which, in the case of the RPFS, would be the fully functioning state represented by a perfect score of 42. In fact, although better than 75 percent of these clients moved up on the scale, none of them reached this ideal end point. In other words, while most of these clients travelled a good way,[3] all of them still had a way to go. Since additional time did not result in additional improvement, some readers might be tempted to conclude that most of these clients had simply gone as far as they could go.

My own interpretation is that these clients have only gone as far as they can go in therapy for the time being. Some of them may continue to improve without further therapy in a suitable community, and others may want to re-enter treatment at a later date. Indeed, my own feeling is that the ideal strategy for most clients would involve a series of widely spaced, relatively brief (10 to 25 sessions), and probably time-limited courses of therapy. With such a strategy, no client would ever need to be permanently consigned to a less than optimal level of functioning, and at the same time, no client would ever need to be perpetually in treatment. Instead, he would return periodically, at points of his own choosing, to assess his status and, if need and desire dictated, to attempt to actualize his potential further. Such a strategy would, of course, place a premium upon speeding up the rate of therapeutic change within each course of treatment. According to Shlien (Shlien, 1957; Shlien, Mosak, and Dreikurs, 1962) and others, time-limits seem to serve precisely this function. According to Wiener (1959), even the arbitrary termination of treatment in potentially interminable cases produces no dire consequences. Thus, it appears as if there is much to gain and nothing to lose from the employment of a periodic rather than a once and for all treatment strategy.

TREATMENT GOALS

One intriguing additional possibility is that constructive changes might be accelerated if clients and therapists achieved an early mutual focus on an especially relevant treatment goal. As a beginning step toward exploring this possibility, two major potential foci of emphasis were delineated in this study, and clients and therapists were queried separately as to which one they regarded as their primary goal. Data summarized in Table 25 indicates that

---

[3] The typical very severely impaired client moved up to the severely impaired category; the typical severely impaired client moved from near the bottom to near the top of that range.

each of these goals was selected with roughly equal frequency by both clients and therapists in this sample. Despite this overall agreement between groups, disagreement within cases was high: therapists' initial goals differed from those of their clients in almost half of the completed cases and in fully two-thirds of the cases which later turned out to be dropouts.

The difference in goal concordance between completed cases and dropouts is even greater when changes in treatment goals during the course of treatment are taken into account. Therapists in this study were asked to indicate, on the Therapists' Outcome Rating Form, what their original goal had been and whether it had remained constant for the duration of the case (see Appendix B). Five therapists listed a different goal at post-therapy than they had listed at pre-therapy, although interestingly enough, only two of them recognized the fact that a change had taken place. Recognized or not, in 4 out of 5 of these cases, the shift corrected an initial disparity by bringing the therapist into belated accord with his clients' initial goal. Thus, if we consider final rather than initial goals, two-thirds of the completed cases are concordant and only one-third are discordant; the reverse is true for dropouts.

Table 25
Client and Therapist Goals and Goal Concordance in
Completed Cases and Dropouts

Completed Cases		n = 30		Dropouts		n = 12	
Client Goals*		Therapist Goals		Client Goals		Therapist Goals	
16	Explore	15	Explore	7	Explore	5	Explore
13	Control	15	Control	5	Control	7	Control
Client-Therapist Goal Concordance-Discordance				Client-Therapist Goal Concordance-Discordance			
Goals concordant: 16 cases				Goals concordant: 4 cases			
Goals discordant: 13 cases				Goals discordant: 8 cases			

*n is 29 rather than 30 in this column because one client refused to select a goal at the outset, insisting that he wanted nothing and was just coming because his mother told him to.

The study was not designed to obtain information on possible shifts in the primacy of client's goals but data is available on the meaningfulness of clients' original choices. Answers to a series of questions on the Clients' Goal Selection Form filled out at pre-therapy indicate that clients felt they understood the alternatives presented and were not simply responding to a forced choice by placing an arbitrary checkmark next to one or the other of the two specified goals. More specifically, of the total entering group of 45 clients, 23 reported that they experienced no difficulty in making a choice; an additional 16 explained that choice was difficult only because they found both goals meaningful and desirable. Only two clients explained their difficulty in terms of a lack of comprehension of the alternatives; three others rejected both goals; one said he did not really know what he wanted.

With this encouragement as to the worth of the data, it was deemed advisable to go ahead with planned tests of the relationship between client and therapist goals and impairment. Results, illustrated in Table 26, are more or less as predicted. Client goals tend to be related to impairment, with more severely impaired clients tending to feel that their need for increased self-control and strengthening is primary, and less severely impaired clients placing greater emphasis on the attainment of increased freedom and expressivity. Therapists' goals, on the other hand, bore no significant relation to their clients' initial impairment, thus providing support for suggestions offered in chapter 5 that therapists are more prone to select treatment goals on a general orientation basis than on a specific deficit basis tailored to the particular needs of each client. However, if changes in therapists' goals are taken into account, the relationship does become significant, indicating that therapists' final goals are not only more acceptable to their clients, but are more appropriate as well.

Table 26
Relation of Clients' and Therapists' Treatment Goals
to Client Impairment at Pre-Therapy

Treatment Goals and Impairment	U	U′	Z or n	Corrected Z	P
Clients' Initial Goals n = 44*	177.5	302.5	−1.473	−1.476	.10
Therapists' Initial Goals n = 45	207.5	298.5	−1.033	−1.036	n.s.
Therapists' Final Goals n = 30	53.5	170.5	14 × 16	−	.01

*n is 44 rather than 45 here because one client refused to select a goal, insisting he didn't want anything.

If a new study of a similar group of clients were to be undertaken at this point, it would be most interesting to allow RPFS results to enter into the process of goal selection and to institute time limits, say, a maximum of six months per case, in an effort to make the therapeutic contract as appropriate and explicit as possible with regard to both the direction and duration of treatment. With such contracts, it seems reasonable to hope for even better results, more satisfactory to all concerned, and with substantial reductions in the amount of time and money required.

DROPOUTS

The above paragraphs conclude our analysis of the results for completed cases. What remains to be done is to analyze the findings with regard to dropouts in this study. Twelve clients fell into this category, effecting a unilateral withdrawal from treatment by failing to return after anywhere from 3 to 19 sessions (the mean number of sessions per dropout was 9.1, and the median was 7). Results of an examination of 22 possible differences between dropouts and completed cases summarized in Table 27 reveal only one significant difference and two trends toward significance. They provide reasonable support for earlier claims with regard to the nonuniqueness of dropouts and their therapists, particularly in light of the fact that probabilities here may be somewhat inflated due to the large number of tests made.

More specifically, dropouts do not differ from other clients in terms of social class, severity of impairment, Klopfer prognostic scores, authoritarianism, Rice Voice Quality, age, race, productivity, hospitalization history, or concurrent treatment. They differ or tend to differ only with regard to their previous therapeutic history: clients who have had prior outpatient psychotherapy are more likely to remain in treatment the second time around, even, or perhaps especially, if they dropped out the first time.

Table 27
Comparison of Dropouts with Completed Cases: Client,
Therapist, and Case Factors

Client Factors	Phi	P	Therapist Factors	Phi	P
1. Social Class	−.048	n.s.	1. Experience	−.161	n.s.
2. Severity of Disturbance	.106	n.s.	2. Democratic Values	.000	n.s.
3. Klopfer Prognosis	−.013	n.s.	3. Concurrent Empathy	.086	n.s.
4. Authoritarianism	.087	n.s.	4. Predictive Empathy	.149	n.s.
5. Rice Voice Quality	.173	n.s.	5. Expectations	.359	.02**
6. Age	−.136	n.s.	6. Whitehorn–Betz Type	−.067	n.s.
7. Race	.013	n.s.	7. Personal Treatment	−.152	n.s.
8. Productivity	.134	n.s.	8. Initial Liking	.013	n.s.
9. Concurrent Treatment	.152	n.s.	9. Initial Interest	.170	n.s.
10. Prior Outpatient Treatment	.312	.10*	10. Initial Understanding	.080	n.s.
11. Prior Hospitalization	.255	n.s.			

Case Factor	Phi	P
Initial Goal Concordance	.307	.10***

*Clients with prior outpatient therapy are less likely to drop out.

**Clients are more likely to drop out if their therapists have low expectations for them.

***Cases where client and therapist goals are concordant are less likely to be dropouts.

Similarly, therapists whose clients drop out of treatment are no different from those whose clients remain in treatment in terms of experience, empathy, Whitehorn-Betz type, democratic values, personal treatment history, or self-rated interest, liking, and understanding for their clients. They differ or tend to differ only in terms of having less positive initial expectations for their clients. Finally, as might be expected on the basis of findings reported earlier in this chapter, cases marked by goal discordance seem more likely to eventuate as dropouts than are cases where the client and therapist have concordant goals.

In summary, these results serve to reinforce the major point of this study, that the untreatable client is, like the unicorn, a mythical beast. In addition, they provide some suggestions to help therapists remove imaginary horns and get on with the business of providing therapy for people of all sorts who need and want such help.

CHAPTER 11

psychotherapy, primary prevention, and professional politics

PSYCHOTHERAPY, CLASS, AND RACE

Results of this research, detailed in the last three chapters and documented in the tables they contain, indicate that individual psychotherapy can be an effective method of helping lower class and severely disturbed clients move toward the fulfillment of their psychological potential. These results also indicate that significant progress in this direction can be made in a period of months rather than years and that genuinely democratic values and a strongly nonauthoritarian stance on the part of the therapist may be the single most important element relevant to such progress. Despite all the detail and all the documentation, some readers may find these results difficult to consider on their merits and may be tempted to dismiss them because they do violence to their conceptions of the poor in general and of the severely disturbed poor in particular.

Two opposite conceptions are prevalent and both are neatly telescoped in the conversation F. Scott Fitzgerald is supposed to have had with Hemingway. They were talking about the rich rather than the poor, but the basic lines of division are the same. Fitzgerald is supposed to have said, "The very rich are different from you and I"; and Hemingway is supposed to have replied, "Yes, they have more money." Today, those on the Fitzgerald side of the debate with regard to the poor argue that they are very different from you and I, so different that individual psychotherapy cannot help them. Such people argue that psychotherapy is an intrinsically middle class method, unsuitable for lower class clients because it calls for the acceptance of delayed rather than immediate gratification and relies heavily on verbal communication—talk, rather than action.

Three of four presuppositions underlie this argument, and all of them are wrong. Presupposition one is that therapy provides only delayed gratification; presupposition two is that the poor have no capacity for delayed gratification; presupposition three is that the poor lack verbal skills because they are generally deficient; and presupposition four, an optional extra for relativists, is that the poor lack verbal skills because they do not value verbal communication, being happily immersed in a different-but-equal, or perhaps superior, nonverbal subculture.

Presupposition one has to do with misapprehensions about the nature of therapy and the role of the therapist. These misapprehensions are based on the exaggeration of an anachronism, the by now legendary blank screen model according to which the therapist was supposed to spend years sitting around saying nothing and trying to look inscrutable while he listened to free associations and tried to fit them together, as though his client were a jigsaw puzzle waiting with inanimate patience to be solved. Good therapists generally and good contemporary therapists particularly are nothing like that (e.g., Alexander, 1963; Matarazzo, 1965; Rogers, 1963). They are real, open and honest human beings, and their therapeutic role is an active one that begins the moment their clients walk in the door. As such, they provide immediate as well as delayed gratification because they have discovered that it is better for all clients, not just poor or severely disturbed ones.

Thus, the poor do not need any great capacity for delayed gratification in order to benefit from psychotherapy, but even if they did, that would not prove an insurmountable obstacle. Contrary to presupposition two, the inability to delay gratification is not really endemic among the lower classes. Often, what looks like inability is a deliberate choice—and a wise one at that. It makes sense to put off a minor immediate reward in favor of a major later one only if one has enough control over one's life circumstances to insure a reasonably stable and predictable future. That, however, is exactly what the poor usually lack.

For them, the future is most often uncertain, unstable, and subject to a multitude of arbitrary external influences: work lay-offs are more frequent and also more devastating since salaries are too low to allow for savings that provide a financial safety margin; the likelihood of illness and injury is greater due to overcrowding, poor living conditions, and the higher incidence of crime in slum neighborhoods; reliance on large impersonal bureaucracies over which one has little control (relief offices, public hospitals, unemployment compensation boards, housing authorities) is greater, and since minority groups are disproportionately represented among the poor, they are more often subjected to prejudice, another arbitrary experience which may be visited upon one at any time without regard to actions under one's own control.

Examples could be multiplied almost indefinitely, but the point seems clear already: in a situation like this, one does well to manage in the present. The future is usually beyond control, and it is therefore sensible to learn to take everything one can get at the moment, lest one forego current satisfactions only to wind up with nothing at all. People who make this sensible choice are not necessarily incapable of making a different choice and opting for delayed gratifications when their circumstances change so that realistic opportunities for delayed rewards are present. Thus, what looks like a psychological deficit or difference in poor people generally turns out to be an adaptive choice for many and an inner necessity regardless of external circumstances for only a few.

In any case, this argument is an academic one—at least in this context—because therapy does not require long-term delays. It does, however, require some verbal communication and thus, a refutation of presuppositions three and four—that middle and upper class people value verbal communication and are skilled at it, whereas lower class people do not value it and are not skilled at it—is not academic but essential. Fortunately, these presuppositions are as preposterous as they are prevalent. They are preposterous because, in reality generally and in America particularly, there is no cultural or subcultural group that does not value human communication, and there is no human group that does not rely heavily on verbal means of achieving such communication.

The poor value verbal communication at least as much as the rich do and, in many instances, more. Afro-Americans, for instance, have an extraordinarily rich oral tradition, expressed through song, story, speech-making, and just plain rapping,. This tradition is as alive today as it has always been, and it lives among the Black poor as well as among the Black rich, as witness such orators as Martin Luther King, Jr., and Malcolm X, and their audiences, audiences which were dominated by those with blue collars and those with no collars at all. Most Blacks value verbal skills and most have them. Those that do not are not reflecting a cultural difference but a failure to be socialized into their own culture.

How did so preposterous a notion as that of the nonverbal poor gain currency? Many poor people, especially many minority group poor people, are convinced that a deep, virulent, and virtually universal strand of prejudice and racism is the real dynamic here, and the only one. In recent years, a significant minority of professionals have come to agree with them, vehemently. With regard to Blacks particularly, a polarization has taken place

between those who see racism everywhere and those who see cultural deprivation everywhere. Some of my colleagues and I have had glimpses of something rather different, and I would like the reader to look at this something
else too, by considering the extended example presented below.

RACISM VERSUS CULTURAL DEPRIVATION: AN EXAMPLE

As part of an effort to ascertain the incidence of symptomatology and its
relation to school adjustment for young children, it was my job, over a period
of four years, to hire and train teams of psychologists to evaluate large
numbers of first graders in a community called Woodlawn.[1] The evaluation
procedure called for the teams to see the children in groups of ten and do the
following: (1) quickly identify each child's name (on a typewritten list) with
his face; (2) turn them all loose for a half hour or so of unstructured play
with blocks, tinker toys, and beads; and (3) call them back and chat briefly
with each about what he had made. Because Woodlawn is a ghetto community on Chicago's southside, virtually all of the children were Black, and
because psychology, like most professions, is a sort of a suburb, complete
with de facto segregation, almost all of the psychologists were white.[2]

Given this situation, initial trial runs of the procedure often followed a
particular pattern. Steps 1 and 2 went smoothly; both the raters and the kids
did what they were supposed to do and had a good time doing it. Step 3 was
a minor disaster. Generally, a child who had built something especially elab-
orate and was especially pleased with it would either volunteer to respond
first or would be chosen first by the psychologist. Asked what he had made,
he would confide that it was a king's castle or a fire station or a candy store,
or maybe a moon rocket—a worthy answer but alas, a totally unintelligible
one.

All small children tend to be somewhat unintelligible, particularly when
speaking to strange adults. They get scared, shy, silly, or excited. They all talk
at once or mumble or giggle or whisper or lisp through their missing teeth,
meanwhile squirming and addressing the floor or the far wall or their shoes or
their navels. In addition, however, these children spoke with a variety of
Black accents, some of which were very unlike the white accents of the
psychologists. This difficulty, superimposed on all the other difficulties, often
made them totally unintelligible, creating a situation that was profoundly
discomfiting to both the psychologists and the children.

---

[1] Findings from this and other methods of evaluation used in the Woodlawn research
are reported and discussed in several other publications: Kellam, Branch, Agrawal, and
Grabill, 1970; Kellam and Schiff, 1967; Kellam, Schiff, and Branch, 1968.

[2] See, for example, the documentation provided by Wispe, Awkard, Hoffman, Ash,
Hicks, and Porter (1969) in their article, The negro psychologist in America.

The psychologists were profoundly discomfited because they felt that they were supposed to understand immediately and that failure to do so was proof of their inadequacy. The children were profoundly discomfited because they felt they were supposed to know how to speak so that the psychologists could understand them and that failure to do so was proof of their inadequacy. Carrying so heavy a freight as a result of an initial misunderstanding and reactions to it, further conversation tended to stagger badly. Usually, the psychologist would ask the child to repeat himself. Usually, the child was even less clear the second time, and the psychologist less free to hear him. On the third go-round, the child often failed to answer at all, and in desperation, the psychologist would try altering the question—from "What did you make" to "What did you make it with," or "What did you play with." And the child, dutiful and subdued, would answer, pointing, "Sticks," or "Blocks."

At this, the psychologist's face would light up because he had understood the word. Seeing this, the child's face would light up because his word had been understood. Problem solved? Well, initially, the children tended to think so, and so, often, did the psychologists. The children, you see, had learned the right answer, the one that worked and saved them from painful discomfort and helpless inadequacy. Thus, each of the waiting and watching children would, in their turn, respond with the magic words. The conversation would go something like this:

"And what did you make, John?"

"A stick."

"Oh? Well, what did you make it with?"

"Sticks."

"Uh huh, did you do anything else, son?"

"No."

"Well, uh, were they any special kind of sticks?"

"Nope."

"Well, did you have a good time doing that?"

"Yep."

"Okay, uh, Betty, how about you? What did you make?"

Enough, we all know Betty's answer. And Wilma's and Stephen's and Charles' and on down the line. And there you have it. Ten new recruits to the nonverbal culture, or ten examples of instant cultural deprivation—readers' choice. Also, several instant racists, psychologists who, with the most open minds and the best wills in the world, have learned first hand about the inadequacy of the children of the poor, about their lack of verbal ability and imagination and their underdeveloped powers of abstraction.

Fortunately, instant cultural deprivation of this sort is instantly reversible—and so is instant racism, providing that the mutual problem underlying both is instantly dealt with. Obviously, one cannot deal with it by making the children instant experts on producing white speech nor by making the psychologists instant experts on understanding Black speech. That is not possible and not necessary. What is possible and necessary is to change the unrealistic expectations with which both parties to the exchange are burdened and to free them to use the realistic know-how they already possess. This can be done quite simply. The psychologists may not be able to hear all of the children all of the time, but they can see them, if they are not made too anxious to look. The children may not be able to make all of the psychologists understand what they are saying all of the time, but they can and do understand what the psychologists are saying, if they are not made too anxious to listen.

To unmake the anxiety, one need only convince the psychologist that it is all right not to understand and that it is not an indication of his inadequacy or the child's. In particular, it is important to convey to the psychologist that he need not and indeed cannot be an expert, instant or long range, on Blackness, although if he relaxes a bit, he may learn something about the subject and even enjoy the process. Teachers are ready at hand. The children, for instance, have been Black all their lives. Even though their lives have only been six years long, that is still a lot of Blackness, considering the fact that they have been Black 365 days a year and 24 hours a day during that entire period. Getting these essential points across to the psychologists, in context, generally took very little time and required much less explicit spelling out than this. Once they had got these essential points, they proved quite capable of taking it from there unaided.

Thus, when John gave up and with a reverse magic wand transformed his superconstruction into a stick, one of our ex-instant racists might look admiringly at the object, which might stand several feet high or contain an intricate pattern or have several moving parts, grin, and tell John the truth, namely, that that was the fanciest, best-looking stick he ever saw. At that point, John's returning sense of pride, competence, and self-esteem was likely to make him begin to grin too. The psychologist would then laugh and say something like: "Sure that's a stick, huh? Sure you're not just teasing me because I didn't understand you the first time, huh?" At which point, John and all of the other children are likely to begin to laugh too, and to teach, and to learn. End of example.

What was the point of it? Was it intended to suggest that there are no culturally deprived children and no bigoted professionals? Hardly. The circumstances of our society being what they are, it is impossible for beleaguered have-nots, struggling under the terrible onus of poverty and discrimination to successfully socialize all of their children to their own or any other culture. It is equally impossible for the professions, functioning in a still dominantly segregated society, which refuses fully and fairly to confront the uglier facts of its history and to make the reparative commitments that such a confrontation would show to be necessary, to avoid turning out any racists. The point is that we have enough real problems, real deprivation, and real bigotry, without creating unreal ones by exaggerating and distorting every minor difficulty and misunderstanding.

Difficulties and misunderstandings treated in this way do not stay minor very long. Fantasies have a way of taking on flesh very quickly. If you doubt that, put the book down and think for a while about what might happen to John, a very bright and adequate little boy, if misunderstandings like the one in the example are not immediately corrected, as they were in the Woodlawn project, but are repeated, again and again, in context after context until he becomes anxious, anxious and angry, every time he thinks about having to talk to a white adult, or even to do something he might be asked to talk about, until he quits talking and doing, stops learning and teaching, and begins to spend all of his time brooding. And think about the decent, well-meaning white professional, confronted with a grown-up John's anger and inadequacy, each feeding the other until John seeks not recognition or reparation but only revenge. How long do you think the psychologist will stay well-meaning? How long will you, or I, or any of us?

PSYCHOTHERAPY, SOCIAL PROBLEMS, AND POLITICS

Individual psychotherapy will not prevent such misunderstandings nor rectify the grim social conditions that make it inevitable that they should arise again and again. It is, however, one way of helping to heal some of the scars produced by such misunderstandings and conditions. Those on the Hemingway side of the debate about the poor say that there are no scars, and that, since it is the social conditions which create these nonexistent scars, they will cease to exist when the millenium comes. To make that happen tomorrow, we must all make war on the status quo today by becoming involved in social therapy rather than psychotherapy.

War against the uglier features of the status quo with regard to poverty and racism is certainly in order, but even in a war, it is usually a good idea to try to treat the wounded, if for no other reason than that if you don't, you may run short of soldiers. The poor are and must be the primary soldiers in the war against poverty, just as Blacks are and must be the primary soldiers in the war against racism. Outsiders do not and cannot fight a war for insiders without transforming the fight into a battle over something else which, whatever its own intrinsic merits, is inevitably more-or-less irrelevant to the original group's cause. This is least true when the original group has the power to hire and supervise outsiders; it is most true when the outsiders are hired and supervised by other outsiders—and true in spades when the outside supervisors have a powerful stake in what the insiders wish to change.

Thus, Daniel Moynihan (1969) and others notwithstanding, maximum feasible participation of the poor is not just a dispensable slogan in the war on poverty and racism. It constitutes the difference between a real war with the potential for achieving major victories for the oppressed and a pseudo-war in which major gains accrue to the frequently well-meaning but almost inevitably misguided functionaries hired by the other side. External obstacles to meaningful participation of the poor in general, and of the Black poor in particular, are enormous and worthy of separate and extended treatment, but internal obstacles are also real and important. Many impoverished Blacks are not effectively involved in the battle against poverty and racism because they are pre-battle casualties of the very system they must fight to change.

Such pre-battle casualties are clearly and demonstrably many times greater among the already outnumbered poor than they are among the affluent (e.g., Dohrenwend and Dohrenwend, 1965; Phillips, 1967; Roman and Trice, 1967). This fact alone makes it evident that Hemingway was wrong in suggesting, by implication, that the poor are different *only* insofar as they lack money, although that is certainly one of the most significant and basic differences, significant precisely because money is a major source of power in modern society and basic because lack of power is causally related to the other differences. The poor exist and are made different from you and me— not so different that we cannot talk to and hence treat them, but different enough so that they more often need treatment—because they lack money and other forms of power, and they lack these essentials because of gross inequities in the distribution of money and other forms of power in American society.

Lack of money and other forms of power make the poor socially impotent to obtain the service, training, and status they want and need. Social impotence is conducive to psychological impotence, which in turn fosters social impotence, and so on and on in a vicious circle which dizzies and imprisons those whirling inside of it. From this analysis, it follows that the poor need to fight against psychological as well as social powerlessness—that is, to fight for freedom, strength, and autonomy—individually and collectively. Programs that help them to do the one help them to do the other and are thus complementary, not competing or conflicting.

Some of the Hemingways doubt this, fearing that psychotherapy is an intrinsically reactionary process in contrast to social therapy, which they view as intrinsically radical. Actually, psychotherapy can be either liberating or imprisoning in its psychological and socio-political effects, and the same thing is true of programs aimed at social rather than individual change. Clear thought on such issues is currently clouded by a tendency to confuse methods that are professionally traditional with ideologies that are politically conservative and to assume that radically different professional methods necessarily bespeak a radical or at least a liberal and liberating social and political ideology.[3] In reality, however, it is not the category of service that determines its effects but the nature of the service, the nature of the system through which service is provided, and the interaction between the two.

Thus, with regard to the nature of service, psychotherapy can involve an effort to free and strengthen individuals so that they may more effectively pursue their own goals, whatever those are.[4] At the other extreme, it can involve crude efforts at indoctrination conducted by reactionaries or other zealots who politicize the treatment process while decrying politics. Similarly, social therapy can help to free and strengthen groups, redressing gross inequities in the distribution of money and other forms of power between them, or it can serve to extend and solidify those disparities by enshrining them in new institutional forms. Despite optimistic claims to the contrary, many social therapeutic innovations in community mental health do not really seem to have the potential for helping to redress significant disparities in money and power in a significant way.

With regard to the redistribution of money, over-optimistic claims are most often based on the notion that hiring the poor to work as community mental health agents constitutes some sort of potential economic panacea. Actually, of course, unless we want to turn the world into a kind of magic mountain or universal clinic, the proportion of poor people we can absorb is quite small compared to the need, and no substitute for helping to open up training for and access to jobs in business, industry, and all the other professions.[5] Moreover, were we to pay adequate wages to all of the nonprofessionals we already employ—janitorial and maintenance staff, aides, cooks, orderlies, security and clerical people, as well as community mental health agents—the proportion of people we could hire with current or foreseeable budgets would be markedly decreased.

Should that happen, our contribution to community mental health would not necessarily be decreased. It would probably be increased because we would then be eliminating the poverty we help to create rather than simply enlarging the ranks of the employed poor and giving some of them a stake in

---

[3] In this context, it seems appropriate to remind readers that Franz Fanon (1963), who was, among other things, a psychotherapist, was hardly a conservative, and Elton Mayo (1933, 1945, 1947), who pioneered social therapy in industry, was not exactly a flaming liberal. See, for example, Bendix and Fisher's (1961) excellent analysis of Mayo's political biases.

[4] Thus, the gentleman in this study who entered psychotherapy as a Black Muslim left it as a Black Muslim. His therapist did not teach him to love white folks, or to renounce self defense, and did not try to. He sought only to help him overcome inner obstacles to his fuller participation in the groups of his choice and succeeded quite reasonably in that quite reasonable task.

[5] Genuine redress of gross inequities would, of course, also require fundamental tax reform and other basic economic changes.

perpetuating the misery of their brothers. Such a shift in salary structure is likely to take place in the near future, not because of far-sighted generosity on the part of professionals, but thanks to expanding and increasingly effective union activity in the service fields. Because there are limits to what the public and the government can reasonably be expected to pay for community mental health services, the needed shift in salary structure may be made more rather than less problematic by the presence of thousands of nonprofessionals recently recruited into the field as community mental health agents. In this changing situation, it is unclear how long newly created roles will remain viable, and there is a very real danger that jobs created in a day will disappear in a day, leaving a sizeable group of people more frustrated and embittered than they were before.

These people are currently playing a wide variety of roles in the field, some useful and some not. Of the useful ones, only some are genuinely new. Indeed, one of the more common tactics is to hire nonprofessionals to offer the poor—guess what—psychotherapy, paying them only a fraction of what even the lowest paid professional earns. If, as seems likely, some of these nonprofessional therapists do as good a job as the professionals, then elementary fairness would seem to require that they receive, if not equal pay for equal work, then at least something roughly comparable. If, as also seems likely, some of these nonprofessionals are not doing as good a job as professionals but are providing a distinctly second-class service, then they should not have less pay but no pay at all—and no jobs in this area. After all, if there are no second-class clients, then there is no need for second-rate therapists.

So much for the redressing of economic inequities via hiring the poor to work for community mental health agencies. The more fundamental problem, however, has to do with the redistribution of power in a broader sense. This problem will not be solved by hiring the poor to work for us, no matter how many we employ or how much we pay them. To help redistribute power, we must reverse present strategies, and instead of hiring and sometimes co-opting the poor to work for us, we must learn to work for them and to create structures that make this possible. We can and should work for the poor as individuals by making first-rate nonindoctrinational psychotherapy available to them on request. We can and should work for the poor as groups by serving as technical experts, at their request, helping them to carry out their own plans to regain control over their communities and their own lives.

Generally, however, we do neither of these things but take an opposite tack, arguing that we cannot treat or otherwise personally relate to the poor as individuals because we are middle class or because we are white, but insisting that we can, nonetheless, select, train, and direct lower-class underlings who do this, while we sit at the lucrative and powerful apexes of the hierarchical heaps we create, determining from on high the destinies of the poor and poorly perceived people down below. My own feeling is that this is precisely the wrong role for middle class professionals and, particularly, for white ones dealing with Blacks. In fact, the central thesis of this book is that the main problem for troubled individuals and troubled communities in our society today is a lack of autonomy, self-control, and self-direction, a lack, in short, of egalitarian democracy and an excess of unresponsive and uninformed authoritarian direction and control.

Large scale community mental health programs which transform potential or existing communities of practitioners into increasingly authoritarian hierarchies with rigidly centralized power structures do not contribute to the solution of this problem for poor people or poor communities. Instead, they create a situation in which the service agencies themselves increasingly mirror the very problems they are supposed to solve, turning professional as well as nonprofessional employees into futile cogs in the bureaucratic machinery that is grinding all of us into creatures who fall sadly short of our full psychosocial potential as creative and adaptive human beings.

SERVICE AND SERVICE DELIVERY SYSTEMS

Bureaucracy is, of course, the modern version of authoritarianism, a version that is rapidly replacing older forms of authoritarianism in the mental health field, transforming service delivery systems in ways that have profoundly adverse effects on those who provide service, on those who receive it, and on the nature of service itself. Ironically, this retrogressive transformation has been greatly accelerated by the progressive emphasis on community mental health because community mental health is a very big job and bureaucracy is usually rationalized in terms of pragmatic necessity as the most efficient way to organize any large group of people to get any big job done.

Actually, as Drucker (1946), Gouldner (1961), Merton (1940), Ullman (1967), and others have pointed out, the relation between bureaucracy and efficiency is complex, questionable, and variable at best, and inverse at worst. In the mental health field, and in similar arenas, it tends to be inverse—so much so that bureaucracy may well be the least efficient way to organize people for their task. To understand why this is so, it is necessary to look more closely at the central features of bureaucracy, the central problems of mental health, and the relation between the two.

According to Weber (1946, 1947), what is central to bureaucracy and serves to distinguish it from other authoritarian hierarchies is the fact that functions are *specialized* and *standardized* by *rationally* allocating tasks and duties in accordance with an overall plan. Officials at the top of the hierarchy construct overall plans by analyzing the collective task into component parts, which are means to the collective end, and lower echelon individuals are then assigned responsibility, not for the collective end but for specific component parts, focusing on means or mean segments and not on ends.

In attempting to understand the implications of such a system of human organization in a field like mental health, it is essential to grasp the underlying assumptions that justify Weber's use of the word "rational" in his characterization of bureaucracy. Assumption one is that there is something approaching a clear, consistent, complete, and generally agreed-upon definition of the collective task, the ultimate end toward which the organization is supposed to be working. Without such a definition of the end, rational specialization of function to accomplish it is impossible. Assumption two is that the end is achievable through standardized means. If it is not, then standardization of function to achieve it cannot be rational.

The ultimate end of mental health systems, whether oriented to communities or to individuals, is to promote better health, or as I prefer to call it, more adequate psychosocial functioning. Alas, as was pointed out in chapter 4, there has been no clear, consistent, reasonably complete, and generally agreed upon definition of adequate psychosocial functioning: that is one of the central problems of the mental health field. Without such a definition, it is not possible to define the collective task or ultimate end. As a consequence, it is not possible to devise a truly rational plan for accomplishing it, let alone to specialize and standardize functions by rationally allocating to each person the responsibility for a component part of the overall plan.

As a result, what actually happens when a mental health system is bureaucratized is that powerful administrators name the collective end without defining it and then construct overall plans cafeteria style by choosing the techniques that they currently prefer and rationalizing these as requisite means to the undefined end. They then proceed to specialize the function of groups of individuals in terms of these techniques by organizing them to create discrete, formal programs, and to standardize the function of individuals within these programs by assigning responsibility for particular technique components or subcomponents to particular individuals. Obviously, generic psychotherapy of the sort practiced in this study is much too nonspecialized a phenomenon to constitute such a program or to lend itself to such subdivision. Typically, when a mental health system is bureaucratized, generic psychotherapy disappears and is replaced by, for example, work therapy programs, family therapy programs, aftercare programs, or crisis programs—programs which are much narrower in scope and much more easily amenable to standardization.

In terms of the logic previously outlined, this process is essentially irrational, as well as undemocratic, and might best be described as a process of substituting means for ends and losing the distinction between them altogether.[6] In the mental health arena, the distinction is peculiarly easy to lose. Those with a positivistic or behavioristic outlook would argue that this is so because it is a soft-headed and essentially meaningless distinction which should not have been made in the first place. Such people recommend that we focus on concrete behavior and forget about abstract definitions of unnecessary concepts like mental health or psychological adequacy.

From their perspective, the ultimate aim of, for example, a work therapy program is to put people to work. The program is therapeutic to the extent that it succeeds in getting its participants employed. Solutions like that seem refreshingly simple and sensible at first glance but tend to disintegrate under a more penetrating second glance—for example, by these standards, slavery was wonderfully therapeutic for American Blacks because it put virtually all of them to work, a proposition that is not only obviously nonsensical but also likely to be every bit as distasteful to behaviorists as it is to other decent and humane people.

Thus, as was pointed out in chapter 4, there is no way of escaping the need for an adequate definition of mental health and no possibility of creating a genuinely rational or meritocratic system of mental health services without making that definition measurable. One must know what the end is (definition) and whether it has been accomplished (measurement).

Some of the nonbehaviorists who have recognized the centrality of this problem have tended to regard it as an insoluble one, stressing the difficulties of definition and measurement in this area and pointing out that because something is ultimately necessary, it does not mean that it is currently possible. Such a viewpoint seems unduly pessimistic. An accurate and measurable definition may be currently and perhaps even ultimately beyond reach, but better approximations than have heretofore been made seem well within the realm of immediate possibility.

To find out whether they are, it is obviously necessary to try. The surprising fact is that attempts at comprehensive definition and measurement such as the one presented in this book have not often been made. There are many reasons for the relative dearth of efforts in this vital area, quite aside from the intrinsic difficulty of the undertaking. For one thing, as long as the medical model held undisputed sway, mental health was commonly viewed as the absence of illness, and the focus of effort was on the delineation of disease patterns or symptom complexes and not on positive definitions of mental health or psychological adequacy as such.

---

[6] The process might also be viewed as an extreme version of what Merton (1940) describes as the displacement of goals, but since in mental health, the goals were never clear in the first place, original avoidance might be a more precise term than the word displacement, with its suggestion of a prior something which has been displaced.

Later, when a number of innovative theorists broke free of the medical model (e.g., Allport, 1955, 1961; Binswanger, 1963; Boss, 1963; Erikson, 1963; Laing, 1968; Maslow, 1954, 1968) and developed positive conceptions of mental health, they tended to do so in ways that made their theories rallying points for the nonmethodologically oriented instead of springboards for serious and sustained measurement efforts.[7] Meanwhile, the methodologically oriented professionals tended to apply their increasingly elegant and sophisticated measurement techniques to substantive issues that were either quite narrow and specific, or theoretically broad but philosophically shallow and superficial. Thus, mental health bureaucracies have tended to operate by naming rather than by defining and measuring their ends, at least in part because comprehensive and measurable definitions were not readily available when community mental health services were being organized.

However, even if adequate definitions are made available and mental health bureaucracies adopt them, they are unlikely to succeed in achieving their newly clarified ends with bureaucratic means, however reoriented. Bureaucratic means are intrinsically unsuited to the achievement of ultimate mental health ends because they are standardized means—the whole point of breaking up tasks into component parts and component parts into subcomponents is to standardize procedures—and standardized procedures are rational only if one is striving to produce a standard product.

In mental health, that is the one thing no one seems to want, at least, not in the 1970s. In 1984, it may be different, but at present, bureaucratic administrators would probably be as appalled as other spectators if the "products" of the services they oversee, the clients, emerged from treatment like so many identical robots rolling off an assembly line. Clients would be even more appalled. Each human being is a unique entity and wants to remain so. People who voluntarily seek treatment may do so because they want to achieve an ultimate end, such as the realization of something like their full share of the universal human potential for adequate psychosocial functioning, but each person wants to achieve his own unique version of that end in his own unique way.

Indeed, one essential test of a reasonable definition of a psychologically adequate human personality is its ability to allow for literally infinite variety, just as a reasonable definition of a physically adequate human face (a forehead, two eyes, a nose, a mouth, cheeks, and a chin) allows for the fact that no two human faces ever are or should be exactly alike. Human personalities, like human faces, are unique in two ways. First, they are unique because each element in the total configuration is a unique version of that element. Second, they are unique because each total configuration is a unique version

[7]Carl Rogers and his followers are the major exceptions to this generalization, having sought consistently to make their conceptions both positive and measurable.

of totality in which the unique versions of elements are combined and interrelated in a unique way.

Thus, each client who comes seeking aid comes as a unique individual seeking aid which is individually tailored to the totality of his needs by a person who is in close enough contact with him to apprehend them and who has the freedom and flexibility to respond to them in a unique way. Distant administrators setting up standardized programs and devising standardized procedures without having direct contact with specific clients cannot possibly even approximate that ideal. The best they can do is to provide a variety of standardized programs and procedures—and that will not solve the problem. No assortment of standardized products is likely to satisfy a person who is looking for a custom-tailored product.

Custom-tailoring requires custom-tailors, individuals who focus on ends and have a maximal amount of freedom and flexibility to adapt and combine old means and to create and dissect new ones, judging their utility solely in terms of the contribution they make or fail to make to the immediate end in question, and helping particular clients or client communities to achieve their particular version of the general end. A practitioner who is a custom-tailor may, if he chooses, specialize in particular sorts of clients—e.g., adults, adolescents, children—but he must take personal responsibility for them as the unique totalities they are, and he must strive, insofar as it is humanly possible, to deal personally with whatever mental health problems they present and to use whatever means seem best to advance that end, judging as best he can in terms of immediate feedback from his clients and altering his actions in terms of it as the relationship develops.

Occasionally, if he feels particularly ill-equipped to deal with a particular problem or to use a particular means which he thinks might be particularly useful for one of his clients, he may enlist the aid of a colleague or two, either as a treatment consultant or as a direct but auxilliary treatment participant, but he must maintain personal contact with the client and he must continue to accept personal responsibility for the case as a whole or transfer the case to someone who will. In other words, he may specialize in certain sorts of clients, but he must be a generalist with regard to the mental health needs of those clients.

When he stops doing that, he stops being a custom-tailor and becomes a relatively mechanical link in an assembly line trying to turn out men like a mass production factory turns out machines. Bureaucratic organization works inevitably to make men machine-like because it works to make concern with ends the official function of a specialized few—administrative planners—and to divert the attention of the even more specialized many—line staff—away from ends and toward means which become more and more narrowly and specifically defined as bureaucratization "progresses." Each narrowing increase in specificity of function reduces the freedom and flexibility of line staff, lessening their ability to be generalists for their clients and to respond to them in a personal, nonstandardized way.

A bureaucratically organized mental health system is not organized around practitioners who are generalists for their clients, nor around clients as unique totalities who require such generalists. It is not organized around concrete, variable people at all but around abstract, standard parts: specific programs organized around specific problems that are dealt with by specific procedures. Programs are formal, discrete entities which replace people as basic units of organization. Lines between programs are clear and sharp, not shifting and fluid, and personnel are horizontally divided up among programs and vertically arranged within them in such a way that each person fills a prearranged position with responsibility *for* some component part of a program and *to* some superior who has responsibility for that component. Clients are then defined in terms of the particular problems around which programs are organized, and they are processed to and through those programs and subjected to the various procedures and techniques which constitute them.

In that reasonably accurate but relatively abstract phraseology, the system tends to sound rather obviously bad and irrelevant, so much so that one might wonder how anyone who was not already badly dehumanized could support it. However, when the names of the programs are filled in, a surprising transformation frequently takes place, and the very same system tends to sound just as obviously good and relevant. A reasonably typical list of core programs might, for example, include all of the programs listed on page 167: (1) an aftercare program; (2) a family therapy program; (3) a work therapy program; and (4) a crisis therapy program. Looked at from the perspective of these labels, in this context, one might abruptly cease wondering how any humane person could support the system and wonder instead what point there is in any humane person's attacking it.

Quite simply, the point is not that aftercare, family therapy, work therapy, and crisis therapy are bad and irrelevant; they are indeed good and relevant, in the abstract. The point is that in the concrete, they should be constantly and fluidly structured and restructured by and for clients and staff. They become bad and irrelevant only when the process is reversed and clients and staff are rigidly restructured in terms of them, or in more Weberian terms, when the intrinsic bureaucratic characteristic of tailoring men to fit jobs instead of jobs to fit men is brought into operation.

To be concrete, consider two final case examples from this research, Mr. Brown and Mr. Grey. These gentlemen raised no particular problems for the nonspecialized therapists in this study. Treatment was custom-tailored to their respective needs. Outcome, in both cases, was reasonably favorable (each improved his total RPFS score by 1.5 points). As noted in chapter 2, however, the unprogrammed, nonbureaucratic milieu which permitted such adjustments is no more, and in light of the developments discussed above, the odds are high that if Mr. Brown and Mr. Grey came seeking treatment today, they would not be confronted by a nonspecialized psychotherapist but by a system of specialized programs. In what follows, an attempt will be made briefly to portray these men and then to consider how they would have fared in a modern mental health bureaucracy.

Mr. Brown was a thirty-year-old man who had never been hospitalized. He was single and lived alone, having migrated to Stock City from his southern birthplace eight years ago, leaving his parents and siblings behind. He shifted from job to job for the first two years after his migration until he found one that he liked. He had worked steadily and competently at it ever since, despite the voices. The voices have sounded in Mr. Brown's ears since early adolescence; they accused him of being rotten and worthless, of doing corrupt and vicious things, and they filled him with shame and guilt and fear. His condition was chronic, not acute. His request for treatment was not precipitated by a crisis but by a sensitive physician, who saw him for a routine checkup, found him physically healthy, but noticed his extreme discomfort and suggested that there were professionals who might help him to lessen it.

Looking from Mr. Brown to the system and back again, there is an obvious lack of fit: aftercare is out because he has never been in; family therapy is impossible for people without families; work therapy would involve a gratuitous rejection of the fact that this is the one successful area of his life. To put him into crisis therapy, one would have first to precipitate the crisis or else treat a fifteen-year-old condition as though it were a sudden emergency, an approach that would probably confuse and frighten him. The simple fact is that nothing in this abstractly relevant system is concretely relevant to Mr. Brown, a fact which Mr. Brown and the staff members who confront him would find hard to ignore. Staff members in a bureaucratic system either would have to put him into an unsuitable program or reject him as an unsuitable candidate, despite his obvious need. Whichever way the decision went, no one directly affected by it would be likely to be pleased.

Some readers might object that the example is unfair because Mr. Brown is atypical or because this hypothetical-typical list of programs is too short. With regard to the first objection, it should be stressed that Mr. Brown is not only atypical, he is unique, and that is exactly why, to echo Leighton's (1959) beautifully selected book title, "his name is legion." To meet the second objection, we can, of course, lengthen the list, but only to a point. There can never be as many programs as there are people and even constant program innovation from the top is unlikely to fit people at the bottom.

When dealing with infinite variety, concrete responsiveness has a permanent edge over abstract relevance which is likely to be obvious to those on the firing line and invisible to those looking down on it.

Even when abstract relevance becomes concrete, it can be problematic in the rigidly programmatic context of a bureaucracy, as witness example two, Mr. Grey. Mr. Grey is also thirty years old, but he has been hospitalized four times and married twice. He lives with his mother, her third husband, and two younger half-sisters, visits one of his ex-wives frequently, and sometimes spends a week or two with a girlfriend. He has never managed to hold a job for more than a few months at a time, has no skills, and is currently unemployed. His stepfather bitterly resents his living there without working and has presented his mother with an ultimatum of the either-he-goes-or-I-go variety. This ultimatum has precipitated a personal crisis for the client, resulting in his first suicide attempt, a near success. Mr. Grey is the opposite of Mr. Brown: he has post-hospital adjustment problems, family problems, work problems, and a real live crisis to deal with. Everything in the system is relevant to his needs, yet the system is not.

Mr. Grey's problems may be divisible into specialized parts in a standardized manner, but Mr. Grey is not. He cannot be in four places simultaneously and his problems did not happen to occur sequentially. To refer him to only one program would be to ignore three of his problems. To focus on all four is to expose him to the difficulty of relating to a succession of four different programs and God knows how many "personnel" within each program. There are, for example, aftercare programs bureaucratically designed to provide "continuity of care" for people released from mental hospitals which involve chains of half a dozen or more "care-takers" for a single individual. Such continuity is a reality from the bureaucratic point of view because the system does not lose track of its clients. From the client's point of view, however, the rapid and confusing succession of new faces and places is more likely to seem like gross discontinuity, and his experience is likely to be shared by the "personnel" who make up the links in the chain of direct but frustratingly attenuated contact with him. Once again, those who must wear the shoe feel the lack of fit.

Thus, dissatisfaction with the system and awareness of its shortcomings[8] is likely to be highest among clients and among those staff members who must deal directly with them. However, in a bureaucracy, these are the people with least power to change the system. Power in a bureaucracy is vested in

---

[8] Dissatisfaction at this level is a constant; clear awareness of its causes is variable because a variety of defense measures may eventually be called into play, protecting those most hurt by the game from too continual and bruising a confrontation with the realities of their predicament. And, of course, bureaucracy fosters and rewards such defenses in the ways that Merton (1940) points out and in some other ways as well.

those who administer the system, administrative specialists who have no direct contact with clients and, unless they are very low level administrators, little or no contact with line staff. Indeed, the higher up a bureaucratic administrator is, the more distant he is from the line of direct action. As we have already seen, the farther one is from that line, the better it tends to look. The net result is a situation in which those with the power to change the system don't feel the need, and those who feel the need don't have the power.

Chester Barnard (1938) and some of his followers see such dilemmas as communication problems and go so far as to suggest that instead of looking at bureaucracy in Weberian terms as an authority system, we might more profitably view it as a communication system. Such a redefinition seems to focus on the problem only to miss the point: bureaucracy is basically a system of authority, not a system of communications, because it is the pattern of authority which determines the pattern of communication and not the other way around.

Of course, those at the top could do an objectively better job of handing down decisions if they had more adequate feedback about what goes on at the bottom, but they still could not be as immediately responsive as those at the bottom. In any case, the problem is largely academic because they are unlikely to get adequate feedback as long as they have such disporportionate power. Moreover, as long as they attain and retain their power independently of the satisfaction of either service personnel or service recipients, they do not really need adequate feedback and are unlikely to want it.

They will not get adequate feedback from clients because they have no contact with clients; they will not get adequate feedback from staff, even if they do have contact with them, because, while messengers bearing bad tidings are no longer literally beheaded, they are not exactly blessed and do sometimes get the figurative ax. At the very least, if they persist with their pervasive tales of woe about the concrete dreariness of a system which positively glows in the abstract, they are likely to be bypassed for promotion. For service personnel, being bypassed for promotion means staying on the firing line where the frustration is highest and the rewards are lowest; thus, truth-telling to one's superiors is negatively reinforced. Even when promotion is not an issue, making the best of a bad system generally means finding loopholes that superiors might close if they knew of their existence. Once again, prudence dictates a high degree of selectivity in choosing what information one may safely pass up to one's superiors.

Bureaucratic administrators, for their part, need not fret too much about their lack of information about how the system really works. Their job security and "success" is not dependent on the esteem or satisfaction of those below them. They are responsible, if at all, to outsiders above them who also view the system abstractly and have even less knowledge about how it actually works. Since it actually works rather badly, because of the very bureaucratic hierarchy atop which these administrators sit, real knowledge may be abstractly desirable, but it is hardly necessary and may be concretely painful. For the bureaucratic mental health administrator, ignorance may indeed be bliss, and there is no ignorance as sincere as motivated ignorance.

Thus, those with minimal power are motivated not to talk, and those with maximal power are motivated not to listen. Power is the primary fact, and as long as it is distributed as it is in a bureaucratic hierarchy, well-meaning efforts at improving the operation of the resultant system by striving for better communication seem doomed to failure. To rectify the situation, restoring meaningful external responsiveness and free and open internal communication, it is necessary to redistribute power, taking it away from administrators who only manage service and dividing it equitably between those who give service and those who receive it.

In other words, it is necessary to replace bureaucracy with democracy, destroying the irrational authoritarian hierarchy and creating in its stead a community of colleagues and their clients who interact freely and flexibly with one another, collaborating in the search for individualized means which are effective in achieving individualized versions of the common end. Democracy is infinitely superior to bureaucracy because it makes such collaborative searches possible, but it does not automatically guarantee their success or allow one to evaluate results and the reasons for them in an objective way. Alas, in the absence of objective evaluation, democracy tends to flounder and ultimately to degenerate into mob rule, stage-managed by actors incapable of solving real problems—and hence unwilling to address them—and intent instead on finding an endless succession of new panaceas to embrace and/or scapegoats to blame and attack.

To protect against such dangers, democracy must be combined with meritocracy in such a way that the following conditions obtain: (1) all participants in the resultant community are left free to choose their own means of achieving mutually agreed-upon ends; (2) all participants are fairly and objectively evaluated in terms of how often and how well they succeed in achieving those ends; and (3) all participants are given honest and meaningful feedback about the results of their efforts and those of others.[9] Under such conditions, everyone has free choice and everyone has reasonably accurate and relevant information on which to base his choices.

From what has been said thus far, it is apparent that, in this formulation, meritocracy provides the information that prevents democracy from degen-

[9] Clients' privacy must, of course, be protected to the extent that they want it protected, but practitioners do not have a comparable right. For us, one of Lord Acton's lesser known axioms seems appropriate: "That which is secret degenerates."

erating into blind mob rule. It is perhaps less apparent, but no less true, that democracy provides something that prevents meritocracy from degenerating into its debased form, arbitrary elitism. The something that genuine democracy provides is power-sharing, which protects true meritocracy by working to ensure equal access to the means of attaining merit and to ensure reasonably relevant and meaningful standards of merit.

Currently, we do not have much democracy or meritocracy, let alone an ideal combination of the two, in our mental health service delivery systems, or in the schools and training institutions that produce the people who staff them. What we have, increasingly,[10] is a bureaucratic system that is neither meritocratic nor democratic. This is a sorry state of affairs, but one that is hardly peculiar to the mental health field. Sadder still is the fact that most of us who have tried to improve conditions have attempted to replace bureaucracy and/or traditional authority with either meritocracy or democracy. That is a losing game because unless those two positive alternatives are combined and kept together each tends to degenerate into their common nemesis, arbitrary authority.

Democracy plus meritocracy may be a winning combination, but it is a hard one to put together and to keep together. The odds seem best in individual therapy, individual classrooms, and other one-to-one and small group relationships. They are longer in universities, training centers, and other large institutions. They are longest of all in poor communities, a differential created by two facts. The opposition to democracy in a university, while formidable enough, is still much less formidable than the opposition ranged against the poor. Second, the power the university community already has relative to its own affairs is so much greater than that which the poor have relative to theirs.

Thus, although the need for democracy and meritocracy, and for programs of primary prevention aimed at helping to achieve these conditions, is enormous in poor communities, the obstacles to the creation and maintenance of such programs are also enormous. Under present conditions, pressures and temptations are fantastic, support is hard to come by, and bitter dissension and distrust are omni-present, making the whole process a bruising and exhausting one. Even if one achieves some measure of success, the financial cost of any sizeable program is likely to be quite high, and the pressures of funding and, especially, of refunding are such as to push action into less relevant and more repressive directions. After all, successful programs of this sort necessarily involve a redistribution of power and that constitutes a direct challenge to the status quo. It should therefore come as no surprise to learn

[10]This is not to suggest a halcyon past. In general, what bureaucratic authority is replacing is traditional authority, as in the process described in chapter 2, or charismatic authority.

that such programs tend not to get refunded or, at least, not until genuine change agents are replaced by more "positive and constructive" leaders and approaches.

No one knows this better than poor people themselves, and the Black poor know it very well indeed. It is one of the major reasons they tend to have so profound a distrust for professionals, Black or white, and their programs. Happily, comparable pressures do not obtain in one-to-one relationships, another fact which poor people are quite capable of grasping, and that is one of the main reasons why it is actually easier to relate to poor people as individuals in psychotherapy, even if one is of a different class or race, than it is to relate to them as groups via large scale community programs.

Speaking chauvinistically and personally as a psychologist, I still hope that we can make a significant contribution to primary prevention for impoverished communities and provide effective psychotherapy for individual members of those communities. However, if primary prevention proves impossible, I would rather see us confine our *professional* efforts to psychotherapy and get out of the social action business altogether than see us hold out false promises or, even worse, become the press agents and technicians for ever newer and more sophisticated forms of distraction, repression, and control. Even if our efforts do end up being restricted mainly to the provision of psychotherapy, we will still have a very big job on our hands.

PSYCHOTHERAPY AGAIN

Psychotherapeutic services for those who need them most have always been in desperately short supply. With the exception of a few settings like the one in which this research was done, the quality of service has tended to be as inadequate as the quantity. This sorry state of affairs has been a constant; only the rationalizations for it have changed over the years. The old rationalization was that the poor and the severely disturbed lacked the capacity to receive help; the new one is that psychotherapy lacks the capacity to provide it—but only for such people. Results, in both cases, are the same. Two classes of service for two classes of people, and when all the extraneous words are stripped away, the divisions do not correspond to neutral differences but to loaded conceptions of superior and inferior which contribute to the already frightening degree of polarization in our society between the fortunate and the unfortunate, the haves and the have-nots.

Results of this research serve to undercut both rationalizations for second-class service and the assumption of immutable inferiority which usually underlies them by demonstrating that the poor and the severely disturbed can and do profit from psychotherapy when they have the benefit of therapists who can deal with them on a respectful and egalitarian democratic basis. The implication of these findings seems clear: psychotherapy should not be dropped from the roster of community mental health services for the poor and the severely disturbed; it should be included and both its quantity and quality should be improved.

Improving the quantity of therapy available to the severely disturbed poor will not be cheap because disporportionate numbers of poor people fall into that category and will continue to do so until there is a significant redistribution of money and power in our society. In the meantime, results of this research indicate that psychotherapy need not be impossibly expensive either, first because we can and should do the job more quickly than most of us have done it in the past; and second, because we can and should discard inappropriate medical models which have operated to retard progress while keeping therapeutic personnel in desperately short supply and the cost of services prohibitively high.

With regard to improving the quality of psychotherapeutic services, suggestions motivating and arising from this research have centered around the need to improve the academic and institutional milieus in which service personnel are trained and employed so as to make them simultaneously more meritocratic and more democratic. Such improvements are not likely to produce therapists who can work equally effectively with all types of clients, but they should help to produce therapists with a greater degree of versatility than is common today and with a greater ability to tell the difference between their own individual preferences and limitations and the nature of reality. For example, there are a lot of clients I, personally, can't treat—genuinely narcissistic characters, for instance—but that says a lot about me and little or nothing about the treatment potential of such clients.

With regard to the issue of client treatability, some further points seem worth stressing. First, while there may be no inherently untreatable clients except for those who genuinely do not want help, there are therapeutic failures, seven of them in this study according to the RPFS, and many, many more in settings across the country. Probably, there always will be some in all client populations, but if we succeed in encouraging a larger and more varied group of therapists to work on a reasonably intensive individual basis with the severely disturbed poor, there should be many fewer failures with such clients than there are now. We should then begin to learn from our failures instead of avoiding our problems by shunning the poor and the severely disturbed or treating them only at a "safe" distance via the direction of nonprofessional intermediaries.

Certainly, in the field of medicine, close and continuing professional contact with "untreatable" patients has proved helpful in gradually transforming more and more of these people into "treatables." In the mental health field, plagued as it is by inappropriate medical analogies, it is striking that this most obvious and most appropriate analogy is conspicuous mainly by its absence. My own feeling is that it makes as little sense for the majority of professional therapists to concentrate on the mildly disturbed and avoid the severely disturbed as it would make for physicians routinely to treat patients with colds and reject cancer victims.

In addition to trying to learn from their experiences, physicians generally treat cancer victims because, even if they cannot always restore them to fully unimpaired functioning, they usually can provide some alleviation of suffering and/or some prevention or retardation of further deterioration. Still another reason is because even unsuccessful treatment is an important professional expression of human concern. All three of these reasons for treating the severely impaired make sense, regardless of whether the impairments in question are physical or psychological. Thus, even if the results of this study had been less positive, the basic recommendation—more and better therapy for those who need it most—might have been the same.

Some readers may find this study and its recommendations disappointing because, in addition to offering no great bargains or panaceas, it offers no specific new treatment techniques or "gimmicks," to use a deliberately loaded word—as deliberate and loaded as the attitude from which it stems. The attitude referred to is a belief that we can and must relate to people of different classes and races as real human beings in contact with other real human beings and not as interchangeable wielders of impersonal techniques being applied to defective or misprogrammed machinery.

This does not mean that greater specificity would not be desirable in this area. Rather, it means that basic therapist attitudes and attributes should be identified first. Then the means by which they are made manifest in the therapeutic situation should be studied, not with a view to helping people act a part they do not feel, but in order to help people who do feel the part to make that fact more readily apparent to those they serve. We should be prepared, however, to discover that the ways of doing that are as varied as human beings themselves, and if so, that infinity is a hard thing to nail down.

appendices

workshop course outline

Psychotherapy Research Workshop
Session Topics and Selected References

The purpose of this outline is to provide a general overview of the major topics we will attempt to deal with in the workshop. In dealing with these topics, we hope to avoid superficiality but, because this is a brief (12 session) workshop, it will not be possible to deal exhaustively with any one topic. References are listed under each topic to make it easier for anyone who is especially interested in any particular topic to pursue the matter more intensively on his own. If you have no particular interest in pursuing any one topic further or find your interest satisfied, for the time being, by what you already know and/or the coverage provided in the workshop sessions, please feel free to ignore the references: There are *NO* required or even "suggested" readings for the workshop.

Guides to the research literature, general communication problems, science and social science, and the issue of influence.

A. Guides to the research literature
   1. *Psychological Abstracts*
   2. *Annual Review of Psychology*
   3. *Contemporary Psychology*

B. General communication problems
   1. Snow, C. P. *The two cultures and a second look.* New York: Mentor Books, 1964.
   2. Bordin, E. S. Curiosity, compassion and doubt: The dilemma of the Psychologist. *Amer. Psychol.* 21 (1966): 116–21.
   3. Chein, I. Some sources of divisiveness among psychologists. *Amer. Psychol.* 21 (1966): 333–42.

    4. Boring, E. G. The psychology of communicating science. In *History, psychology and science*, R. I. Watson and D. T. Campbell (eds.). New York: Wiley, 1963.

C. Science and social science
    1. Bachrach, A. J. *Psychological research: An introduction.* New York: Random House, 1962.
    2. Whitehead, A. N. *Science and the modern world.* New York: Mentor Books. 1948.
    3. Langer, S. *Philosophy in a new key.* New York: Mentor Books, 1948.
    4. Gendlin, E. *Experiencing and the creation of meaning.* Glencoe, Ill.: Free Press, 1962.

D. Contrasting attitudes towards scientific influence
    1. Szasz, T. S. *Law, liberty and psychiatry.* New York: Macmillan, 1963.
    2. Skinner, B. F. *Walden Two.* New York: Macmillan, 1948.
    3. Szilard, L. My trial as a war criminal. In *The Voice of the Dolphins.* New York: Simon and Schuster, 1961.

E. Research on influence
    1. Asch, S. E. Effects of group pressure upon the modification and distortion of judgments. In *Readings in social psychology*, G. E. Swanson, T. M. Newcomb, and E. L. Hartley (eds.). 2d ed. New York: Henry Holt, 1952.
    2. Clark, K. E. and Clark, M. P. Racial identification and preference in Negro children. In *Readings in social psychology*, G. E. Swanson, T. M. Newcomb, and E. L. Hartley (eds.). 2d ed. New York: Henry Holt, 1952.
    3. Solomon, P., Kubzansky, P. E., Leiderman, H., Mendelson, J. H., Trumbull, R., and Wexler, D. *Sensory deprivation.* Cambridge, Mass.: Harvard University Press, 1961. (See especially the introduction by D. O. Hebb.)

F. Research as an influence
    1. Clark, K. E., and Clark, M. P. *Brown* v. *Board of Education,* United States Supreme Court, 1954.
    2. Stanton, A. H., and Schwartz, M. S. *The mental hospital.* New York: Basic Books, 1954.
    3. Hollingshead, A. B., and Redlich, F. C. *Social class and mental illness.* New York: Wiley, 1958.
    4. Harrington, M. *The other America: Poverty in the United States.* New York: Macmillan, 1963.
    5. Rioch, M. J., Elkes, C., Flint, A. A., Usdansky, B. S., Newman, R. G., and Silber, E. National Institute of Mental Health pilot

study in training mental health counselors. *Am. J. Orthopsychiat.* 33 (1963): 678–89.
6. Holzberg, J. D., Knapp, R. H., and Turner, J. L. Companionship with the mentally ill: Effects on the personalities of college students. *Psychiat.* 29 (1966): 389–405.

II. Individual therapy: pros and cons

A. Research in the 50s.
1. Eysenck, H. J. The effects of psychotherapy: An evaluation. *J. Consult. Psychol.* 16 (1952): 319–24.
2. Rosenzweig, S. a. transvaluation of psychotherapy—A reply to Hans Eysenck. *J. Abnorm. Soc. Psychol.* 49 (1954): 298–304.
3. Rogers, C. R., and Dymond, R. F. *Psychotherapy and personality change.* Chicago: University of Chicago Press, 1954.
4. Rosenthal, D., and Frank, J. D. Psychotherapy and the placebo effect. *Psychol. Bull.* 53 (1956): 294–302.

B. Issues in the 60s: Supply and demand
1. Dohrenwend, B. P., and Dohrenwend, B. S. The problem of validity in field studies of psychological disorder. *J. Abnorm. Psychol.* 70 (1965): 52–69.
2. Schofield, W. *Psychotherapy: The purchase of friendship.* Englewood Cliffs, N.J.: Prentice-Hall, 1964.
3. Rioch, M. The fiddlers of X. *Psychother.* 1 (1964): 88–90.
4. Albee, G. W. No magic here. *Contemporary Psychology* 10 (1965): 497–98.
5. Albee, G. W. The Psychological Center must precede the development of a language for professional psychology. Paper presented at the 74th Annual Convention of the American Psychological Association, New York, 1966.

C. Issues in the 60s: Radical alternatives to therapy
1. Cumming, J., and Cumming, E. *Ego and milieu.* New York: Atherton, 1962.
2. Brager, G. New concepts and patterns of service: The Mobilization for Youth Program. In *Mental health of the poor,* F. Riessman, J. Cohen, and A. Pearl (eds.). Glencoe, Ill.: Free Press, 1964.
3. Kellam, S. G., and Schiff, S. K. The Woodlawn Mental Health Center: A community mental health center model. *Soc. Serv. Rev.* 40 (1966): 255–63.

III. Evaluating the effectiveness of treatment: The outcome problem

A. Defining outcome in relation to goals
1. Freud, S. Analysis terminable and interminable. In *Therapy and technique,* P. Rieff (ed.). New York: Collier Books, 1963.

2. Alexander, F. Psychoanalysis and psychotherapy. In *The scope of psychoanalysis*, F. Alexander (ed.). New York: Basic Books, 1961.

3. Colby, K. *A primer for psychotherapists.* New York: Ronald Press, 1951. (See especially pp. 3–5.)

4. Rogers, C. R. Psychotherapy today or where do we go from here? In *Psychotherapy research: Selected readings*, G. E. Stollak, B. G. Guerney, and M. Rothberg (eds.). Chicago: Rand McNally, 1966.

B. Problems in the measurement of outcome

1. Rogers, C. R., and Dymond, R. F. *Psychotherapy and personality change.* Chicago: University of Chicago Press, 1954. (See Chapters 1 and 17.)

2. Cartwright, D. S., and Roth, I. Success and satisfaction in psychotherapy, *J. Clin. Psychol.* 13 (1957): 20–26.

3. Rice, L. N. Therapist's style of participation and case outcome. *J. Consult. Psychol.* 29 (1965): 155–60.

4. Gaylin, N. L. Psychotherapy and psychological health: A Rorschach function and structure analysis. *J. Consult. Psychol.* 30 (1966): 494–500.

IV. Determinants of therapeutic effectiveness: Client and therapist factors

A. Client factors

1. Gallagher, E. B., Sharaf, M. R., and Levinson, D. J. The influence of patient and therapist in determining use of psychotherapy in a hospital setting. *Psychiat.* 28 (1965): 297–310.

2. Overall, B., and Aronson, H. Expectations of psychotherapy in patients of lower socioeconomic class. *Am. J. Orthopsychiat.* 33 (1963): 421–30.

3. Riess, F., and Brandt, L. W. What happens to applicants for psychotherapy? *Comm. Ment. Health J.* 17 (1965): 175–80.

4. Klopfer Rorschach prognostic rating scale.

5. Cartwright, R. D. Two conceptual schemes applied to four psychotherapy cases. Paper presented at the A.P.A. convention, 1963.

B. Therapist factors

1. Fiedler, F. E. A comparison of therapeutic relationships in psychoanalytic, non-directive and Adlerian therapy. *J. Consult. Psychol.* 14 (1950): 436–45.

2. Heine, R. W. A comparison of patients' reports on psychotherapeutic experience with psychoanalytic, non-directive and Adlerian therapists. *Amer. J. of Psychother.* 7 (1953): 16–23.

3. Cartwright, R. D., and Lerner, B. Empathy, need to change, and improvement with psychotherapy. *J. Consult. Psychol.* 27 (1963): 138–44.

4. Truax, C. B., and Carkhuff, R. R. For better or for worse: The process of psychotherapeutic personality change. In *Recent advances in behavioral change.* Montreal: McGill University Press, 1964.

research forms

Therapist's Self-Description Form

Date_____

1. Therapist's name _____
   Age_____   Sex _____   Race_____
   Marital Status_____   # of children _____

2. Professional Affiliation

   a) social worker _____   e) highest degree _____
   b) psychologist _____   f) date earned _____
   c) psychiatrist _____   g) If working towards an advanced
   d) other   _____   degree, date expected_____

3. a) Basic therapeutic orientation or school. (Please pick *one* generally recognized label; be as specific as you can and do *not* write eclectic.)____
   _____

   b) How well do you feel the label you've just selected for yourself really describes your position?
      _____Quite well; I'm a fairly orthodox practitioner.
      _____Only moderately well; I use a modified version of that general approach.
      _____Rather poorly; I'm really pretty eclectic and find it hard to attach any single label to myself.

4. Changes in orientation and orthodoxy over time
   a) Would you have given the same answer to question 3a. above at all points in your career?
      Same _____   Different _____
   If you checked "different" please indicate below what other orientation(s) you subscribed to in the past and give a rough chronology, e.g., did the change(s) take place early or late in your career, recently, or long ago, etc.

Previous Orientation(s)_____

_____

_____

Chronology_____

_____

_____

b) Would you have given the same answer to question 3b. above at all points in your career?

Same_____   Different_____

If you checked different, please indicate below the nature, direction, and timing of the difference.

From_____ to_____

Chronology _____

_____

_____

5. Experience as an individual therapist (include *all* experience as a therapist).

a) Years as a therapist_____
b) Years at this institution_____
c) Years as a supervisor of individual therapy_____
d) Please estimate the total number of clients with whom you have attempted individual therapy_____
e) Estimate what percentage (of 5d. above) were lower class_____
f) Estimate what percentage (of 5d. above) were severely disturbed, e.g., psychotics, psychotic characters, borderline psychotics, character disorders, addictions, perversions._____
g) Estimate what percentage (of 5d. above) were either lower class *or* severely disturbed but not both_____
h) Estimate what percentage (of 5d. above) were both lower class *and* severely disturbed_____
i) Estimate what percentage (of 5d. above) were neither lower class *nor* severely disturbed, e.g., middle or upper class *and* moderately or mildly disturbed, e.g., neurotics, maladjustments, situational reactions in otherwise healthy personalities._____

6. Self evaluation and preferences

a) In terms of my skill as a therapist, I think I am generally:

_____Somewhat better with severely disturbed clients than with moderately or mildly disturbed ones.

_____Not quite as good with severely disturbed clients as with moderately or mildly disturbed ones.

_____ About the same with severely disturbed clients as with moderately or mildly disturbed ones.

b) In general, I like working with severely disturbed clients:

_____ Somewhat more than with moderately or mildly disturbed ones.

_____ Somewhat less than with moderately or mildly disturbed ones.

_____ About the same as with moderately or mildly disturbed ones.

c) In terms of my skill as a therapist I think I am generally:

_____ Somewhat better with lower class clients than with middle or upper class ones.

_____ Not quite as good with lower class clients as with middle or upper class ones.

_____ About the same with lower class clients as with middle or upper class ones.

d) In general, I like working with lower class clients:

_____ Somewhat more than with middle and upper class ones.

_____ Somewhat less than with middle and upper class ones.

_____ About the same as with middle and upper class ones.

7. Work experience, preferences and expectations:

a) Have conducted group therapy

Yes _____ No _____

b) Have conducted couples or family therapy

Yes _____ No _____

c) Will probably want to experiment with these and/or other modifications of the conventional two-person therapy situation in the future.

Yes _____ No _____

d) Have been involved in some form of community work.

Yes _____ No _____

e) Will probably want to involve myself in some aspects of community work in the future.

Yes _____ No _____

f) Regardless of other experience and interests, I feel that my main professional interest has been in individual therapy.

Yes _____ No _____

g) Regardless of other experience and interests, I feel that my main professional interest will continue to be in individual therapy.

Yes _____ No _____

h) If I were starting my career all over again, I would choose to be

_____ A member of the same profession.

_____ A member of some other profession (please specify).

8. Therapist's personal treatment history (experience as a client).

a) Current treatment:

None _____   date started _____

Individual_____   # of months to date_____
Group_____   # of sessions per week _____
Other (please specify)_____
Your therapist's profession _____
Your therapist's orientation_____
b) Previous treatment (if more than one prior course of treatment, start
   with most recent and end with first treatment experience).
   None_____   # of years ago_____
   Individual _____   # of months duration _____
   Group_____   # of sessions per week _____
   Other (please specify) _____
   Your therapist's profession _____
   Your therapist's orientation_____
   Your evaluation of this course of treatment:
      Maximally helpful to me_____
      Moderately helpful to me_____
      Minimally helpful to me_____
c) Previous treatment
   Individual_____   # of years ago_____
   Group_____   # of months duration _____
   Other_____   # of sessions per week _____
   Your therapist's profession _____
   Your therapist's orientation_____
   Your evaluation of this course of treatment:
      Maximally helpful to me _____
      Moderately helpful to me _____
      Minimally helpful to me_____
d) Previous treatment
   Individual _____   # of years ago_____
   Group_____   # of months duration _____
   Other_____   # of sessions per week _____
   Your therapist's profession _____
   Your therapist's orientation_____
   Your evaluation of this course of treatment:
      Maximally helpful to me_____
      Moderately helpful to me_____
      Minimally helpful to me_____
e) Previous treatment
   Individual_____   # of years ago _____
   Group_____   # of months duration _____
   Other_____   # of sessions per week_____
   Your therapist's profession _____
   Your therapist's orientation_____
   Your evaluation of this course of treatment:
      Maximally helpful to me_____
      Moderately helpful to me_____

Minimally helpful to me————————

f) Attitudes towards your total experience as a client.
   On the whole I feel that my own treatment has been:
   Maximally helpful to me————————
   Moderately helpful to me————————
   Minimally helpful to me————————

g) On the whole, my own treatment:
   Fulfilled my initial expectations ———————————————
   Caused me to modify my initial expectations ——————————
   Disappointed my initial expectations ———————————————

h) If I should decide to enter treatment at some future time, all other things being equal, I would prefer to have my therapist be:
   A member of my own profession————————————————
   A member of some other profession (please specify)————————
   The best qualified person regardless of profession ————————

9. Your position on therapeutic issues: Please indicate the extent to which you either agree or disagree with each of the following statements by placing one of the following marks next to each.

   +3 agree strongly   -3 disagree strongly
   +2 agree moderately   -2 disagree moderately
   +1 agree slightly   -1 disagree slightly

   ————a) Successful completion of personal treatment should be a mandatory requirement for all therapists

   ————b) Ideally, close supervision of individual therapy should be provided for all therapists on all or most of their cases at all stages of their career.

   ————c) There are some cases which should not be treated by nonmedical therapists without psychiatric supervision.

   ————d) Heads of treatment facilities for the mentally ill should generally be medically trained.

   ————e) If they had had a successful treatment experience, most political radicals of both the right and the left would change their views on society and its ills.

   ————f) Patients can profitably decide many things in inpatient settings with patient government systems but decisions about discharges and passes should be made only by the professional staff.

   ————g) Nonpsychotic adults convicted of offenses like prostitution and homosexuality need help whether they know it or not and therefore the courts should make outpatient treatment mandatory for them.

   ————h) Involvement of the poor in programs planned for their welfare is essential, but, because they are mainly oriented to immediate gratification, it is unrealistic to give them top level decision-making powers in planning such programs because long range goals would inevitably suffer.

_____i) Most people who are very concerned about possible threats to civil liberties involved in large scale community mental health programs are either naive or reactionary.

_____j) To co-ordinate service and facilitate effective mental health programs on a community-wide basis, any properly qualified professional should have access to any information about a client in the hands of any other properly qualified professional without either having to obtain the client's consent.

10. Comments: (Please use the space below to report on your reactions to this questionnaire as honestly and critically as you can and to add any additional information on your professional attitudes and background you consider important.)

Therapist's Description of Client Form

Date _____

1. Case identification:
   a) Client's name _____
   b) Therapist's name _____

2. Intake data:
   a) date of request for help _____
   b) date of first interview _____
   c) date of therapeutic contract _____
   d) number of sessions prior to therapeutic contract:
      1) with therapist _____ 2) with intake person(s) other than therapist _____
   e) referral source (please be as specific as you can) _____ _____

3. General description of client:
   a) sex _____   d) marital status _____
   b) age _____   e) # of children _____
   c) race _____   f) religion _____

4. Social class items:
   a) education _____
   b) occupation _____
   c) employed _____ unemployed _____
   d) major source of income _____
   e) amount of income _____
   f) Is client head of household? Yes _____ No _____
   g) If you checked "No" above, please answer the following:
   h) Relationship of head of household to client _____

   i) Head of household's education _____

   j) Head of household's occupation _____

   k) Is head of household employed? Yes _____ No _____

5. Severity of disturbance:
   a) very severe, e.g., psychotic, psychotic character, or borderline psychotic

     _____

   b) severe, e.g., character disorder or neurotic character, addiction, perversion_____

   c) moderate, e.g., neurotic, any type_____

   d) mild, e.g., maladjustment, situational reaction in an otherwise healthy person _____

6. Primary treatment goal: (Select only one)
   a) ego strengthening, improved contact with reality, more adequate defenses and emotional control_____

   b) deep level exploration, improved contact with self, greater emotional freedom and expressivity _____

7. Previous treatment:
   a) none _____
   b) outpatient:
      1) type(s) of therapy_____
      2) # of courses of therapy_____
      3) duration and dates of each course_____
   c) inpatient:
      1) type(s) of therapy_____
      2) # of hospitalizations_____
      3) duration and dates of each hospitalization _____

8. Concurrent treatment:
   a) none_____
   b) drug therapy_____
   c) group therapy_____
   d) family therapy_____

   e) activities _____
   f) day center_____
   g) other (please specify) _____
      _____

9. Personality characteristics and attributes: please indicate below whether you feel your client is high, medium or low on each of the following items:
   a) preoccupation with somatic complaints _____
   b) tendency to externalize blame   _____
   c) guardedness, suspicion   _____
   d) tendency to act out   _____
   e) introspectiveness   _____
   f) general ego strength   _____
   g) sophistication with regard to therapeutic process_____
   h) verbal fluency and articulateness   _____
   i) experienced anxiety   _____

j) genuine motivation for change _____

k) estimated intelligence _____

10. Therapist's estimate of prognosis:

_____a) Very good; I feel pretty certain that I can help this client.

_____b) Good; I feel that I can probably help this client.

_____c) Fair; I feel that the odds are 50/50.

_____d) Guarded; there's an outside chance but I feel the odds are against it.

_____e) Very guarded; I feel that this client will probably drop out or otherwise frustrate my attempt to help him but I plan to try anyway.

11. Please estimate your subjective, gut-level reaction to this client in terms of the following:

a) Degree of liking he invokes in you. High____ Medium____ Low____

b) Degree of interest he arouses in you. High____ Medium____ Low____

c) Degree of emotional transparency he has for you, e.g., degree to which you feel you can accurately sense what he is feeling.
High____ Medium____ Low____

12. Comments: (About your client, this questionnaire, or life in general.)

Client's Treatment Goal Form

Date_____

Client_____

Therapist_____

Please read both statements below and place a check next to the one which best describes the main thing you hope to get out of treatment.

1) I hope to understand myself better and to be more in touch with my own feelings. _____

2) I hope to get rid of unpleasant symptoms and to be more in control of myself. _____

Was it hard to decide which statement to check? Yes_____ No_____

If you answered yes, please indicate why by checking one of the following:

I really want both of those things _____

I don't really want either of those things _____

I'm not sure what I want _____

I know what I want but I don't know what those two statements mean

_____

How long do you think treatment will take?_____

Therapy Attendance Record

Termination:

Therapist's name _____ Mutual decision_____
Client's name_____ Client's decision_____
Date of 1st session_____ Therapist's decision_____
Number of sessions per week_____ External factors_____
Date of last session_____ (e.g., death, hospitalization, move to
another city, etc.)

Appointments Scheduled

Instructions: Place a check in the "kept" column if session was held as scheduled. If session was not held as scheduled, place either a T or a C in either the "cancelled" or "failed" column, depending on whether the therapist or the client cancelled or failed. (Cancelled means that one party notified the other in advance that he would not be able to attend the session as scheduled. Failed means that one party simply failed to show up for a scheduled appointment, without giving the other party prior notification).

#	Date	Kept	Cancelled	Failed	#	Date	Kept	Cancelled	Failed	#	Date	Kept	Cancelled	Failed
1					31					61				
2					32					62				
3					33					63				
4					34					64				
5					35					65				
6					36					66				
7					37					67				
8					38					68				
9					39					69				
10					40					70				
11					41					71				
12					42					72				
13					43					73				
14					44					74				
15					45					75				
16					46					76				
17					47					77				
18					48					78				
19					49					79				
20					50					80				
21					51					81				
22					52					82				
23					53					83				
24					54					84				
25					55					85				
26					56					86				
27					57					87				
28					58					88				
29					59					89				
30					60					90				

Therapist's Outcome Rating Form

Date_____
Client_____
Therapist _____

Section I: In making these ratings of the outcome of your case, please do *not* try to compare your client with other clients or with some abstract norm representing optimal mental health. Instead, compare him as he is now with the way he was at the beginning of therapy. In other words, it is amount of change, not absolute degree of health which we are trying to assess.

A. Global Rating. In general, this client has shown:
  1) a great deal of positive change _____
  2) a fair amount of positive change_____
  3) a small amount of positive change_____
  4) positive change in some areas, negative in others_____
  5) no significant change_____
  6) a deterioration_____

B. Specific Rating 1. In terms of ego strength, contact with reality, adequacy of defense and emotional control, this client has shown:
  1) a great deal of positive change_____
  2) a fair amount of positive change_____
  3) a small amount of positive change _____
  4) positive change in some areas, negative in others_____
  5) no significant change _____
  6) a deterioration_____

C. Specific Rating 2. In terms of deep level exploration, contact with self, emotional freedom, and expressivity, this client has shown:
  1) a great deal of positive change_____
  2) a fair amount of positive change_____
  3) a small amount of positive change_____
  4) positive change in some areas, negative in others_____
  5) no significant change_____
  6) a deterioration_____

Section II: As you know, clients and therapists do not always agree in their evaluation of outcome: therapists sometimes feel that positive changes have taken place even though the client does not and, conversely, therapists sometimes feel that little or no change has taken place even though the client is enthusiastic. Accordingly, we have reprinted the six-degree outcome scale in slightly altered form below. This time, please rate the case as you think the client would rate it were he asked to fill out this form.

    Compared to the way I felt when I first came here I now feel:

      1) very much better_____
      2) pretty much better_____
      3) a little better_____
      4) better in some ways, worse in others_____
      5) about the same_____
      6) worse than before_____

III. At the start of treatment, you were asked to select one of two goals for this client, either the one implied in item IB or IC in the preceding part. Did whichever one you chose remain your major goal for this client throughout treatment or did your goal change as therapy progressed? (If you can't remember which goal you originally chose for this client, please indicate that below also.)

IV. On the preceding page, you were asked to describe the outcome of your case, first in the researcher's terms and then in the client's terms. In this section, please describe the outcome of this case in your own terms. (If you want more space, use the back of the page as well as the space below.)

V. Finally, please comment on the research procedure in relation to this case: Did it have any effects on treatment and, if it did, were they positive effects, negative effects, or some of each?

Client's Outcome Rating Form

Date_____
Client_____
Therapist_____

We are trying to learn more about helping people so that we can do as good a job as possible. You can help us by giving your opinion of the results of your therapy. Please read all six of the statements listed below and check the one that best describes the way you feel now as compared to the way you felt when you first came here. Neither your therapist nor any other person who knows you will be allowed to see your answers. Please be absolutely frank and give your honest opinion.

I feel:

      1) very much better_____
      2) pretty much better_____

3) a little better _____
4) better in some ways, worse in others _____
5) about the same _____
6) worse than before _____

RPFS Score Sheet

Client's Name _____ Scorers Initials _____
Date of Client's Rorschach _____ Scoring Date _____

STRUCTURE SCORE

COMPONENTS	FINDINGS	POINTS
P		
Bizarreness		
F+%		
B+%		
Pure C, Y, T, & V		
Disturbed M		
Affective ratio & approach type		
Preoccupation & primary space		
	TOTAL STRUCTURE SCORE _____	

FUNCTION SCORE

COMPONENTS	FINDINGS	POINTS
M		
C, CF, & FC		
B%		
R		
Content Categories		

Z - Simple W

TOTAL FUNCTION SCORE_____

TOTAL COMBINED SCORE
(STRUCTURE PLUS FUNCTION)_____

APPENDIX **C**[1]

client factors in relation to client and therapist outcome ratings

In this study, it was predicted that clients who received high prognostic ratings on any one of eleven factors commonly assumed to be related to therapeutic outcome would not show any greater gains on the RPFS than clients who received low prognostic ratings on those same eleven factors. Results, reported in chapter 9, were as predicted with the single, partial exception of Rice Voice Quality: Clients who received high prognostic ratings on this measure tended to achieve more favorable outcomes as measured by corrected RPFS gain scores but not by raw RPFS gain scores.

Table 28 indicates that results would not have been dramatically different even if more traditional measures of outcome had been used. Six client factors are unrelated to improvement as measured by both clients' outcome ratings and therapists' outcome ratings. They are social class, authoritarianism, Rice Voice Quality, age, race, and productivity. Four additional client factors are either unrelated to improvement or related in a manner opposite to conventional expectations. According to clients' outcome ratings, Klopfer Prognosis, concurrent treatment, and prior therapy are unrelated to improvement, and severity of impairment is inversely related (low prognostic clients do better than high prognostic ones). According to therapists' outcome ratings, three of these factors are inversely related to improvement and one is unrelated: low prognostic clients on the Klopfer Scale tend to do better than high ones, clients receiving therapy alone tend to do better than those receiving concurrent treatment (drug or activities therapy), clients who have had previous therapy do better than those in therapy for the first time, and

Table 28
Client Factors in Relation to Client and
Therapist Outcome Ratings

Client Factors	Client Outcome Ratings		Therapist Outcome Ratings	
	Phi	P	Phi	P
1 Social Class	.027	n.s.	.059	n.s.
2 Severity of Disturbance	.302	.05*	.089	n.s.
3 Klopfer Prognosis	.067	n.s.	.218	.10*
4 Authoritarianism	.202	n.s.	.073	n.s.
5 Rice Voice Quality	.053	n.s.	.171	n.s.
6 Age	.015	n.s.	.048	n.s.
7 Race	.086	n.s.	.015	n.s.
8 Productivity	.067	n.s.	.073	n.s.
9 Concurrent Treatment	.095	n.s.	.309	.05*
10 Prior Outpatient Therapy	.202	n.s.	.218	.10*
11 Prior Hospitalization	.308	.05*	.365	.025

*Significant in the opposite direction: Low prognostic clients tended to do better than high prognostic clients.

more severely disturbed clients do no better and no worse than less severely disturbed ones.

The eleventh and final client factor, prior hospitalization, is an especially interesting one because it relates to client and therapist outcome ratings in two opposite ways. Clients who had been hospitalized were more likely to be highly pleased with the results of their therapy than other clients. However, therapists were less likely to be highly pleased with the success of their efforts with those clients. Taking into account the fact that previously hospitalized clients did no better and no worse than other clients in terms of RPFS outcome ratings, the most reasonable interpretation here might be that ex-inmates were made a bit over-optimistic by the fact that someone had been willing to treat them without shipping them off to an institution, whereas therapists of ex-inmates were a bit over-pressimistic about what they had accomplished with people who had a history of institutionalization. All in all, the conclusion that nonclassical clients in this study were helped by psychotherapy would appear to be a valid one, regardless of the outcome measure used.

$\mathbf{C}^2$

therapist factors in relation to client and therapist outcome ratings

With regard to the five therapist factors hypothesized to be positively related to improvement, results detailed in chapter 9 indicate that only one, democratic values, is associated with RPFS outcome in a positive way. Table 29 below indicates that democratic values are still positively related to outcome as measured by therapists' ratings but are unrelated to outcome as measured by clients' ratings. Thus, the significance of this factor would have received at least partial support even if more traditional measures of outcome had been used.

A second hypothesized positive factor, one which failed to relate to RPFS outcome, also failed to relate to outcome as measured by clients' ratings but did tend to relate to outcome as measured by therapists' ratings. The factor in question is experience; therapists high on it showed a tendency to rate their own cases as more improved. However, since the tendency is slight and since neither RPFS outcome ratings nor client outcome ratings support it, this may just mean that more experienced therapists tend to be more confident about their work than less experienced ones. The remaining three hypothesized positive factors which failed to relate to RPFS outcome also failed to relate to client and therapist outcome ratings, and one, Truax Concurrent Empathy at pre-therapy, showed a slight tendency to be inversely related to outcome as measured by therapists' outcome ratings.

Our heretofore unsupported faith in the importance of empathy does, however, receive some unexpected encouragement from the fact that therapists' initial self-rated sense of understanding for their clients did relate to outcome, not as measured by their own ratings (a possible halo effect, had it

Table 29
Therapist Factors in Relation to Client and
Therapist Outcome Ratings

Therapist Factors	Client Outcome Ratings		Therapist Outcome Ratings	
	Phi	P	Phi	P
1 Experience	.067	n.s.	.218	.10
2 Democratic Values	.107	n.s.	.347	.05
3a Concurrent Empathy	.220	n.s.	.275	.10*
3b Concurrent Empathy	.236	n.s.	.181	n.s.
4a Predictive Empathy	.100	n.s.	.051	n.s.
4b Predictive Empathy	.115	n.s.	.155	n.s.
5 Expectations	.081	n.s.	.099	n.s.
6 Whitehorn–Betz Type	.067	n.s.	.029	n.s.
7 Personal Treatment	.071	n.s.	.066	n.s.
8 Initial Liking	.009	n.s.	.029	n.s.
9 Initial Interest	.375	.025*	.230	.10*
10 Initial Understanding	.333	.05	.154	n.s.

a = Empathy at pre-therapy
b = Empathy at post-therapy
*Significant in the opposite direction: Low prognostic therapists tended to do better than high prognostic therapists.

occurred) or by RPFS ratings, but by client ratings. Ironically, this extremely simple, subjective measure of empathy was the only one of the three measures of empathy used in this study which was not hypothesized to be positively related to outcome. I stand corrected and will treat it with more respect in the future.

All other therapist factors predicted to be unrelated to outcome were unrelated except for one which was inversely related, according to clients' ratings and tended to be inversely related according to therapists' ratings as well. This factor is therapists' initial, self-rated interest in their clients, a simple, subjective measure that is too puzzling in its implications to be readily interpretable at this point.

references

Adams, H. B., Cooper, G. D., and Carrera, R. N. The Rorschach and the MMPI: A concurrent validity study. *Journal of Projective Techniques* 27(1963): 23-34.

Adorno, T. W., Frenkel-Brunswik, E., Levinson, D. J., and Sanford, N. *The authoritarian personality*. New York: Harper and Row, 1950.

Albee, G. W. *Mental health manpower trends*. Monograph series, no. 3, Joint Commission on Mental Illness and Health. New York: Basic Books, 1959.

Albee, G. W. No magic here. *Contemporary Psychology* 10 (1965): 497-98.

Albee, G. W. The Psychological Center must precede the development of a language for professional psychology. Paper presented at the 74th Annual Convention of the American Psychological Association, New York, 1966.

Albee, G. W. The relation of conceptual models of disturbed behavior to institutions and manpower requirements. In *Manpower for mental health*, F. N. Arnhoff, E. A. Rubinstein, and J. C. Speisman (eds.). Chicago: Aldine, 1969.

Alexander, F. Psychoanalysis and psychotherapy. In *The scope of psychoanalysis*, F. Alexander, (ed.). New York: Basic Books, 1961.

Alexander, F. The dynamics of psychotherapy in the light of learning theory. *American Journal of Psychiatry* 120 (1963): 440-48.

Allport, G. W. Foreward. In *An experiment in the prevention of delinquency: The Cambridge-Somerville Youth Study*, E. Powers and H. Witmer (eds.). New York: Columbia University Press, 1951.

Allport, G. W. *Becoming: Basic considerations for a psychology of personality*. New Haven: Yale University Press, 1955.

Allport, G. W. *Pattern and growth in personality*. New York: Holt, Rinehart and Winston, 1961.

Amble, B. R., and Moore, R. The influence of a set on the evaluation of psychotherapy. *American Journal of Orthopsychiatry* 36 (1966): 50-56.

Arnhoff, F. N., Rubinstein, E. A., and Speisman, J. C. *Manpower for mental health*. Chicago: Aldine, 1969.

Asch, S. E. Effects of group pressure on the modification and distortion of judgments. In *Readings in social psychology*. G. E. Swanson, T. M. Newcomb, and E. L. Hartley (eds.). 2d ed. New York: Henry Holt, 1952.

Astin, A. W. The functional autonomy of psychotherapy. *American Psychologist* 16 (1961): 75–78.

Auble, D. Extended tables for the Mann-Whitney statistic. *Bulletin of the Institute of Educational Research at Indiana University* 1, no. 2, 1953.

Auld, F., and Myers, J. K. Contributions to a theory for selecting psychotherapy patients. *Journal of Clinical Psychology* 10 (1954): 56–60.

Avnet, H. H. How effective is short-term therapy? In *Short-term psychotherapy*, L. R. Wolberg (ed.). New York: Grune and Stratton, 1965.

Bachrach, A. J. *Psychological research: An introduction*. New York: Random House, 1962.

Baez, V. W. Influence of biased psychological reports on teacher behavior and pupil performance. In *Proceedings of the 76th Annual Convention of the American Psychological Association*, 1968.

Bailey, M. A., Warshaw, L., and Eichler, R. M. A study of factors related to length of stay in psychotherapy. *Journal of Clinical Psychology* 15 (1959): 442–44.

Barnard, C. I. *The function of the executive*. Cambridge, Mass.: Harvard University Press, 1938.

Barret-Lennard, G. T. Dimensions of therapist response as causal factors in therapeutic change. *Psychological Monographs* 76 (1962): 1–36.

Barron, F. Some test correlates of response to psychotherapy. In *Basic readings on the MMPI in psychology and medicine*, G. S. Welsh and W. G. Dahlstrom (eds.). Minneapolis: University of Minnesota Press, 1956.

Barron, F., and Leary, T. F. Changes in psychoneurotic patients with and without psychotherapy. *Journal of Consulting Psychology* 19 (1955): 239–45.

Beck, S. J., Beck, A. G., Levitt, E. E., and Molish, H. B. *Rorschach's Test I. Basic processes*. 3d ed. New York: Grune and Stratton, 1961.

Bendix, R., and Fisher, L. H. The perspectives of Elton Mayo. In *Complex organizations.*, A. Etzioni (ed.). New York: Holt, Rinehart and Winston, 1961.

Berg. I. A., and Adams, H. E. The experimental bases of personality assessment. In *Experimental Foundations of clinical psychology*, A. J. Bachrach (ed.). New York: Basic Books, 1962.

Bergin, A. E. The effects of psychotherapy: Negative results revisited. *Journal of Counseling Psychology* 10 (1963): 244–50.

Betz, B. J. Experiences in research in psychotherapy with schizophrenic patients. In *Research in psychotherapy* H. H. Strupp and L. Luborsky (eds.). Vol. 2. Washington, D.C.: American Psychological Association, 1962.

Betz, B. J. Bases of therapeutic leadership in psychotherapy with the schizophrenic patient. *American Journal of Psychotherapy* 17 (1963): 196–212.

Betz, B. J. Differential success rates of psychotherapists with "process" and "nonprocess" schizophrenic patients. *American Journal of Psychiatry* 19 (1963): 1090–91.

Binswanger, L. *Being-in-the-world: Selected papers of Ludwig Binswanger*, Jacob Neddleman (trans. and ed.). New York: Basic Books, 1963.

Blau, P. M. *The dynamics of bureaucracy*. Chicago: University of Chicago Press, 1963.

Bloom, B. L. Prognostic significance of the underproductive Rorschach. *Journal of Projective Techniques* 20 (1956): 366–71.

Bordin, E. S. Curiosity, compassion and doubt: The dilemma of the psychologist. *American Psychologist* 21 (1966): 116–21.

Boring, E. G. The psychology of communicating science. In *History, psychology and science*, R. I. Watson and D. T. Campbell (eds.). New York: Wiley, 1963.

Boss, M. *Psychoanalysis and daseinsanalysis.* New York: Basic Books, 1963.

Brager, G. New concepts and patterns of service: The Mobilization for Youth Program. In *Mental health of the poor*, F. Riessman, J. Cohen, and A. Pearl (eds.). Glencoe, Ill.: Free Press, 1964.

Brager, G., and Purcell, F. P. (eds.). *Community action against poverty.* New Haven: College and University Press, 1967.

Brandt, L. W. Rejection of psychotherapy. *Archives of General Psychiatry* 10 (1964): 310–13.

Brazier, A. M. *Black self-determination: The story of the Woodlawn Organization.* Grand Rapids, Michigan: Eerdmans, 1969.

Burnham, R. J., and Hartsough, D. M. Effects of experimenter's expectancies (the "Rosenthal effect") on children's ability to learn to swim. Paper presented at the meeting of the Midwestern Psychological Association, Chicago, May, 1968.

Butler, J., and Fiske, D. W. Theory and techniques of assessment. *Annual Review of Psychology* 6 (1955): 327–56.

Cappon, D. Results of psychotherapy. *British Journal of Psychiatry* 110 (1964): 35–45.

Carkhuff, R. R. Training in counseling and therapeutic practices: Requiem or reveille? *Journal of Counseling Psychology* 13 (1966): 360–67.

Carkhuff, R. R., and Truax, C. B. Training in counseling and psychotherapy: An evaluation of an integrated didactic and experiential approach. *Journal of Consulting Psychology* 29 (1965): 333–36.

Carson, R. C. *Interaction concepts of personality.* Chicago: Aldine, 1969.

Cartwright, D. S. Effectiveness of psychotherapy: A critique of the spontaneous remission argument. *Journal of Counseling Psychology* 2 (1955): 290–96.

Cartwright, D. S., Kirtner, W. L., and Fiske, D. W. Method factors in changes associated with psychotherapy. *Journal of Abnormal and Social Psychology* 66 (1963): 164–75.

Cartwright, D. S., and Roth, I. Success and satisfaction in psychotherapy. *Journal of Clinical Psychology* 13 (1957): 20–26.

Cartwright, R. D. Predicting response to client-centered therapy with the Rorschach PR Scale. *Journal of Counseling Psychology* 5 (1958): 11–15.

Cartwright, R. D. Two conceptual schemes applied to four psychotherapy cases. Paper presented at the American Psychological Association Convention, 1963.

Cartwright, R. D. Psychotherapeutic processes. *Annual Review of Psychotherapy* 19 (1968): 387–416.

Cartwright, R. D., and Lerner, B. Empathy, need to change and improvement with psychotherapy. *Journal of Consulting Psychology* 27 (1963): 138–44.

Cartwright, R. D., and Vogel, J. D. A comparison of changes in psychoneurotic patients during matched periods of therapy and no therapy. *Journal of Consulting Psychology*, 24 (1960): 121–27.

Caudill, W. *The psychiatric hospital as a small society.* Cambridge, Mass.: Harvard University Press, 1958.

Chein, I. Some sources of divisiveness among psychologists. *American Psychologist* 21 (1966): 333–42.

Chomsky, N. *American power and the new mandarins.* New York: Pantheon Books, 1969.

Clark, K. E., and Clark, M. P. Racial identification and preference in Negro children. In *Readings in social psychology.* G. E. Swanson, T. M. Newcomb, and E. L. Hartley (eds.). 2d ed. New York: Henry Holt, 1952.

Cloward, R., and Ohlin, L. *Delinquency and opportunity: A theory of delinquent gangs.* Glencoe, Ill.: Free Press, 1960.

Colby, K. *A primer for psychotherapists.* New York: Ronald Press, 1951.

Colby, K., Watt, J. B., and Gilbert, J. P. Therapeutic person-computer conversation. In *Psychotherapy research: Selected readings,* G. E. Stollak, B. G. Guerney, and M. Rothberg (eds.). Chicago: Rand McNally, 1966.

Cronbach, L. J. Processes affecting scores on "understanding others" and "assumed similiarity." *Psychological Bulletin* 52 (1955): 177–93.

Cumming, J., and Cumming, E. *Ego and milieu.* New York: Atherton, 1962.

DeCharms, R., Levy, J., and Wertheimer, M. A note on attempted evaluations of psychotherapy. *Journal of Clinical Psychology* 10 (1954): 233–35.

Denker, P. G. Results of treatment of psychoneurosis by the general practitioner: A follow-up study of 200 cases. *New York State Journal of Medicine* 46 (1946): 2164–66.

Dohrenwend, B. P., and Dohrenwend, B. S. The problem of validity in field studies of psychological disorders. *Journal of Abnormal Psychology* 70 (1965): 52–69.

Drucker, P. *Concept of the corporation.* New York: John Day Co., 1946.

Endicott, N. A., and Endicott, J. "Improvement" in untreated psychiatric patients. *Archives of General Psychiatry* 9 (1963): 575–85.

Endicott, N. A., and Endicott, J. Prediction of improvement in treated and untreated patients using the Rorschach Prognostic Rating Scale. *Journal of Consulting Psychology* 28 (1964): 342–48.

Erikson, E. H. *Childhood and society.* New York: Norton, 1963.

Errera, P., McKee, B., Smith, D. C., and Gruber R. Length of psychotherapy: Studies done in a university community psychiatric clinic. *Archives of General Psychiatry* 17 (1967): 454–58.

Eysenck, H. J. The effects of psychotherapy: An evaluation. *Journal of Consulting Psychology* 16 (1952): 319–24.

Eysenck, H. J. The effects of psychotherapy. In *Handbook of abnormal psychology,* H. J. Eysenck (ed.). New York: Basic Books, 1960.

Eysenck, H. J. The outcome problem in psychotherapy: A reply. *Psychotherapy: Theory, Research and Practice* 3 (1964): 97–100.

Fairweather, G. W., and Simon, R. A. A further follow-up comparison of psychotherapeutic programs. *Journal of Consulting Psychology* 27 (1963): 186.

Fanon, F. *The wretched of the earth.* New York: Grove Press, 1966.

Faris, R. E. and Dunham, H. W. *Mental disorders in urban areas.* Chicago: University of Chicago Press, 1939.

Federn, E. The therapeutic personality as illustrated by Paul Federn and August Aichorn. *Psychiatric Quarterly* 36 (1962): 29–43.

Federn, P. *Ego psychology and the psychoses.* New York: Basic Books, 1952.

Feifel, H., and Eells, J. Patients and therapists assess the same psychotherapy. *Journal of Consulting Psychology* 27 (1963): 310–18.

Fiedler, F. E. A comparison of therapeutic relationships in psychoanalytic, non-directive and Adlerian therapy. *Journal of Consulting Psychology* 14 (1950): 436–45.

Fiedler, F. E. The concept of the ideal therapeutic relationship. *Journal of Consulting Psychology* 14 (1950): 239–45.

Fiske, D. W., and Baughman, E. E. Relationships between Rorschach scoring categories and total number of responses. *Journal of Abnormal and Social Psychology* 48 (1953): 25–32.

Fiske, D. W., Cartwright, D. S., and Kirtner, W. L. Are psychotherapeutic changes predictable? *Journal of Abnormal and Social Psychology* 69 (1964): 418–26.

Fiske, D. W., Hunt, H. F., Luborsky, L., Orne, M. T., Parloff, M. B., Reiser, M. F., and Tuma, A. H. Planning of research on effectiveness of psychotherapy. *Archives of General Psychiatry* 22 (1970): 22–32.

Fiske, D. W., and Maddi, S. R. *Functions of varied experience.* Homewood, Ill.: Dorsey Press, 1961.

Fonda, C. The white-space response. In *Rorschach psychology*, Maria A. Rickers-Ovsiankina (ed.). New York: Wiley, 1960.

Freud, S. The theory of the libido: Narcissism. In *A general introduction to psychoanalysis*, J. Riviere (trans.). New York: Permabooks, 1935.

Freud, S. On narcissism: An introduction (1914). In *Collected papers*, E. Jones (ed.). Vol. 4. New York: Basic Books, 1959a.

Freud, S. Psychoanalysis (1922). In *Collected papers*, E. Jones (ed.). Vol. 5. New York: Basic Books, 1959b.

Freud, S. Analysis terminable and interminable. In *Therapy and technique*, P. Rieff (ed.). New York: Collier Books, 1963.

Freud, S. Turnings in the ways of psychoanalytic therapy (1919). In *Therapy and technique*, P. Rieff (ed.). New York: Collier Books, 1963.

Friess, C., and Nelson, M. J. Psychoneurotics five years later. *American Journal of Mental Science* 203 (1942): 539–58.

Fromm-Reichman, F. *Principles of intensive psychotherapy.* Chicago: University of Chicago Press, 1950.

Gallagher, E. B., Sharaf, M. R., and Levinson, D. J. The influence of patient and therapist in determining use of psychotherapy in a hospital setting. *Psychiatry* 28 (1965): 297–310.

Garfield, S. L., and Affleck, D. C. Therapists' judgments concerning patients considered for psychotherapy. *Journal of Consulting Psychology* 25 (1961): 505–9.

Gaylin, N. L. Psychotherapy and psychological health: A Rorschach function and structure analysis. *Journal of Consulting Psychology* 30 (1966): 494–500.

Gendlin, E. *Experiencing and the creation of meaning.* Glencoe, Ill.: Free Press, 1962.

Glover, E. Research methods in psychoanalysis. *International Journal of Psychoanalysis* 33 (1952): 403–9.

Goffman, E. *Asylums.* New York: Doubleday, 1961.

Goldman, R. K., and Mendelsohn, G. A. Psychotherapeutic change and social adjustment: A report of a national survey of psychotherapists. *Journal of Abnormal Psychology* 74 (1969): 164–72.

Goldstein, A. P. Patient's expectancies and nonspecific therapy as a basis for (un)spontaneous remission. *Journal of Clinical Psychology* 16 (1960): 399–403.

Goldstein, A. P. *Therapist-patient expectancies in psychotherapy.* New York: Pergamon Press, 1962.

Gouldner, A. E. Red tape as a social problem. In *Reader in bureaucracy,* R. K. Merton, A. P. Gray, B. Hockey, and H. C. Selvin (eds.). Glencoe, Ill.: Free Press, 1952.

Gouldner, A. E. Metaphysical pathos and the theory of bureaucracy. In *Complex organizations,* A. Etzioni (ed.). New York: Holt, Rinehart and Winston, 1961.

Graziano, A. Clinical innovation and the mental health power structure. *American Psychologist* 24 (1969): 10–18.

Greenson, R. Empathy and its vicissitudes. *International Journal of Psychoanalysis* 41 (1960): 418–24.

Grey, A. Social class and the psychiatric patient: A study in composite character. *Contemporary Psychoanalysis* 2 (1966): 87–121.

Harper, R. A. *Psychoanalysis and psychotherapy: 36 systems.* Englewood Cliffs, N.J.: Prentice-Hall, 1959.

Harrington, M. *The other America: Poverty in the United States.* New York: Macmillan, 1963.

Hartmann, H. Ego psychology and the problem of adaptation. In *Organization and pathology of thought,* D. Rapaport (ed.). New York: Columbia University Press, 1951.

Heilbrunn, G. Results with psychoanalytic therapy. *American Journal of Psychotherapy* (1963): 427–35.

Heine, R. W. An investigation into the relationship between changes and the responsible factors as seen by clients following treatment by psychotherapists of the psychoanalytic, Adlerian and non-directive schools. Unpublished doctoral dissertation, University of Chicago, 1950.

Heine, R. W. A comparison of patients' reports on psychotherapeutic experience with psychoanalytic, non-directive and Adlerian therapists. *American Journal of Psychotherapy* 7 (1953): 16–23.

Henry, W. E., Sims, J. H., and Spray, S. L. *The fifth profession.* San Francisco: Jossey-Bass, 1971.

Hollingshead, A. B., and Redlich, F. C. *Social class and mental illness.* New York: Wiley, 1958.

Holzberg, J. D., Knapp, R. H., and Turner, J. L. Companionship with the mentally ill: Effects on the personalities of college students. *Psychiatry* 29 (1966): 398–405.

Hunt, J. M., Ewing, T. N., LaForge, R., and Gilbert, W. M. An integrated approach to research on therapeutic counseling with samples of results. *Journal of Counseling Psychology* 6 (1959): 46–54.

Hunt, R. G. Social class and mental illness: Some implications for clinical theory and practice. *American Journal of Psychiatry* 116 (1960): 1065–69.

Imber, S. D., Frank, J. D., Nash, E. H., Stone, A. R., and Gliedman, L. H. Improvement and amount of therapeutic contact: An alternative to the use of no-treatment controls in psychotherapy. *Journal of Consulting Psychology* 21 (1957): 309–15.

Imber, S. D., Nash, E. H., and Stone, A. R. Social class and duration of psychotherapy. *Journal of Clinical Psychology* 11 (1955): 281–84.

Jensen, A. R. The Rorschach technique: A re-evaluation. *Acta Psychologica* 22 (1964): 60–77.

Jensen, A. R. How much can we boost I.Q. and scholastic achievement? *Harvard Educational Review* 39 (1969): 1–23.

Johnson, E. Klopfer's prognostic rating scale used with Raven's progressive matrices in play therapy prognosis. *Journal of Projective Techniques* 17 (1953): 320–26.

Jones, M. *The therapeutic community*. New York: Basic Books, 1953.

Katz, M. M., Lorr, M., and Rubinstein, E. A. Remainer patient attributes and their relation to subsequent improvement in psychotherapy. *Journal of Consulting Psychology* 22 (1958): 411–13.

Kellam, S. G., and Branch, J. D. An analysis of basic problems and an approach to community mental health. In preparation, 1970.

Kellam, S. G., Branch, J. D., Agrawal, K. C., and Grabill, M. E. Strategies in urban community mental health. In preparation, 1970.

Kellam, S. G., and Schiff, S. K. The Woodlawn Mental Health Center: A community mental health center model. *The Social Service Review* 40 (1966): 255–63.

Kellam, S. G., and Schiff, S. K. Adaptation and mental illness in the first-grade classroom of an urban community. *Psychiatry Research Report No. 28*, American Psychiatric Association, 1967.

Kellam, S. G., and Schiff, S. K. An urban community mental health center. In *Mental health and urban social policy*, L. J. Duhl and R. L. Leopold (eds.). San Francisco: Jossey-Bass, 1968.

Kellam, S. G., Schiff, S. K., and Branch, J. D. The Woodlawn community-wide school mental health program of assessment, prevention and early treatment. In *Reports from the Rockton Conference*, Midwest Annual Regional Conference, School Social Work, 1968.

Kelley, E. L. Theory and techniques of assessment. *Annual Review of Psychology* 5 (1954): 281–310.

Kemp, D. E. Correlates of Whitehorn-Betz AB Scale in a quasi-therapeutic situation. *Journal of Consulting Psychology* 30 (1966): 508–16.

Kiesler, D. J. Some myths of psychotherapy research and the search for a paradigm. *Psychological Bulletin* 65 (1966): 110–36.

Klopfer, B., Ainsworth, M., Klopfer, W., and Holt, R. *Developments in the Rorschach technique*. Vol. 1. New York: World Book Co., 1954.

Knapp, P. H., Levin, S., McCarter, E. H., Wermer, H., and Zetzel, E. Suitability for psychoanalysis: A review of one hundred supervised analytic cases. *Psychoanalytic Quarterly* 29 (1960): 459–77.

Kogan, L. S., Hunt, J. M., and Barteline, P. *A follow-up study on the results of social casework*. New York: Family Association of America, 1953.

Kohut, H. Introspection, empathy and psychoanalysis. *Journal of the American Psychoanalytic Association* 7 (1959): 459–87

Laing, R. D. *The politics of experience*. New York: Ballantine Books, 1968.

Landis, C. Statistical evaluation of psychotherapeutic methods. In *Concepts and problems of psychotherapy*, L. E. Hinsie (ed.). New York: Columbia University Press, 1937.

Langer, S. *Philosophy in a new key*. New York: Mentor Books, 1948.

Leighton, A. H. *My name is legion: Foundations for a theory of man in relation to culture*. New York: Basic Books, 1959.

Lerner, B. Rorschach movement and dreams: A validation study using drug-induced dream deprivation. *Journal of Abnormal Psychology* 71 (1966): 75–86.

Lerner, B. Dream function reconsidered. *Journal of Abnormal Psychology* 72 (1967): 85–100.

Lerner, B. A new method of assessing perceptual accuracy on the Rorschach. *Journal of Projective Techniques* 32 (1968): 533–36.

Levinson, B. M. The dog as co-therapist. Paper presented at American Psychological Association Convention, 1961.

Lindsay, J. S. The length of treatment. *British Journal of Social and Clinical Psychology* 4 (1965): 117–23.

Lohrenz, J. G., Hunter, R. C., and Schwartzman, A. E. Factors relevant to positive psychotherapeutic responses in university students. *Canadian Psychiatric Association Journal* 11 (1966): 38–42.

Lorr, M., Katz, M. M., and Rubinstein, E. A. The prediction of length of stay in psychotherapy. *Journal of Consulting Psychology* 22 (1958): 321–27.

Lorr, M., and McNair, D. M. Correlates of length of therapy. *Journal of Clinical Psychology*, 20 (1964): 497–504.

Lorr, M., McNair, D. M., Michaux, W. M., and Riskin, A. Frequency of treatment and change in psychotherapy. *Journal of Abnormal and Social Psychology* 64 (1962): 281–92.

Luborsky, L. A note on Eysenck's article, "The effects of psychotherapy:An evaluation." *British Journal of Psychology* 45 (1954): 129–31.

Luborsky, L. Psychotherapy. *Annual Review of Psychology* 10 (1959): 317–44.

Marris, P., and Rein, M. *Dilemmas of social reform: Poverty and community action in the United States*. New York: Atherton, 1967.

Maslow, A. *Motivation and personality*. New York: Harper, 1954.

Maslow, A. *Toward a psychology of being*. Princeton, N.J.: Van Nostrand, 1968.

Matarazzo, J. D. Psychotherapeutic processes. *Annual Review of Psychology* 6 (1956): 181–224.

May, P. R., and Tuma, A. H. Choice of criteria for the assessment of treatment outcome. *Journal of Psychiatric Research* 2 (1964): 199–209.

Mayo, E. *The human problems of an industrial civilization*. New York: Macmillan, 1933.

Mayo, E. *The social problems of an industrial civilization*. Boston: Harvard University Press, 1945.

Mayo, E. *The political problems of an industrial civilization*. Boston: Harvard University Press, 1947.

McNair, D. M., Callahan, D. M., and Lorr, M. Therapist "type" and patient response to psychotherapy. *Journal of Consulting Psychology* 26 (1962): 425–29.

McNair, D. M., and Lorr, M. Three kinds of psychotherapy goals. *Journal of Clinical Psychology* 20 (1964): 390–93.

McNair, D. M., Lorr, M., and Callahan, D. M. Patient and therapist influences on quitting psychotherapy. *Journal of Consulting Psychology* 27 (1963): 10–17.

Meehl, P. E. Psychotherapy. *Annual Review of Psychology* 6 (1955): 357-78.
Meehl, P. E. Cognitive activity of the clinician. *American Psychologist* 15 (1960): 19-27.
Merton, R. K. Bureaucratic structure and personality. *Social Forces* 17 (1940): 560-68.
Michael, S. T. Social class and psychiatric treatment. *Journal of Psychiatric Research* 5 (1967): 243-54.
Miles, H. H. W., Barrabe, E., and Finesinger, J. E. Evaluation of psychotherapy. *Psychosomatic Medicine* 13 (1951): 82-105.
Mindess, H. Predicting patients' responses to psychotherapy: A preliminary study designed to investigate the validity of the Rorschach prognostic rating scale. *Journal of Projective Techniques* 17 (1953): 327-34.
Molish, H. B. "Doubtless there are other paths." *Journal of Projective Techniques* 31 (1967): 3-6.
Molish, H. B. The quest for charisma. *Journal of Projective Techniques* 33 (1969): 103-17.
Moynihan, D. P. *Maximum feasible misunderstanding: Community action in the war on poverty.* New York: Free Press, 1969.
Muench, G. A. An investigation of the efficacy of time-limited psychotherapy. *Journal of Counseling Psychology* 12 (1965): 294-98.
Nichols, R. C., and Beck, K. W. Factors in psychotherapy change. *Journal of Consulting Psychology* 24 (1960): 388-99.
Orlinsky, N., Chairman. Psychotherapy and community mental health: Unplanned obsolescence? Symposium presented at the 74th American Psychological Association Convention, 1966.
Overall, B., and Aronson, H. Expectations of psychotherapy in patients of lower socioeconomic class. *American Journal of Orthopsychiatry* 33 (1963): 421-30.
Paul, G. L. Strategy of outcome research in psychotherapy. *Journal of Consulting Psychology* 31 (1967): 109-18.
Peter, L. J., and Hull, R. *The Peter principle.* New York: Morrow, 1969.
Phillips, L. Socioeconomic factors and mental health. *American Journal of Orthopsychiatry* 37 (1967): 410-11.
Raimy, V. C. (ed.). *Training in clinical psychology.* (Boulder Conference) Englewood Cliffs, N.J.: Prentice-Hall, 1950.
Raines, G. N. (Chairman). Discussion of paper presented by B. J. Betz. *Psychiatric Research Reports* 5 (1956): 106-17.
Rapaport, D. The structure of psychoanalytic theory: A systematizing attempt. *Psychological Issues* 2 (1960): 1-158.
Rice, L. N. Therapist's style of participation and case outcome. *Journal of Consulting Psychology* 29 (1965): 155-60.
Rice, L. N., and Wagstaff, A. K. Client voice quality and expressive style as indexes of productive psychotherapy. *Journal of Consulting Psychology* 31 (1967): 557-63.
Riess, B. F., and Brandt, L. W. What happens to applicants for psychotherapy? *Community Mental Health Journal* 1 (1965): 175-80.
Rioch, M. J. The fiddlers of X. *Psychotherapy: Theory, Research and Practice* 1 (1964): 88-90.
Rioch, M. J., Elkes, C., Flint, A. A., Usdansky, B. S., Newman, R. G., and Silber, E. National Institute of Mental Health pilot study in training

mental health counselors. *American Journal of Orthopsychiatry* 33 (1963): 678–89.

Rogers, C. R. An overview of the research and some questions for the future. In *Psychotherapy and personality change*, C. R. Rogers and R. F. Dymond (eds.). Chicago: University of Chicago Press, 1954.

Rogers, C. R. The necessary and sufficient conditions of therapeutic personality change. *Counseling Center Discussion Papers*, University of Chicago, 2, no. 8 (1956).

Rogers, C. R. The actualizing tendency in relation to "motives" and to consciousness. In *Nebraska Symposium on Motivation*, M. R. Jones (ed.). Lincoln, Nebraska: University of Nebraska Press, 1963.

Rogers, C. R. The concept of the fully functioning person. *Psychotherapy: Theory, Research and Practice* 1 (1963): 17–26.

Rogers, C. R. Psychotherapy today or where do we go from here? In *Psychotherapy research: Selected readings*, G. E., Stollak, B. G. Guerney, and M. Rothberg (eds.). Chicago: Rand McNally, 1966.

Rogers, C. R., and Dymond, R. F. *Psychotherapy and personality change*. Chicago: University of Chicago Press, 1954.

Rogers, C. R., Gendlin, E. T., Kiesler, D. J., and Truax, C. B. *The therapeutic relationship and its impact: A study of psychotherapy with schizophrenics*. Madison, Wis.: University of Wisconsin Press, 1967.

Rokeach, M. *The open and closed mind*. New York: Basic Books, 1960.

Roman, P. M., and Trice, H. M. *Schizophrenia and the poor*. Ithaca, N.Y.: Cornell University Press, 1967.

Rosenthal, D., and Frank, J. D. Psychotherapy and the placebo effect. *Psychological Bulletin* 53 (1956): 294–302.

Rosenthal, R. *Experimenter effects in behavioral research*. New York: Appleton-Century-Crofts, 1966.

Rosenthal, R., and Jacobson, L. *Pygmalion in the classroom: Teacher expectation and pupils' intellectual development*. New York: Holt, Rinehart and Winston, 1968.

Rosenzweig, S. A transvaluation of psychotherapy—A reply to Hans Eysenck. *Journal of Abnormal and Social Psychology* 49 (1954): 298–304.

Sanders, M. K. *The professional radical: Conversations with Saul Alinsky*. New York: Harper and Row, 1970.

Sanford, N. Clinical methods: Psychotherapy. *Annual Review of Psychology* 4 (1953).

Schafer, R. Generative empathy in the treatment situation. *Psychoanalytic Quarterly* 28 (1959): 342–73.

Schofield, W. *Psychotherapy: The purchase of friendship*. Englewood Cliffs, N.J.: Prentice-Hall, 1964.

Searles, H. *Collected papers on schizophrenia and related subjects*. New York: International Universities Press, 1965.

Sechahaye, M. A. *Symbolic realization*. New York: International Universities Press, 1951.

Sheehan, J., Frederick, C., Rosevear, W., and Spiegelman, M. A validity study of the Rorschach prognostic rating scale. *Journal of Projective Techniques* 18 (1954): 233–39.

Shlien, J. M. Time-limited psychotherapy: An experimental investigation of practical values and theoretical implications. *Journal of Counseling Psychology* 4 (1957): 318–22.

Shlien, J. M., Mosak, H. H., and Dreikurs, R. Effect of time limits: A comparison of two psychotherapies. *Journal of Counseling Psychology* 9 (1962): 31–34.

Silberman, C. E. *Crisis in black and white.* New York: Random House, 1964.

Singer, J. L., and Opler, M. K. Contrasting patterns of fantasy and motility in Irish and Italian schizophrenics. *Journal of Abnormal and Social Psychology* 53 (1956): 42–47.

Skinner, B. F. *Walden Two.* New York: Macmillan, 1948.

Smith, M. B. The revolution in mental health care—A "bold new approach?" *Trans-Action* 5 (1968): 19–23.

Snow, C. P. *The two cultures and a second look.* New York: Mentor Books, 1964.

Solomon, P., Kubzansky, P. E., Leiderman, H., Mendelson, J. H., Trumbull, R., and Wexler, D. *Sensory deprivation.* Cambridge, Mass.: Harvard University Press. 1961.

SPSSI. Council statement on race and intelligence. *Journal of Social Issues* 25 (1969): 1–3.

Stanton, A. H., and Schwartz, M. S. *The mental hospital.* New York: Basic Books, 1954.

Stieper, D. R., and Wiener, D. N. The problem of interminability in outpatient psychotherapy. *Journal of Consulting Psychology* 23 (1959): 237–42.

Strupp, H. H. Psychotherapy. *Annual Review of Psychology* 13 (1962).

Strupp, H. H. The outcome problem in psychotherapy revisited. *Psychotherapy: Theory, Research and Practice* 1 (1963): 1–13.

Sullivan, H. S. *Schizophrenia as a human process.* New York: Norton, 1962.

Sullivan, P. L., Miller, C., and Smelser, W. Factors in length of stay and progress in psychotherapy. *Journal of Consulting Psychology* 22 (1958): 1–9.

Szasz, T. S. The myth of mental illness. *American Psychologist* 15 (1960): 113–18.

Szasz, T. S. *Law, liberty and psychiatry.* New York: Macmillan, 1963.

Szilard, L. My trial as a war criminal. In *The Voice of the Dolphins.* New York: Simon and Schuster, 1961.

Thelen, M. H., Varble, D. L., and Johnson, J. Attitudes of academic clinical psychologists toward projective techniques. *American Psychologist* 23 (1968): 517–21.

Truax, C. B. The empirical emphasis in psychotherapy: A symposium. Effective ingredients in psychotherapy: An approach to unraveling the patient-therapist interaction. *Journal of Counseling Psychology* 10 (1963): 256–63.

Truax, C. B. A scale for the rating of accurate empathy. In *The therapeutic relationship and its impact: A study of psychotherapy with schizophrenics.* C. R. Rogers, E. T. Gendlin, D. J. Kiesler, and C. B. Truax (eds.). Madison, Wis.: University of Wisconsin Press, 1967.

Truax, C. B., and Carkhuff, R. R. For better or for worse: The process of psychotherapeutic change. In *Recent advances in behavioral change.* Montreal: McGill University Press, 1964.

Truax, C. B., and Carkhuff, R. R. Experimental manipulation of therapeutic conditions. *Journal of Counseling Psychology* 29 (1965): 119–24.

Truax, C. B., Wargo, D. G., Frank, J. D., Imber, S. D., Battle, C. C., Hoehn-Saric, R., Nash, E. H., and Stone, A. R. Therapist empathy, genuineness and warmth and patient therapeutic outcome. *Journal of Consulting Psychology* 5 (1966): 395–401.

Tucker, L. R., Damarin, F., and Messick, S. A base-free measure of change. *Psychometrika* 31 (1966): 457–73.

Ullman, L. P. *Institution and outcome.* London: Pergamon Press, 1967.

Van der Veen, F. Basic elements in the process of psychotherapy. *Journal of Consulting Psychology* 31 (1967): 295–303.

Ward, C. H., and Richards, J. C. Psychotherapy research: Inertia, recruitment, and national policy. *American Journal of Psychiatry* 124 (1968): 1712–14.

Waterson, D. J. Problems in the evaluation of psychotherapy. *Bulletin of the Menninger Clinic* 18 (1954): 232–41.

Webb, E. J., Campbell, D. T., Schwartz, R. D., and Sechrest, L. *Unobtrusive measures: Nonreactive research in the social sciences.* Chicago: Rand McNally, 1966.

Weber, M. *The theory of social and economic organization.* A. M. Henderson and T. Parsons (trans. and eds.). Glencoe, Ill.: Free Press, 1946.

Weber, M. Bureaucracy. In *From Max Weber: Essays in Sociology,* H. H. Gerth and C. W. Mills (trans. and eds.). New York: Oxford University Press, 1947.

Weinman, B., Sanders, R., Kleiner, R., and Wilson, S. Community based treatment of the chronic psychotic. *Community Mental Health Journal* 6 (1970): 13–21.

White, R. W. Motivation reconsidered: The concept of competence. In *Functions of varied experience,* D. W. Fiske and S. R. Maddi (eds.). Homewood, Ill.: Dorsey Press, 1961.

White, R. W. Ego and reality in psychoanalytic theory. *Psychological Issues* 3, no. 3. Monograph 11. New York: International Universities Press, 1963.

Whitehead, A. N. *Science and the modern world.* New York: Mentor Books, 1948.

Whitehorn, J. C., and Betz, B. J. Further studies of the doctor as a crucial variable in the outcome of treatment with schizophrenic patients. *American Journal of Psychiatry* 117 (1960): 215–23.

Wiener, D. N. The effect of arbitrary termination on return to psychotherapy. *Journal of Clinical Psychology* 15 (1959): 335–38.

Will, O. A. Process, psychotherapy and schizophrenia. In *Psychotherapy and the psychoses,* A. Burton (ed.). New York: Basic Books, 1961.

Williams, M. R. Unpublished material from the files of DART (Deprived Areas Recreation Team) and PSA (Professional Skills Alliance), Detroit, Michigan.

Winder, A., and Hersko, M. The effect of social class on the length and type of psychotherapy in a Veterans Administration Mental Hygiene Clinic. *Journal of Clinical Psychology* 11 (1955): 77–79.

Wispe, L. G., Awkard, J., Hoffman, M., Ash, P., Hicks, L. H., and Porter, J. The Negro psychologist in America. *American Psychologist,* 24 (1969): 142–50.

Wispe, L. G., and Parloff, M. B. Impact of psychotherapy on the productivity of psychologists. *Journal of Abnormal Psychology* 70 (1965): 188–93.

Zubin, J. Classification of the behavior disorders. *Annual Review of Psychology* (1967).

author index

subject index